THE FILM DIRECTOR'S TEAM

By Alain Silver &
Elizabeth Ward

SILMAN-JAMES PRESS
Los Angeles

First Silman-James edition

Material from *Angie* reproduced with the permission of Paramount
Pictures Corp.

This book is sponsored by the Special Projects Committee of the
Directors Guild of America, Inc. George L. George, General Editor.
The opinions expressed herein are those of the authors and not
necessarily those of the Directors Guild of America, Inc.

Library of Congress Cataloging-in-Publication Data

Silver, Alain, 1947-
The film director's team / Alain Silver and Elizabeth Ward
p.   cm.
Ward's name appears first on the earlier edition.
Includes index.
1. Motion pictures—Production and direction.
I. Ward, Elizabeth, 1952- . II. Title
PN1995.9.P7W36   1993   791.43'0233—dc20   92-41670

ISBN: 1-879505-11-8

Cover design by Heidi Frieder

Printed in the United States of America

SILMAN-JAMES PRESS
1181 Angelo Drive
Beverly Hills, CA 90210

THE FILM DIRECTOR'S TEAM

dedicated to the memory of
George L. George
a lifelong commitment to film literacy
and
Wallace C. Worsley
a consummate professional

Contents

Acknowledgments

For this Second Edition, the authors would like to express their continued appreciation to the Directors Guild of America, particularly George L. George, David Shepard, and Selise Eiseman for their support and assistance. Thanks also to Creature Features for permission to use forms from *The Creature Wasn't Nice* a.k.a. *Spaceship* as examples and to all those involved in the production, especially Mark Haggard, Bruce Kimmel, Ned Topham, Patrick Regan, Lise C. Cook, Sharon Gerhard, and Bob Hoover. (*Spaceship* is available on videotape from Vestron.) The *Angie* samples are courtesy of Paramount Pictures. Others were prepared for Island Pictures, Hemdale, Guber-Peters Television, Kings Road, Imagination Productions, Premiere Pictures, Thrill Me Productions, Michael Schultz, Ben Myron, Tom Laughlin, Frank Laughlin, James Allard, Ron Walsh, and Milton Bagby.

We would also like to thank the production managers and assistant directors who gave of their time to participate in the panel discussion, especially, for his candor, the late Xavier Reyes. Many other DGA members have offered suggestions and encouragement, among them Scott U. Adam, David A. Nicksay, Richard Abramitis, the late John Quill, and Barbara Gelman. Finally, Peter Jensen held the Steadicam; Dianne Edwards helped prepare the transcript of the panel discussion; Elizabeth Stanley provided updated information on the Training Program; India Brookover-Coleman loaned a pencil; and Linda sharpened it.

Preface

This book attempts to define and illustrate the functions and responsibilities of those persons who are part of the motion picture director's team. Specifically, this concept is used to refer to production managers and assistant directors working on motion pictures. We hope that the practical and theoretical material in our exposition will prove useful both to working professionals as a reference to tools and methodology and to students and novices as a detailed procedural guide. The underlying problem, as the reader will discover, is that whether the medium is feature films or long- and short-form television, whether the budget is measured in thousands or millions of dollars, the filmmaking process resists standardization.

This book is concerned with the total work of the production manager and the assistant director, the entire scope of their job functions and the pertinent aspects of the job functions of other film professionals who interact with them. In order to delineate and exemplify all the knowledge and skills which the production manager and assistant director bring to the film production process, we have approached the concept of the directorial team from three slightly different perspectives. The first surveys the history, development, and current practice of the two job functions in general terms. The second perspective is chronological and follows the directorial team in practical detail by surveying its members' evolving responsibilities through the various phases of an actual production. The final perspective is applied, based on a panel discussion with production managers and assistant directors and presenting their individualized approaches to the work. As with three camera angles, these perspectives may "pan" or "tilt" and occasionally overlap. Obviously, our intention in using this method is not to be redundant but to explore and reveal to the reader as fully as possible the depth and complexity of the work of the production manager and assistant director and their involvement in successful filmmaking.

It is not our purpose to delve into the same areas covered by previously published books that take the general concept of filmmaking as their subject. The elements of physical production, such as camera, lighting, sound, makeup, costuming, and the like, will enter into our discussion but only from the point of view of experts in the management and direction of the entire process—not from the vantage point of professionals involved in individual elements. We assume that our readers have a rudimentary knowledge of how these elements combine to produce a film and of the key personnel involved. Should a reader discover an unfamiliar term for a technician or a technical procedure, we have included a Glossary.

I
General Concepts

A useful definition of the role of the production manager and assistant director in the filmmaking process will require, quite understandably, some clarification of that process itself. Coverage of "Hollywood" by the print media and television has given most people a notion of what film directors and film producers do. For many if not most filmgoers, the title cards for director of photography, editor, and art director have been effectively demystified. Even the credits for such formerly arcane jobs as gaffer or key grip, credits which were originally intended to be appreciated only by peers in the film industry, can be understood by anyone after limited investigation. Yet the actual process by which all these people and their technical skills come together to fashion a motion picture, the process of production, is apparent neither in the credits nor in the motion picture itself. For those who think in terms of causality, it is no secret that the prime movers in production, those who make the key decisions, are the directors and producers. However, their work and their responsibilities, from the broadest considerations of script and casting to the finest points of camera placement and cutting, control rather than define the actual work of making a motion picture.

Some of those involved in this work have, in moments of triumph and exasperation alike, compared it to a battle. For some, unfortunately, belief in this analogy has led to deplorable belligerence. Most film-makers recognize only one enemy: time. Its weapons are the unforeseen events which cause delay. From this viewpoint, there may be parallels between a shooting schedule or *call sheet* and the plans for a military campaign. The analogy is also apt on other levels, for it is reasonably safe to assume that neither a battle nor a motion picture production have ever gone exactly as planned and for many of the same reasons. In filmmaking, the plan of attack drawn up by the production manager and assistant directors can never be more than a reasoned estimate of the time required for certain maneuvers. They can never anticipate the delays inflicted by illness, accident, mechanical breakdown, or inclement weather. The ability to respond to such setbacks—to improvise a flanking action—may be the most elusive and invaluable of the production manager's and assistant directors' skills. Other analogies highlight other aspects of film production. The planning and construction of buildings requires a similar diversity of craftsmen working in concert. Transportation industries need efficient deployment of personnel and equipment to minimize "downtime." Either may employ production control specialists to track deadlines and quotas or an industrial relations department to arbitrate salaries and working conditions. All these analogies are apt but imperfect, not only because filmmaking spans all these considerations and more but also because they fail to reveal the most individual, perhaps unique, challenges of motion picture production.

A popular film industry truism holds that filmmaking is a series of compromises. To a certain extent, all creative or manufacturing endeavors must involve compromises, singly or in series. All these activities have their particular mediators or managers positioned between the designers and decision makers (directors and producers) and the employees (the film crew). Some in the film industry take its industriousness literally and are most comfortable regarding themselves as bosses or workers—each in an adversary relationship with the other. For most, however, film is like the other fine arts in that it affords its practitioners, at all levels, a medium for creative expression. Like the other fine arts, a film also must be sold to support its creators. This is not of direct concern to the production manager and assistant director; selling remains the realm of agents, distributors, exhibitors, and other entrepreneurs. It may appear that the job skills of the production manager and assistant director, which are to manage and assist only during the short-term preparation for and execution of the production process, fall within a narrow range. Moreover, there are few vestiges of the precise work of these professionals in the final product offered to the consumer. A finished motion picture does not reveal whether it was completed on schedule and on budget any more than individual scenes disclose whether its actors were ever *in meal penalty* or *on forced call,* phrases and conditions with which even the frequent filmgoer is unlikely to be familiar. The amount of time required to bring a project from initial conception to exhibition in theaters or on television may be quite protracted—several years is not uncommon. Proportionately, the few weeks or months during which the production manager is on salary and the even briefer period of employment for the assistant directors may belie their significance in the total process of filmmaking.

THE STUDIO SYSTEM

The evolution of this process can be the basis for a current definition of those who control its operation. The film industry, like most others, came into being to meet a demand by consumers for a product. Although some competition over patents and procedures, and debates over formats and applications continue to this day, the mechanical standardization of the motion picture has long since been established. (Unlike, for example, the home videotape industry which retains two major, incompatible ½-inch tape formats or, more recently, diverse, competing videodisk systems.) The next stage in the development of an industry is procedural; but although certain standard operating procedures have evolved, considerable diversity remains among the methods in film production.

This diversity may well be more of a factor today than it was during the entrenched period when the studio system dominated production. Whether or not he originated the idea, Thomas Ince initiated the studio operation. The consequences of Ince's efforts in the 1920s still pervade the film business, but most pertinent to this discussion is the emergence of the production manager. For Ince, who was intent on personally supervising all the pictures made under his banner, the studio system was devised as a way of maintaining tight control over a growing number of projects. There were two concepts of major importance to the success of Ince's system: departmentalization and estimating. The former was simply the breakdown of all the major facets of filmmaking—including pre- and post-production— into manageable units. The story department, camera department, editorial department *et al.* were each headed by a studio employee who had a line relationship to the studio head. These department heads kept Ince informed of the status of all his projects as they progressed from story development through principal photography to final assembly. The departments also had an estimating function, not merely in terms of cost analysis but also in the larger sense of anticipating production needs. Once a script had been approved, each department head was required to review it and report on the manpower and equipment allocations it might entail. Clearly, even a man of prodigious energy and analytical ability, as Ince was reputed to be, would be hard-pressed to digest daily departmental reports on more than a few projects, either planned or in production. Thus, another link in the chain of command evolved—the line producer. As the title implies, this position involves a line responsibility. In the traditional studio system each project was assigned a producer, whose supervisory function extended to all departments, but only insofar as their work might contribute to his or her project. The line producer is still common to the industry. Outside the studio framework, however, it is no longer clear whether this person has a line responsibility to a supervising producer, an executive producer, a production vice-president, an executive in charge of production, a chief executive officer, a board chairman, or all or none of the above. Under Ince and such well-known heirs of his system as Louis B. Mayer, Jack Warner, and Darryl Zanuck, the dichotomy between the aesthetic and technical considerations of production led to a split in job functions and chain of command. As the producer became increasingly associated with creative aspects, his primary line responsibility to the studio head shifted towards quality control, specifically the performance of the writer, director, and actors. As cost control becomes a secondary consideration for the line producer, an immediate subordinate directly responsible for the cost-efficient performance of any production unit was needed, a person who was, in effect, a unit production manager.

THE DIRECTOR'S ASSISTANT

It is ironic that while the director of motion pictures and television programs has long enjoyed a public awareness of his or her job function and authority equal to and often greater than that of the producer, there is virtually no public awareness of the work of the director's first and second assistants. Like that of unit production manager (UPM), the position of assistant director (AD) was created by and has evolved with the industry's production needs. In its earliest manifestations, the assistant director was just that, a sort of *aide-de-camp* and nothing more. As the details of filmmaking—from getting actors to setting props to rolling camera and cuing action—became too complex for the director, they were delegated first to an assistant and through that person to an expanding film crew. The most publicized directors of the silent period, such as D .W. Griffith, helped to increase both the number and the duties of their assistants. Griffith's intricate staging of epic scenes relied heavily on assistant directors both to help set the movements of the background action and to progress efficiently through the numerous setups which the scenes required. Eventually, this developed into a line relationship between director and first assistant.

At its simplest level of operation, the filmmaking process begins with a decision by the director of what scenes are to be shot on a given day. This is communicated to the first assistant, who must then synthesize these scenes to be shot into a work sequence for cast and crew. The notation and dissemination of this work sequence on a call sheet is carried out by the second assistant director. In the traditional studio system, the assistant directors were, in turn, assisted by a production clerk, who functioned as a liaison with the production manager and/or production department and who kept a record of hours worked, material expended, and other details affecting costs. Some production systems today assign the production clerk's duties to a third assistant director. In the United States, the work of the production clerk has simply been assimilated by the second assistant, who now records all the pertinent details of work performed in a daily Production Report. Remarkably, neither the critical set functions nor the responsibilities of the assistant directors to oversee them have changed significantly over the last fifty years since the standardization of the sound motion picture. The first assistant, and such additional second assistants[1] as may be needed still run the set for the director, still formalize and track the day's work, still bring the actors to the set, still stage the background action using extra players.

At this point, it may not be clear to the reader in what way or from what perspective the functions of the production manager and the assistant directors are related. The unit production manager or

---

[1] Most feature and television productions do employ assistant director trainees who, while in training to become second assistants, are available to aid in set operations. See Appendix II. Some producers alternatively hire production assistants for this purpose, although such a practice is disapproved by the Directors Guild of America and is a formal violation of their collective bargaining agreement.

UPM[2] is responsible to the producer for hiring personnel and supervising production from a cost control standpoint. How does that relate to assisting a director on the set? Actually, there would seem to be potential conflict between those administering the budgetary limitations of a given motion picture and those assisting the director in realizing his or her creative goals. How then, as regards most of the features and filmed television produced in the United States, did the director, the assistant directors, and the unit production managers all come to be members of the same guild?

THE DIRECTOR'S TEAM

Production managers were not always part of the Directors Guild of America (DGA). They were admitted into the collective bargaining unit in 1964, whereas assistant directors became part of the original Screen Directors Guild in 1937, the year after it was formed. Before this is interpreted as the inappropriate grafting of a management branch onto a creative trunk, it should also be noted that, in the Eastern United States, second assistant directors were not always part of the DGA but transferred their affiliation from the International Alliance of Theatrical and Stage Employees in 1964. Past allegiances or lack of them aside, there are few today who would assert that the production manager has a lesser place in a directors union than the assistant director. The DGA itself has formally recognized a progression in its own contractually defined industry experience roster from second assistant to first to unit production manager with each advance in grade being permitted only after fulfillment of a minimum number of working days at the lower level of responsibility.[3]

More significant than the Directors Guild hierarchy is the actual interface between these job functions during production. For without

---

[2] Although many productions, particularly in filmed television, have both production managers and unit production managers, the duties are the same and the two terms as well as the abbreviation UPM are often interchanged in film industry practice. This book will also freely interchange them.

[3] Specifically, the DGA Basic Agreement calls for 520 days worked before a second assistant may move up on a regular basis to first and for 260 days as a first assistant before moving up to UPM. Needless to say, the minimum pay scales increase commensurately.

a firm grasp of set operations based on previous time spent *working the
set*, the unit production manager may not possess the knowledge
prerequisite to effective budgeting, scheduling, and cost control. Conversely, for the assistant director on the set to fulfill the basic duty of
planning and accomplishing the day's work within the parameters of
schedule and budget, that person must have a fundamental knowledge
of production costs from pay scales and overtime factors on cast and
crew to facilities and equipment charges. Without such knowledge,
it might be difficult to react decisively to the shifting demands of
production and to make the fine distinction between what the production must have and what it might forego without sacrificing quality.

It is in this distinction that the potential for divided allegiances
usually resides. The producer, the director, the production manager,
the assistant directors, all share a basic, functional responsibility: the
production of a motion picture—but the specific concerns attached to
this responsibility are variable. Specifics of quality and cost entail
chances for conflict that are quite marked. In the classic studio system
of Ince's devise, with the producer as the ultimate fiscal voice and the
director as the aesthetic one, the key line relationships might have
been drawn in parallel chains of command:

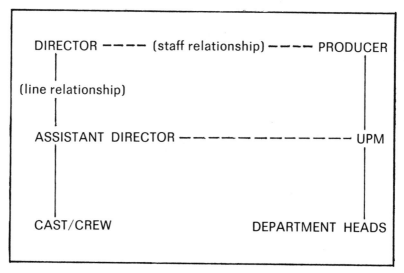

Obviously, this diagram is very simplified. If one extrapolates a staff
or consulting relationship between the director/producer and the
assistant director/production manager tiers, however, it does approximate the original studio system's operative method. It is also clear that

the classic system and its method are gone. Not only is it common for the producer's primary interest to shift from cost to quality, but also the assistant director's line or command relationship to the director is undercut by the limitations of schedule and budget. Today, it might be more accurate to diagram the line and staff relationships in a production unit as:

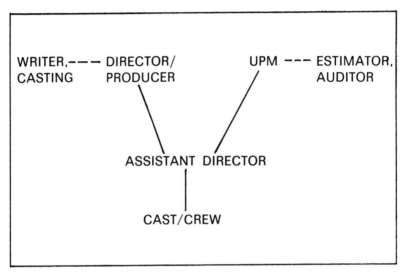

Again, a chart such as this depends on some oversimplification; but it does graphically reveal that the assistant director is the nexus for potential conflict and split allegiances.

The likelihood of a division of loyalties is increased by the hiring practices of the film business. This is particularly true in one-camera, episodic television where the assistant directors divide their allegiances among the producers, actors, and crew who work with them during the entire season and the directors who may be hired for only one episode, in what industry jargon dubs a *guest shot*. Given these circumstances, it is understandable that some producers and production supervisors in episodic television regard the very term assistant director as a misnomer. Their belief is that the first loyalty of the set ADs should be to the production company which hired them and that their *de facto* function is to be the producer and/or production company's field representative. The question of who hires whom has thus always been and will likely continue to be the governing factor in the political infrastructure of the film industry both on and off the set. Although this organizational dynamic certainly is not unique to motion pictures

—it may actually be difficult to cite any business enterprise in which it is not a governing factor—the working conditions of the set test the soundness of this infrastructure in ways that may well be unique.

DEFINITIONS

At the core of the question is the director and that position's function. Most readers will have encountered some form of the stereotype film director. This is not a man in puttees and beret with a megaphone under his arm or any such that have suffered the distortion of numerous parodies. A more accurate stereotype reveals the fundamental control of the director, not just over camera placement and cast performance but over all the details of filmmaking. A film set is not a locus in which a caricature indulges aesthetic whim, but where a professional uses his or her training to direct a group of subordinate talents in the creation of a motion picture. In practical terms, the director's function and relationship to the film crew is roughly equivalent to that of the captain of a vessel, for, except where it may be voluntarily subrogated, the director's authority over the set is complete. It would be too facile to extend this analogy and regard the first assistant as first mate. Too facile because the first assistant is not merely a backup or an adjutant to the director ready to assume command in an emergency; the duties of the first assistant extend beyond mere adjutancy.

How far-reaching and complex the duties of both assistant director and production manager are and how critical their efficient performance of those duties is to successful motion picture production are questions to be fully answered later in this study. At this point, the best way to recapitulate and establish a theoretical base may be simply to reproduce the most widely recognized articulation of those duties which is contained in the DGA Basic Agreement. Article One, section two of that Basic Agreement includes the following under the heading, "Definition of Employees Recognized":

The Unit Production Manager, under the supervision of the Employer, is required to coordinate, facilitate and oversee the preparation of the production unit or units (to the extent herein provided) assigned to him [sic], all off-set logistics, day to day production decisions, locations, budget schedules and per-

sonnel. Without limitation, among the duties which the employer must assign to the UPM or 1st Assistant Director are the supervision of or participation in the following:
1. Prepare breakdown and preliminary shooting schedule.
2. Prepare and coordinate the budget.
3. Oversee preliminary search and survey of all locations and the completion of business arrangements for the same.
4. Assist in the preparation of the production to insure continuing efficiency.
5. Supervise completion of the production report for each day's work, showing work covered and the status of the production, and arrange for the distribution of that report in line with the company's requirements.
6. Coordinate arrangements for the transportation and housing of cast, crew and staff.
7. Oversee the securing of releases and negotiations for locations and personnel.
8. Maintain a liaison with the local authorities regarding locations and the operation of the company.

The Basic Agreement also defines first and second assistant directors:

The 1st Assistant Director, alone or in conjunction with the UPM organizes pre-production, including organizing the crew, securing equipment, breaking down the script, preparing the stripboard and a shooting schedule. During production he or she assists the director with respect to on-set production details, coordinates and supervises crew and cast activities and facilitates an organized flow of production activity. The 1st assistant director may be assigned responsibilities of the UPM. His other prime responsibility is to service and assist the director. Without limitation, among the duties which the employer must assign to the 1st assistant director or the UPM are the supervision of participation in the following:
1. Prepare breakdown and stripboard; prepare shooting schedule keeping the same within time limitations imposed by budget, cast availability and the requirement of complete coverage of the script.
2. If delegated by the UPM or in the absence of the UPM, oversee the search, survey and management of locations and ascertain the specific requirements of those locations as they might affect the production.
3. Check weather reports.

4. Prepare day-out-of-day schedules for talent employment and determine the cast and crew calls.
5. Supervise the preparation of the call sheet for the cast and crew.
6. Direct background action and supervise crowd control.
7. May be required to secure minor cast contracts, extra releases, and on location to obtain execution of contracts by talent.
8. Supervise the functioning of the shooting set and crew . . .

The 2nd assistant director is the one who is assigned by the employer as an assistant to the first assistant director in conducting the business of the set or the location site. Without limitation, among the duties which the employer must assign to the 2nd assistant director are the supervision of or participation in the following:

1. Prepare the call sheet.
2. Prepare the daily production report.
3. Distribute scripts and script changes to cast and crew and give call to cast and crew.
4. Communicate advance scheduling to cast and crew.
5. Aid in the scouting, surveying and managing of locations.
6. Facilitate transportation of equipment and personnel.
7. May be required to secure execution of minor cast contracts, extra releases, and, on occasion, to secure execution of contracts by talent. (Can also be delegated to 1st assistant and UPM.)
8. Function as supervisor during studio or location wrap.
9. Schedule food, lodging and other facilities.
10. Maintain liaison between UPM or production office and the first assistant director.
11. Assist in the direction of background action and the supervision of crowd control.
12. Supervise and direct the work of any trainee assigned to the picture.

The foregoing description is not intended, nor shall it be construed, either to enlarge or diminish the duties of UPMs, 1st and 2nd assistant directors or other personnel as such duties are presently and were heretofore customarily performed in the motion picture industry.

WORKING CONDITIONS

Although the concept of "duties . . . customarily performed" might appear to be an afterthought, it is actually the basis for all of the DGA contract's definitions. The definition of Director is little more than this concept: "A Director is one who directs the production of motion pictures, as the word 'direct' is commonly used in the motion picture industry." What this introductory section has attempted to elucidate is that the words "production manager" and "assistant director" are also part of common use and are governed by customary performance to which any abstractions or definitions must be accountable. As the Basic Agreement of the DGA stresses, the key role of the so-called director's team is management and supervision. If the list of duties in the Basic Agreement is an indicator, then the production manager and the assistant director must function as a unit, for each is highly dependent on the other for guidance and/or information. Nor is it merely a question of recognizing duties; effective management and supervision depends on organizing needs according to priorities and on the communication of those priorities. These are the methods implicit in the Basic Agreement's definitions and contained, in the broader sense, in the notion of customary performance or working conditions.

As in any industrial process, customary performance or working conditions not only create and sustain the required job function but continue to exercise a preemptive control over them. Many DGA members bristle if they hear a production manager or assistant directors assert that something is not their job. For if the director is regarded in the common usage of the business simply as "one who directs the production of motion pictures," then the production manager and assistant directors must be, as part of the director's team, aware of and able to control all aspects of that production without limitation. Accordingly, although there are many technical aspects of filmmaking that are not part of the production manager's or assistant directors' jobs, there are few if any which are outside their purview.

In an industry that resists standardization, working conditions can become the main element affecting production procedures. As has already been mentioned, the demands of episodic television can divide an assistant director between a theoretical loyalty to the director and a practical loyalty to the production company. When working conditions dictate that a difficult episode entails several, grueling eighteen-hour workdays which threaten both budget and morale, the allegiances of production manager and assistant director to the notion of a director's team can be severely tested. The DGA has attempted to alleviate some of the potential conflict in its 1981 Basic Agreement by securing the director's right to select the first assistant—but only in feature films and long-form television.

It seems clear that, whether the production is governed by the DGA contract or is non-union, working conditions depend most heavily on the basic hiring entity, i.e., the production company. That production company, whether a major studio or a small independent, initially establishes working conditions by designating the context of the production. Context is what hangs in the balance between the script with its implicit requirements and the budget with its explicit limits. This will be examined in detail in succeeding portions of this study. Secondary working conditions derive not only from the script and budget but also from the policies of the production company, policies that the production manager and assistant director must know and respect. Universal Studios, for example, publishes its own film production guide for production managers and assistant directors, which expands considerably on the duties listed in the DGA Basic Agreement. In the Universal guide there are twenty-four, eleven, and twenty-three responsibilities given for the UPM, first assistant, and second assistant, respectively. Some of these are merely details of paperwork peculiar to Universal; but others, such as UPM item 24: "Prepare listing of screen credits," which is usually undertaken by an associate producer, are slightly at variance with customary performance.

In sum, production manager and assistant directors must be aware of the underlying complexity of their job functions, of its roots in the studio system, of the current requirements established by individual employers, and of the rights secured through DGA collective bargaining. Perhaps the most fundamental working condition for production managers and assistant directors is being part of a directorial team. In practice, most production managers do delegate a portion of their arbitrarily defined work to a location manager or a production coordinator, leaving them to order meals or negotiate a location use fee. In a demanding situation, the first and second assistant directors may well rely on trainees or production interns to help collect extra vouchers or give calls. Ultimately, however, as the forthcoming portions of this book should underscore, only the production managers and assistant directors are part of that directorial team, only they have a lineal participation in the director's authority and a true share in its attendant obligations.

II

Industry Methods— Preproduction

The typical film or television production situation consists of six phases that are common to many industries in which a group of individuals collaborates to manufacture a product for public consumption. These phases are: development; preproduction; production; post-production; distribution; and exhibition. Although this study is directly concerned with only two of these phases, preproduction and production, it may be useful to clarify each of them.

Development involves conceptualizing and selling the narrative, whether fiction or nonfiction, whether feature film, television series, or special event. The written format, which may be an outline, treatment, or full script, constitutes the basic property, which may be presented to investors, producers, and/or production companies. A significant corollary to securing financing for a property is the desired production value. In determining the amount of money and time to be expended in a given property's manufacture, the producers must also determine the visible quality required for the finished film to appeal successfully to consumers and return a profit.

- *Preproduction* is the planning period immediately preceding the manufacture of the given property. It also entails securing and organizing the personnel and equipment needed for production.
- *Production* is commonly referred to as shooting or filming. It could also be described as the manufacture of the raw product.
- *Post-production* actually completes the manufacturing process. The motion picture is edited and combined with music and sound effects that refine the results of the production period into the finished form.
- *Distribution* is the delivery of the product by those who license and control its availability to consumers, whether theatrical distributors, network or cable system suppliers, or syndicators.

15

- *Exhibition* is consumption of the product by the audience that buys a ticket, subscribes to a cable system, or tunes in to commercial television.

Simplistic as these distinctions may seem, they are the basis for all the contending spheres of interest and influence in the film industry. Although an increasing number of production managers are also participating in post-production and occasionally serving as associate producers, it remains generally true that they and assistant directors are involved only in phases two and three of a given property's manufacture. This restriction colors both their job function and their allegiances.

INITIATING PRODUCTION

To be a producer is to have a stake in the creation and/or profits of a particular project. On a theoretical level, someone must produce the elements needed to initiate production. These elements include working capital, a property (novel or script), and attachments (directors and actors). It is common for motion pictures and television programs to credit a variety of producer types, from the executive or supervising producers to the associate or assistant producers. It is possible to generalize about their respective functions. Executive producers most often raise money, supervising producers oversee episodic television, associate producers are concerned with post-production, etc. It is not our purpose to make fine distinctions about the job functions of producers, but rather to use the term generically. Producer as a term represents any combination of real persons and organizations who exist as the primary financing entities and supervising authorities for motion pictures and television. As such, they are the employers of the production manager and assistant directors on any particular project.

HIRING THE PRODUCTION MANAGER

The production manager is hired directly by the producer and/or studio production supervisor. In certain kinds of studio operations, the production supervisor is the production manager in charge of all television projects and the one who hires unit production managers for each show. Whatever their actual title, these supervising production managers oversee the various production manager and assistant director units on individual projects.

The unit production manager is generally the first person to be hired once a project secures financing or studio approval. In practical terms, certain key artistic and technical personnel such as the director, production designer, or cinematographer may already be on staff and in consultation with the producer. A production that entails unusual requirements—from exotic locations to difficult special effects—will often hire specialists to work on such problems in advance of the production manager. Nonetheless, the UPM as the manager of the entire crew will begin to supervise all the *below-the-line* activities from his or her first day of employment.

THE LINE

The distinction between above-the-line and below-the-line can significantly affect the supervisory duties of the production manager and assistant directors. Simply stated, the line is drawn across the center of all the budget forms in use in the industry. Above this line are the personnel considered part of the creative side of the project: the talent. This includes the writers, director, producer, and actors.[1] Below-the-line personnel are the craftspeople and technicians who make up the crew. This includes the production staff (production manager and assistant directors). In theory, the producer is responsible for hiring and supervising the talent which is above-the-line; the production manager does likewise for those below-the-line. However, once actors report, while details of performance remain the exclusive concern of the director, their work times—like all others on the set— are determined by the production manager and assistant directors.

If the line is occasionally blurred or exaggerated, its intent remains straightforward: to establish a hierarchy of values that elevates creative concerns over technical ones. In practice, the production manager and assistant directors may have to walk the line like a tightrope balancing between accommodating both creative and tech-

[1] It also includes certain ancillary personnel such as the secretaries or assistants to the talent. Some budgets place stand-ins and extras above-the-line; others, below. (*See* sample forms.)

nical needs. Under ideal circumstances, the relationship between the talent above and the staff below depends on communication that is both imaginative and practical. The director, producer, and actors need technical awareness to manipulate creatively all that is available to them. The crew must understand creative goals in order to implement them. The instruments of communication are, of course, the production manager and assistant directors.

The production manager and assistant directors, in turn, rely on their own kind of creative thinking. They are not hired to make aesthetic contributions but for their managerial expertise over a creative environment. Both the production staff and the production operating staff (that is, the crew) will quickly discern the attitudes of those "above-the-line." Directors and producers who are open to suggestions may find the key technicians quite willing to contribute ideas. Conversely, directors and producers not desiring unsolicited counsel will seldom receive any. Whether the aesthetic atmosphere of a given set is open or closed will depend entirely on the above-the-line attitude. The production manager and assistant directors must gauge that attitude and service it.

PRODUCTION VALUE

Typically, the production manager's first task after being hired is to complete a first draft budget. Often, a supervising production manager attached to a studio or major independent may have consulted during the developmental stage of a project and roughly estimated costs before the final go-ahead has been given by the financing entity. Whatever the projected total cost of a feature or the median episode budget for a television series, the UPM is responsible for the first completely detailed budget. There are some production managers who specialize in producing budget breakdowns on a free-lance basis. In most instances, the completion of the budget is the first step in the management of a given production through the completion of principal photography. In the case of a series, the production manager will redraft the median episode budget and reuse those fixed elements, e.g., base salaries or weekly rental costs, that remain constant for each episode.

In order to compile a first draft budget, the UPM requires a script and three essential pieces of information: 1) the time allotted for production, expressed in shooting days; 2) the funds allocated for above and below the line; and (3) the production value which the producer expects to derive from the two first factors. The governing equation is simple but internally mutable:

$$Time + Money = Production\ Value$$

The preproduction choices, whether they imply traveling to distant parts of the globe to make *Lawrence of Arabia* or reconstructing Las Vegas on a studio lot as in *One from the Heart,* are predetermining influences, as one might expect. Production value, therefore, is a single concept which must accommodate both aesthetic choices and commercial viability. Simplistically, production value is a conspicuous display of expense in an effort to give the audience value for the price of admission. Whether that value means paying for the rights to a literary best-seller, employing star actors, exotic locations, elaborate effects, or all of these combined, there is nothing cynical or dishonorable in the desire to make the most efficacious use of available funds, so that both producer and audience get what they pay for. Of course, those productions which are too conspicuous in their quest for production value risk criticism or failure for not achieving the potential of their creative and technical elements and disappointing the viewer. From this standpoint of audience expectations and accepting that audiences approach filmgoing from a somewhat informed perspective, neither low budgets nor short schedules necessarily handicap film or television production. Rather, it is the poor use of whatever time and money are available that is more likely to dissatisfy the viewer.

Understanding the production value equation as it applies to a particular production is an interpretive and cognitive communication among the producer, the director, and the UPM.[2] Transforming the abstraction of a script into a budget and schedule which conform to available resources is the production manager's creative contribution

---

[2] In theory, the producer is responsible for defining the desired production value. Only rarely is the producer a mere spokesperson for the director, who is often mistaken by those outside the industry as being singlehandedly responsible for the successful achievement of the film's quality or artistic merit. In fact, the director does assume as part of his or her job function many prerogatives with regard to a project's creative aspects. Nonetheless, the only secure assumption, unless the director shares or has sole producer credit, is that the director is an employee whose control may be restricted by the need to interpret and actualize the producer's original concepts.

to preproduction. The success of that contribution can only be measured by testing the production manager's blueprint against other possible models and ultimately in actual production. The tools for this process are not mysterious. They are the script, the production manager's analytical ability, and a few pieces of paperwork.

READING THE SCRIPT; THE BUDGET

In reading the script, the production manager must "break down" the intricate format into its component information. It is this information which must be transposed into the time and money side of the production equation. A typical format with which the reader may already be familiar is the annotated partial page from *The Creature Wasn't Nice* shown on the following page.

Ideally, the production manager will have a final draft script from which to produce a first draft budget expeditiously. As previously mentioned, there are occasions when a producer or production company is waiting to make a final decision on proceeding with a project, and there may be considerable pressure to be more than expeditious. Many if not most production managers prefer to break down the script in full detail before undertaking the budget. Some will not proceed without first establishing a complete production board. It is quite possible, however, to produce a budget without a full breakdown or board or even a final draft script. It is actually possible to produce a budget from a treatment or a mere narrative concept.[3] Given the total monies and/or total days, a first draft budget may be devised to indicate unusual requirements from supplementary personnel to large expendables. The basis of this draft may be a review of the story line in whatever form it exists and rough notes.

There is a diversity of budget forms in common use, and specific accounting categories and numerical codes may vary from company to company. Of the forms illustrated here, the simplest makes only one division—the traditional line across the page—and uses somewhat unwieldy letter subcodes within its twenty-two principal accounting

[3] This is not uncommon. The concept of packaging in the film industry tends to regard creative personnel as bankable elements. In the search for financing on a project, the budget top-sheet is often part of the investment prospectus.

Scene #	Interior or Exterior	Setting	Time

49.   INT. SCREENING ROOM—SPACESHIP—DAY   49.

Annie, John, Jameson, Rodzinski enter
and sit in comfortable modernistic   *Action*
chairs. Rodzinski takes the chair next   *described*
to Annie. She pointedly gets up and
sits on the other side of the room.
Rodzinski starts to move again. Jameson stops him with a glare.

JAMESON ————————————— *character speaking*

Roll it, Max. ————

———— *dialogue*

The lights dim, as Max projects a
prevue of coming attractions. And we:

CUT TO:

scene shift

categories. This form and its top sheet retain certain advantages which
will be detailed in the following, but the user should be wary of
several archaisms. For instance, in category #12 (Editing and Laboratory) there are still subheads for such items as "separation masters"
from the long-extinct three-strip Technicolor® process. The major
studios and many independents use variants of a more modern form
with four- or five-digit encoding. The first two identify major cate-

gories and the remaining two or three, subheads. Above-the-line remains unchanged but below-the-line is further divided into direct production costs, post-production, or editing costs, and such ancillary other costs as insurance, overhead, publicity, and the like. This latter form yields superior segregation of budget details and, when incorporated into a computerized accounting system, is much easier to access. There is a drawback for an independent production which may have contracted with payroll or production payment services to handle cash disbursement in that the major categories such as camera, wardrobe, lighting, and so on, combine both salaries and equipment. Even in a computerized system, this combination is analogous to the cliched mixture of apples and oranges, and it may require more detailed and complex cost reporting. As might be expected, equipment does not earn overtime or meal penalties nor does it benefit from payments on its behalf for social security, health plans, or workmen's compensation. In a production which must come in on budget and which depends on regular cost reports for review by the production manager to determine if adjustments are needed, analysis of overages is substantially simplified by segregating salaries (where overtime is the usual nemesis) from rentals and expendables (where unforeseen extras or inordinate consumption are likelier problems).

Both budget forms treat fringes almost as afterthoughts; neither has printed entries for estimated overtime. Many budget preparers prefer to enter their fringe allowances within each category. Except in a non-union project, where most deals are made for a flat daily or weekly rate, overtime may be anticipated in a number of ways. Major features often guarantee their personnel an overtime payment—a twelve-hour guarantee is fairly common—and do not budget additional payment beyond that amount. In episodic television, a typical system is to budget a total number of man-hours as the average amount which each show should require. An allocation for a one-hour "action" show with three or four location days in its schedule of seven shooting days might be eighty-eight hours. These man-hours are computed by factoring the overtime into straight time. For example, 11 total hours equals 8 hours at straight time plus 3 hours at time-and-one-half or 8 hours plus 4.5 hours (3 times 1.5) for a total of 12.5 man-hours. Seven such days would equal 87.5 hours. Productions using IATSE crews face escalating costs whenever a crew works more than twelve total hours (including meal periods) in the studio or fourteen hours (including travel time) on a location. The *golden time* which goes

PICTURE BUDGET DETAIL

TITLE	"THE CREATURE WASN'T NICE"		PICTURE NO.	Budget #2
		DATE PREPARED	January 16, 19 81	

ACCOUNT NUMBER	DESCRIPTION		TOTAL	TOTALS	TOTALS
1	Story		37,500 00	(12,500 00)	25,000 00
2	Continuity and Treatment				2,026 00
3	Producer				52,490 00
4	Director				48,170 00
5	Cast				254,251 00
6	Bits				
7	Extras				6,100 00
	Sub Total				388,027 00
8	Production Staff Salaries				60,275 00
9	Production Operating Staff				149,160 00
10	Set Designing				99,750 00
11	Set Operation Expenses				69,586 00
12	Cutting - Film - Laboratory				163,250 00
13	Music				32,000 00
14	Sound				42,500 00
15	Transportation - Studio				17,625 00
16	Location				4,000 00
17	Studio Rental				56,600 00
18	Tests and Retakes				2,500 00
19	Publicity				4,100 00
20	Miscellaneous				9,425 00
21	Insurance - Taxes - Licenses and Fees				68,383 00
22	General Overhead				82,448 00
	Sub Total				861,602 00
	Contingency @ 10%				125,000 00
	Grand Total				1,374,629 00

Approved _____ Mark Haggard _____ Producer

Prepared From ____ 95 ____ Page Script Dated ____ -- ____

____ 25 ____ Day Shooting Scheduled at ____ Laird International ____ Studio

Director ____ Bruce Kimmel ____

Budget by ____ Alain Silver ____

```
                    PICTURE BUDGET DETAIL


TITLE:                                        DATE:


ABOVE THE LINE COSTS:

1100 - STORY AND SCREENPLAY
1200 - PRODUCERS UNIT
1300 - DIRECTION
1400 - CAST
1500 - FRINGE BENEFITS

      'SUB-TOTAL

BELOW THE LINE COSTS:

1999 - TRAVEL/LIVING EXPENSES
2000 - PRODUCTION
2100 - EXTRA TALENT
2200 - SET DESIGN
2300 - SET CONSTRUCTION
2400 - STRIKING
2500 - SET OPERATING EXPENSES
2600 - SPECIAL EFFECTS
2700 - SET DRESSING
2800 - PROPERTY
2900 - WARDROBE
3100 - MAKE-UP/HAIRDRESSING
3200 - LIGHTING
3300 - CAMERA
3400 - PRODUCTION SOUND
3500 - TRANSPORTATION
3600 - LOCATION EXPENSES
3700 - FILM/LABORATORY
4000 - SECOND UNIT
4100 - TESTS
4200 - MISCELLANEOUS EXPENSES
4300 - FRINGE BENEFITS

4500 - FILM EDITING
4600 - MUSIC
4700 - SOUND
4800 - POST-PROD. LABORATORY
4900 - TITLES
5200 - POST-PROD. FRINGE BENEFITS

6700 - INSURANCE
6800 - GENERAL EXPENSES/OFFICE
6900 - PUBLICITY

      SUB-TOTAL

      CONTINGENCY

      TOTAL BUDGET
```

PRODUCTION BUDGET

PRODUCTION #
_____

DATE
_____

TITLE: _____

_____ Remarks: _____

Travel Days: _____
Rehersal Days: _____
Distant Location Shooting: _____
Local Location Shooting: _____
Stage Shooting: _____
Total Days: _____
Crew Daily Pay Hours: _____

Executive Producer _____
Producer _____
Director _____
Start Prod. _____
Finish Prod. _____
Total Prod. Days _____
Answer Print Date _____
Based On _____
Script Dated _____
Script Pages _____

ACCT. NO.	DESCRIPTION	PAGE NO.	BUDGET	TOTALS
1100	Story & Other Rights	1		
1200	Continuity & Treatment	1		
1300	Direction & Supervision	1		
1400	Cast, Day Players, Stunts	2/3		
1500	Travel & Living	3		
1600		3		
1900	Fringe Benefits	3		
	TOTAL ABOVE THE LINE			
2000	Production Staff	4		
2100	Extra Talent	5		
2200	Art Direction	6		
2300	Set Construction	7		
2400	Set Striking	7		
2500	Set Operations	8		
2600	Special Effects	9		
2700	Set Dressing, Oper. & Strike	10		
2800	Property, Oper. & Strike	11		
2900	Men's Wardrobe	12		
3000	Women's Wardrobe	13		
3100	Makeup & Hairdressing	14		
3200	Elect., Rig, Oper. & Strike	15		
3300	Camera Operations	16		
3400	Sound Operations	17		
3500	Transportation	18		
3600	Location	19/20		
3700	Prod. Film & Laboratory	21		
3800	Stage Facilition	22		
3900	Process - Rear Projection	22		
4000	2nd Unit. Miniatures, Special Effects	23/24		
4100	Tests	24		
4400	Fringe Benefits	24		
	TOTAL PRODUCTION PERIOD			
4500	Editing	25		
4600	Music	25		
4700	Post Production Sound	26		
4800	Post Production Film & Lab.	26		
4900	Main & End Titles	26		
5900	Fringe Benefits	26		
	TOTAL EDITING PERIOD			
6500	Publicity	27		
6700	Insurance	27		
6800	Miscellaneous	27		
7400	Fringe Benefits	27		
7500	Fees & Charges	27		
	TOTAL OTHER CHARGES			
	ABOVE-THE-LINE			
	BELOW-THE-LINE			
	DIRECT COSTS			
	OVERHEAD FEE			
	COMPLETION FEE			
			TOTAL	
	DEFERMENTS TOTAL			
			TOTAL NEGATIVE COST: (Deferments Included)	

into effect after these maximums of twelve and fourteen hours multiplies the basic rate by a factor of two and two-and-one-half, respectively. Additionally, there are "meal penalties," premium payments which are assessed for every hour past six worked without a meal break, and "forced call" payment when the rest period between workdays is less than a minimum amount. Finally, there may be added expenses as night premiums for work performed after 8 P.M. or hazardous work adjustment which are self-explanatory. Although it is possible to make a detailed, day-by-day estimate of such costs, many budget preparers even when making guaranteed deals or using an episodic television structure will simply add a markup of five, fifteen, twenty percent or more to cover potential salary overages.

Some budget preparers do not bother to consider overtime in their first draft; few overlook fringe benefits. Even a non-union production must deal with governmental fringes: the employer's share of social security (FICA) and state and federal unemployment and disability insurance as well as workmen's compensation which, whether through private or governmental carriers, involves an annual minimum plus percentages of salaries. For members of the various guilds and the International Alliance of Theatrical and Stage Employees (IATSE), there are also health and welfare, pension, and vacation and holiday payments.[4] To some, the very term "fringe" benefit may imply a cost of small significance. The realization that typical fringes for a union employee may total thirty percent certainly belies insignificance.[5]

Given these various considerations, it remains to outline the fundamental or operative method of the budget. The basic elements of all the accounting categories are benignly commonplace: time, rate, and quantity. The total cost of cast, crew, equipment, stage or location rental, film—all are governed by a combination of these factors. As has been mentioned, the rates for the above-the-line personnel are the province of the producer; but even at a preliminary stage, the produc-

---

[4] Vacation and holiday pay may seem a strange concept to the reader. It is an attempt to compensate for the intermittent nature of employment in the film industry, where most are not on payroll long enough to enjoy the benefits of holidays or qualify for vacation days, and pays a percentage of earnings as vacation/holiday compensation.

[5] IATSE fringes are actually paid on the basis of payroll hours worked. SAG and DGA fringe is a percentage of salaries paid not to exceed predetermined maximum amounts.

tion manager may expect to receive reasonably accurate estimates of what the talent will be paid. Below-the-line, whether or not guild and union minimums are to apply, the production manager is normally responsible for negotiating and must anticipate what overscale or flat deals will be made. Once the various rates are determined, the number of days or weeks that individuals will work yields the total salaries. For the cast, consideration must be given not just to shooting days but also to rehearsals, hold days, and even post-production looping. For the crew, prep time and wrap time before and after shooting must be included. These will vary according to department from weeks or months for a production designer to as little as one day for a makeup artist or no days for a camera operator. The cost of production equipment and even expendables, from coffee and donuts to gasoline, is similarly reckoned by calculating quantity and/or rate over time.

Laboratory costs and the editing period as a whole are a bit more complex. Television productions have a tight quota of rawstock, but even large budget features must begin with an initial purchase of a given amount of film, which the budget preparer must estimate. Moreover, printed takes which determine the film needed for dailies may vary considerably, so that the budget preparer must rely heavily on experience and normal ratios in his or her estimates. In episodic television, the length of the editing period is strongly influenced by the need to meet an *air date*. In features, while the producer or production company may have a hoped-for release date, it is common to permit the director and editor to proceed at their own pace and to complicate the process with *temp dubs*, previews, and recuts. Both situations may result in unforeseen costs. (In television, more personnel and more overtime may be needed for a difficult episode to make its air date.) On a major feature, budgeted weeks of salaries and rentals may stretch to months.[6]

There are two major categories which require more information than just time, rate, and quantity. These are location and the ancillary or other charges which vary from one budget form to the next. Location falls into two types: local and distant. A local location allows daily

[6] If there is any consolation for the overages unforeseen by production managers in large-budget feature films, it may well be provided by those production companies who forego their services within a few weeks of the end of shooting and spare them from having to witness the substantial cost overruns of a prolonged editing period.

commuting during shooting.[7] The distant location is a shooting site sufficiently distant from the production company's studio or home base that the cast and crew must be provided with overnight accommodations. Both locations entail several expenses such as meals, site rentals, and government permits in addition to travel cost whether that is transport vehicle rental and gasoline or reimbursement of mileage costs to personnel on a report to, i.e., having cast and crew drive themselves to location rather than providing cars and buses (see footnote 7). Distant location further entails commercial air fares, lodging, and *per diem* payments for meals and incidental expenses. Under union conditions, distant location means a six-day workweek but also higher weekly minimum rates and payment for Sunday as a *carry day*.[8] Being distant from the studio call also means distance from post-production facilities and an attendant need for liaison with editorial, so that the director may have access to dailies as soon as possible.

Ancillary charges such as insurance, overhead, completion, and accounting fees are extremely variable. The major varieties of insurance can be flat rate or based on a percentage of actual capital value. This latter method will often involve a post-production audit by the insurance underwriters. No matter how low the production budget, insurance should not be regarded as totally optional. Workmen's compensation and general liability insurance are usually required of

---

[7] Obviously, even a local location could be many miles from a studio or home base. The industry unions permit their members to report to or drive directly to a location as long as they are compensated for vehicle costs. Typical payment is thirty cents per mile, mileage being based on the round-trip distance from the studio or home base to the location. Major cities have designated studio zones to prevent abusive practices. In Los Angeles, the studio zone is a circle with a radius extending thirty miles from the headquarters of the Motion Picture Association of America in West Hollywood. Although local locations may be established beyond this zone, employees may not be required to report there but must be transported. For budgeting purposes, this distinction creates different pay and penalty conditions. A *report to* is a studio day, i.e., work time begins when employees arrive at the work site and golden time begins after twelve hours. A *bus to* is a location day, i.e., the travel time spent riding in a company vehicle to location is considered work time but golden time does not begin until after fourteen hours.

[8] Sunday is a carry day because the employee, though not at work, is required to be away from home. If work is actually performed on a Sunday, it becomes a double-time day.

the employer by law. Despite their implicit liability, film laboratories will offer nothing more than fresh rawstock to compensate for any footage ruined by processing errors, hence the advisability of negative and faulty stock insurance. The major options in insurance are the coverage limits and deductibles. Since some premiums may not be finalized until principal photography is completed, a first draft budget may use a percentage of the total budget to approximate premium costs. Between two and three percent is common.

Overhead is also a percentage of total budget. Originally, overhead was used by the major studios to reflect the value of support given to a production by the physical plant and the departmental structure. For example, five different shooting companies at work on a studio lot will share the use of the switchboard, operations office, power plant, security guards, and the like. While the term overhead is still used for such facilities charges at major studios, many independents are also adding overhead to their budgets. Often, this kind of overhead is used to represent the value of production supervision provided by the company. Neither of these overheads should be confused with contingency, although some budget forms make contingency a subcategory of general overhead. As the word implies, contingency is an additional sum (usually ten percent of budget) which represents a cash reserve. This reserve is often needed to prevent depletion of production monies by unforeseen expenses that cause budget overruns. The contingency percentage may be applied to the total budget, to below-the-line costs, or to selected categories only.[9]

In its turn, contingency should not be mistaken for a completion fee or completion bond. Almost all major studios and independents bond themselves by using the value of their capital assets to guarantee completion of a given project. A budget for a production which will make use of funds from private or non-film-industry sources may have to allow for other kinds of bonding. An independent company wishing

[9] Because the overscale payments to the above-the-line talent may be quite substantial and out of proportion to the maximum hourly overtimes, many budget preparers consider a ten percent contingency on these amounts as concomitantly out of proportion. For example, the costar of a highly rated half-hour series might be paid $30,000 per week. This could produce a contingency of $3,000 per week. Overtime for such a person occurs after ten hours on any day; but because of maximums set by the Screen Actors Guild, even four hours of such overtime would be only $636.40. Despite such situations, most budget preparers apply the ten percent contingency to the total amount both above- and below-the-line.

to employ guild or union members but having no performance history may have to post completion monies in an escrow account. For example, *The Creature Wasn't Nice* was produced by Creature Features, a joint venture formed solely to produce this film. Before Creature Features received full signatory status through the SAG and DGA business offices, various salaries had to be guaranteed.[10] Such escrow payments are different from a formal completion bond. Full indemnification can be provided by a bonding company, which underwrites the completion of production for a fee, typically six percent of the total budget. This figure may be discounted or increased depending on the liability which the bonding agent foresees in a particular project. It is not unusual for a bonding company to decline to guarantee completion on a project which it regards as underfinanced or too hazardous. When granted, the bond itself often contains a performance clause. Such a clause gives the bonding company the right to take control of a production and make any changes they deem fit to personnel or schedule if there are indications that the budget— *not* including contingency—has been or will be exceeded.

Such a sobering prospect, regardless of whether a given production is formally bonded, underscores the need for accurate budget preparation. No budget, no matter how well researched or detailed, is more than figures on a page. Its purpose is to provide a fiscal outline which meshes with the precondition of funds available. If a budget preparer's first draft produces a top sheet total that is higher or lower than the producer or production company have allowed, there are a few obvious alternatives. Increase the funding; reduce script requirements or shooting days; reduce the above-the-line or talent costs— which latter alternatives may entail a consequent loss of production value. These alternatives, however, are not direct concerns of the

---

[10] Money for the lead players was placed in escrow accounts and proof provided to SAG. Money for supporting cast salaries and fringes was sent directly to SAG and held in trust by them until proof of payment to their members was received. In contrast to escrow payment, this meant that supporting cast salaries were actually disbursed twice and that twice the amount allocated for such payments was tied up for twelve weeks before the trust payment was refunded by SAG. An alternate method of escrow was permitted by the DGA. Full salaries were paid in advance into a payroll service trust account from which weekly disbursements were made. Budget preparers anticipating such salary bonds should make budgetary allowances for deposits.

budget preparer. If the first draft budget is not satisfactory, it is a straightforward procedure for the budget preparer to revise it based on the producer's or production company's dictates. Adjustments may be made category by category until the total is right. This does not, however, mean right as opposed to wrong because value judgments are not part of the budget preparer's function. A production budget merely reveals whether the production of a given motion picture for a given amount of money in a given number of days is feasible. Discounting the well-published budgetary overruns of several recent productions as extraordinary, common sense suggests that an average production will remain feasible within a range of potential total costs. Accordingly, a project reasonably budgeted at $5 million might also be produced with some greater degree of difficulty for $4 million or with relative ease for $6 million. Perhaps the ultimate responsibility of the production manager in preparing a budget is to assess where within that range of feasibility a project falls and to communicate to the producer or production company just what degree of difficulty a budget contains. The reputation of a production manager may justifiably rise or fall with the accuracy of his or her assessments in this regard.

COST REPORTING

The accuracy of these assessments is, of course, subject to regular review. In episodic television using computerized reports, the production manager and series estimator or accountant often generate a daily cost run. In features, a weekly summary of cost broken down by major categories is usually sufficient. Whatever form is used and whether machine processed or hand prepared, it should conform to the final or revised budget in totals and account designations. The production manager as budget preparer must not only review the form and produce updated completion estimates but also must initiate any changes in operation to contain overruns. In this sense, the cost report supersedes the budget during the production phase, which underscores the need for compatibility between the two forms, as in the illustration from *The Creature Wasn't Nice.*

cc: Alain Silver
    Ned Topham   "THE CREATURE WASN'T NICE"
    Mark Haggard   COST REPORT on 6-12-81

BUDGET CATEGORY	COST TO DATE	EST. TO COMPLETE	EST. TOTAL	TOTAL BUDGET	OVER/ (UNDER)
STORY	25,000	---	25,000	25,000	---
CONTINUITY	571	---	571	2,026	(1,455)
PRODUCERS UNIT	39,894	17,596	52,490	52,490	---
DIRECTOR	48,056	---	48,056	48,170	(114)
CAST	244,544	---	244,544	254,241	(9,697)
EXTRAS	4,165	---	4,154	6,100	(1,935)
Total Above the Line	357,230	17,596	374,826	388,027	(13,201)
PRODUCTION STAFF	59,739	---	59,739	60,275	(536)
PRODUCTION OPERATING STAFF	163,379	---	163,379	149,160	14,219
SET CONSTRUCTION	109,198	---	109,198	99,750	9,448
SET. OPER. EXPENSES	77,962	---	77,962	69,586	8,376
CUTTING/FILM/LAB	51,432	105,000	156,432	163,250	(6,818)
MUSIC	8,057	25,000	33,057	32,000	1,057
SOUND	1,186	38,750	39,936	42,500	(2,564)
STUDIO TRANS.	23,219	---	23,219	17,625	5,594
LOCATION	4,624	---	4,624	4,000	624
STUDIO RENTALS	47,298	---	47,298	56,600	(9,302)
TESTS & RETAKES	0	2,500	2,500	2,500	---
PUBLICITY	4,409	500	4,909	4,100	809
MISCELLANEOUS	3,957	5,000	8,957	9,425	(468)
INSUR./TAXES/FEES	49,719	11,432	61,151	68,383	(7,232)
GENERAL OVERHEAD	56,589	19,500	76,089	82,448	(6,359)
Total Below the Line	660,768	207,682	868,450	861,602	6,848
Total Above the Line	357,230	17,596	374,826	388,027	(13,201)
TOTAL PRODUCTION	1,017,998	225,278	1,243,276	1,249,629	(6,353)
EXECUTIVE SUPERVISION & EXEC. PRODUCER EXPENSE	21,288				
TOTAL EXPENDITURES	1,039,286				

CASH ON HAND   4,877.78

SCRIPT BREAKDOWN

As has been noted, the chronology of budget preparation and script breakdown will depend on the most pressing needs of the preproduction. Although the budget may be prepared without a complete breakdown, ideally the script breakdown will come first. To return to the illustration from *The Creature Wasn't Nice*, the annotated page 39 from the actual breakdown script has been reproduced. From this script, information is then transferred to "breakdown sheets." Several formats are in use for the breakdown sheet (*see* Appendix I), but the differences are mainly in the manner in which the information is arrayed on the page. The function of the breakdown sheet, as the name implies, is to break down the information contained on the script page into its component physical requirements. These requirements are then regrouped on the breakdown page by department or other appropriate category.

Obviously, the starting point is the script page. In the illustration from *The Creature Wasn't Nice*, the page has been marked for breakdown. The bar lines drawn across it have divided the page into discrete scenes. Dashes have been used to underscore the characters appearing in each scene. Further underlining and slash marks have been used for key props and effects, both actual and possible (those with a question mark). Finally, words have been added in caps to indicate particulars which are not on the script page, but which the breakdown preparer knows are pertinent. In this case, the facts that the screening room is aboard the spaceship and the lighting is "day interior" and that "ATMOS" or atmosphere persons walking in the background will be used in the exterior scenes.

Although each scene begins with a verbal description of locale, the key to its identification from the beginning of preproduction to the completion of post-production will be its scene number. Because everyone in the cast, production crew, and editorial staff will organize their work according to scene numbers, these must remain constant. Insertions of new material as well as deletions or revisions of the final script made after its distribution to cast and crew could cause considerable confusion if its pages and scenes were renumbered. On the sample page, the existence of scene 50A reflects the addition of new material after the script's final draft: in this instance, a portion of what was originally scene 50, a street exterior, was broken off and relocated to a different exterior, City Mall. As scene 51 on the following page remains unchanged, the "A" suffix is used to accommodate the creation of a new discrete unit. However, even if scene 51 had been deleted, its number would not have been reassigned to scene 50A to avoid any possibility of confusion.[11]

The breakdown sheets illustrated here are those actually used with page 39 of the final draft of *The Creature Wasn't Nice*. This script page is noted on the top line after "Script Breakdown." Each breakdown sheet is assigned its own "BD PG#," which simply follows the sequence of the script. On line 3, the set description from the script is entered. The storyday is a concept not used by all breakdown preparers, it refers to the day on which the action occurs in the narrative time of the script and which may be significant for matching costumes, props, and the like. While scene 49 occurs on storyday 10, the subsequent scenes are part of a film-within-a-film and have no storyday per se.

The pages entries are actually a rough measure of running time. It is usual to relate the verbal length of the script to an anticipated running time for the finished film in minutes. The number of scenes is not a useful criterion as they vary in content within a given script. Nor are lines of dialogue a reliable indicator, although they contribute to the real length of the script as expressed by page-count. The progress of a production is normally gauged in terms of both scenes *and* pages photographed. The convention in the film industry is to equate one full page of script with approximately one minute of expected screen time. Since individual scenes may run more or less than a single page,

---

[11] Several methods are used to deal with revisions to the final shooting script and to underscore or highlight the changes. Scene numbers which are deleted are not removed entirely from the script but simply marked OMITTED. When entire pages are removed the numbers are run on from the last actual page, e.g., page 26 may become page 26–29 to indicate that three pages of material have been excised. Lines containing additions or deletions are flagged by the use of asterisks in the right margin. The pages on which these changes occur are normally printed on colored paper. A typical sequence of page colors beginning with a white final draft is blue, yellow, green, pink, goldenrod, etc., with the sequence of colors being repeated as needed. Additionally, revised pages may be dated in the upper right-hand corner: "Rev. 2/2/82," which further distinguishes them. Added pages and scene numbers typically use capital letter suffixes: "50A," "50B," "50C," etc. Because the script supervisor will also use letter suffixes to distinguish master scenes and coverage during actual shooting, some revised scripts employ letter prefixes ("A50," "B50"), but this is less common.

49. INT. SCREENING ROOM (SPACESHIP/DAY)   49.

2/8

Annie, John, Jameson, Rodzinski enter and sit in comfortable, modernistic chairs. Rodzinski takes the
chair next to Annie. She pointedly gets up and sits
on the other side of the room. Rodzinski starts to
move again. Jameson stops him with a glare.

              JAMESON
   Roll it, Max.

Max works?

The lights dim, as Max projects a prevue of coming
attractions. And we:

Projector?
Screen?

                      CUT TO:

ATMOS

50. EXT. CITY STREET (THE SCREEN) - DAY   50.

4/8

A modernistic car SCREECHES around a corner.

              NARRATOR
   He's back!

The car SCREECHES to a stop. *sound only/ tires smoke?*

              NARRATOR
   In his boldest, most exciting
   adventure yet!

Driver?

The door opens, and an OLD MAN of about eighty emerges
from the car.

              NARRATOR   *"Clint" wig*
   Clint Eastwood, as the dirtiest cop
   of them all in "The Dirty Cop Strikes
   Back!"

                      CUT TO:

50A. EXT. CITY MALL - DAY   *ATMOS*   50A.

2/8

The Old Man is walking down a causeway with a cane.

              NARRATOR
   He's rough. . .

A YOUNG PUNK walks by the Old Man and stops him.

             YOUNG PUNK
   Hey, you old fart. . .

The Old Man smacks the Punk in the face with his cane.
The stunned Punk falls to the ground. The Old Man smacks
him again.

                      (CONTINUED)

SCRIPT BREAKDOWN: p. 39   B.D. PG. # 45

TITLE: CREATURE   DIRECTOR: KIMMEL

SET   INT SPACESHIP –   (D)N   STORYDAY 10   PAGES 2/8
              SCREENING RM.

SCENE # 49

SYNOPSIS

        AT THE MOVIES

CAST	COS#	PROPERTY AND DRESSING	
1 ANNIE		SCREEN, CHAIRS	
2 JOHN			
3 JAMESON		WARDROBE	MAKEUP AND HAIR
4 RODZINSKI			
5		CAMERA	PROCESS & PLATES/EDITOR
6			
7			
8		ELECTRICAL/GRIP/CRANE	SPECIAL EFFECTS SMOKE FOR
9		LIGHTS DIM	PROJECTOR BEAM (?)
10		PROJECTOR BEAM (?)	MAX (?)
11		SOUND/MUSIC	LOCATION
12			
13		COMMUNICATION	PERMITS
14			
15		LIVESTOCK	SPECIAL NOTE
16			
17			
18		TRANSPORTATION AND VEHICLES	
19			
20			
21			
22			
23			
24			
25			

ATMOSPHERE: ⊖   STANDINS 4   REGULAR   BITS   WELFARE WORKER

SCRIPT BREAKDOWN: P. 39   B.D. PG. # 46

TITLE: CREATURE   DIRECTOR: KIMMEL

SET EXT CITY ST.   (D)/N   STORYDAY X   PAGES 4/8

SCENE # 50

SYNOPSIS   OLD MAN ARRIVES

CAST	COS#	PROPERTY AND DRESSING	
1		CANE	
2			
3		WARDROBE	MAKEUP AND HAIR POMPADOUR
4			WIG
5			
6		CAMERA	PROCESS & PLATES/EDITOR
7			
8 OLD MAN		ELECTRICAL/GRIP/CRANE	SPECIAL EFFECTS
9		CHAPMAN (?)	TIRES SMOKE (?)
10			
11		SOUND/MUSIC	LOCATION
12			CYPRESS J.C.
13		COMMUNICATION	PERMITS
14		WALKIE TALKIES/BULLHORN	
15		LIVESTOCK	SPECIAL NOTE
16			
17			
18		TRANSPORTATION AND VEHICLES	
19		MODERNISTIC CAR	
20			
21			
22 STUNT DRIVER (?)			
23			
24			
25			

ATMOSPHERE: TBA STANDINS 1   REGULAR   BITS   WELFARE WORKER

SCRIPT BREAKDOWN:	P 39-39A		B.D. PG.# 47

TITLE: CREATURE		DIRECTOR: KIMMEL

SET   EXT CITY MALL   (D)/N   STORYDAY   X   PAGES 4/8

SCENE #   50 A

SYNOPSIS   CANING A PUNK

CAST	COS#	PROPERTY AND DRESSING CANE	
1			
2		WARDROBE	MAKEUP AND HAIR
3		BREAKAWAY PUNK	POMPADOUR WIG
4		JACKET (?)	
5		CAMERA	PROCESS & PLATES/EDITOR
6			
7			
8 OLD MAN		ELECTRICAL/GRIP/CRANE	SPECIAL EFFECTS
9		CHAPMAN (?)	
10		SOUND/MUSIC	LOCATION
11			CYPRESS J.C.
12			
13 PUNK		COMMUNICATION	PERMITS
14		WALKIE TALKIES / BULLHORN	
15		LIVESTOCK	SPECIAL NOTE
16			
17		TRANSPORTATION AND VEHICLES	
18		ELECTRIC CART (BG)	
19			
20			
21			
22			
23			
24			
25			

ATMOSPHERE: TBA STANDINS 2   REGULAR   BITS   WELFARE WORKER their length is measured in pages and fractions of pages. The standard procedure in computing the page-count is to divide each page into eighths. This, rather than tenths or even fifths, may appear to be an unusual base number for fractioning. In practice, eighths are much more easily visualized, since they are the end product of a natural progression from halves and quarters. Also, since few scenes divide themselves perfectly into fractional units, the breakdown preparer must frequently round off the page-count. In the illustration, scene 49 is 2/8, scene 50 is 4/8, and scene 50A is 2/8. In terms of the physical space which these scenes actually occupy, the more accurate ratio would be 3/10, 4/10, and 3/10, respectively. The breakdown preparer could have made scenes 50 and 50A 3/8 of a page each. A certain amount of judgment is required, and the interior action and amount of voice-over dialogue suggests that scene 50 will physically occupy more running time.

In addition to its scene number(s), each unit on the breakdown sheet is also identified by a brief synopsis of its narrative content. The intent is not to describe the action in any detail but to find the particular moment or moments which distinguish the unit from the others in the script. Hence in the samples, "At the Movies," "Old Man Arrives," and "Caning a Punk" are events unique to scenes 49, 50, and 50A, respectively. It is unnecessary to add that in scene 49 Annie and Rodzinski have a problem with their seating arrangements, unless there should be other sequences "At the Movies" which need to be differentiated from scene 49.

The cast or characters are assigned numbers during the breakdown process. As with scene numbers, these should not be altered or reassigned as they will be used extensively later in the production board and on call sheets to identify the script's characters.[12] The assignment of the numbers is usually left to the discretion of the breakdown preparer. A few persons prefer to assign numbers chronologically according to the order in which characters appear in the script. Much more typical is an assignment based on the character's importance in the script. Another frequent consideration is the billing of the actor playing the part. This was the case with *The Creature Wasn't Nice,* where five parts of fairly equal script prominence were numbered to reflect the order of screen credit of the actors.

---

[12] If a character is the same but the name is changed for some reason (e.g., "Jameson" becomes "Johnson"), the cast number is retained.

The various boxes on the right side of the breakdown sheet are for script details which are peculiar to the scene being broken down. Obviously, such items as camera, sound, makeup, wardrobe, etc., will be needed for every scene filmed. It is only necessary for the breakdown preparer to isolate special or unusual elements. These elements are both explicit and implicit in the script. Scene 49 calls for action involving chairs and a screen. These are the minimum requirements of set dressing, from which the production designer must extrapolate. There is an explicit visual effect (the lights dimming) which must be accomplished by the set electricians. Implicit in this is the possibility that the beam of the movie projector should be visible and that smoke may be needed to enhance its visibility. As this need has not yet been confirmed by the director or producer, the entries are flagged with question marks. In the exterior scene 50, the breakdown preparer knows from the script that a cane and modernistic car will be required. At the time of script breakdown, the production manager had already learned that a special wig would be used on the actor portraying the old man. Still questionable are special effects, a stunt driver, and camera crane (Chapman). The breakdown preparer is also certain that there will be atmosphere visible in the scene's background. What remains to be determined (TBA) is how many.

When these question marks will be answered is uncertain. Some information such as the special wig had already been communicated to the production manager at the time of the breakdown. What the question marks indicate are decisions not yet made by the director and producer, but which the budget preparer cannot ignore. In fact, as the information is carried from notes on the script margins, to breakdown sheets, to shooting schedule, to call sheet, the decision may or may not be made at any point along the way. Most important from the standpoint of the production manager and assistant directors is that the process allows for various possibilities of which the technicians involved have been apprised. As long as this procedure is followed, the director and producer may delay their decision until the moment of filming, or until post-production, as a scene such as the car screeching to a halt may be filmed both with and without smoking tires and the final selection made during the editing process.

THE PRODUCTION BOARD

The Production Board is a graphic representation of the entire script. Cardboard strips encoded with information from the breakdown sheets are laid out in a flat frame. Once the production manager or other breakdown preparer has reduced the script information to breakdown sheets, it is possible to arrange the script's basic units into a shooting sequence. On a feature film, where the number of breakdown sheets is typically between one and three hundred, the physical problem of manipulating this unwieldy stack of letter-size sheets of paper is readily apparent. By transferring the most pertinent details of the breakdown sheets onto thin strips and arraying these within a frame, it is possible to view the entire film. Not only do the strips laid side by side present a continuum of the entire production; but they also constitute a flexible tool, for the strips can be rearranged at will to accommodate the changing needs of preproduction and production.

Each vertical strip is used to represent the continuous action of a master scene. This master may consist of one or several actual scene numbers from the script, as it is the usual practice to break down the script in terms of continuous action even if the writer has included individually numbered close-ups or cutaways in the script.[13] The strips are lined to form boxes for encoding information. A header on the left side of the board acts as a key or legend to the entries in the boxes. With the information filled in and laid out, the board resembles a mosaic, as each unit contributes to forming the whole picture.

In the illustration from *The Creature Wasn't Nice*, the top portion of the header has been amended to key the top five boxes on each strip. The first number entered is the page number of the breakdown sheet on which the strip is based. When the board is finalized, these will be used to rearrange the breakdown sheets for use in typing the shooting schedule. Other boxes are used to indicate day or

---

[13] As none of the master scenes in *The Creature Wasn't Nice* contained extensive indications of coverage, there are few examples of strips with more than one scene number. There are some, however, that reflect the director's preproduction decision to shoot certain establishing shots or reoccurring action from the same angles. It may be noted that some designations are for a portion of a scene only, e.g., "98 pt." This commonly refers to action which overlaps two sets either because of intercutting (a frequently seen example would be a telephone conversation) or actual set design.

Production Board #2

Title: "THE CREATURE WASN'T NICE"
Director: BRUCE KIMMEL
Producer: MARK HAGGARD
Asst. Dir.:

Script Dated 2/24/81

Date / BREAKDOWN PAGE	49	47	46	48	47A	2	59	87	66	5	18	41	52	81	10	43
Day or Nite	D	D	D	D	D											
Period PAGES	7/	4/	4/	1/	6/	1/	2/	1/	1/	14/	1/	1/	1/	1/	2/	7/
Sequence																
Prod. No. SCENE #	53	50A	50	52	51	2	70 (98PT)	103 (48PT)	76PT	5	19	43	62	96	10	45 PT
Scene Description	EXT STREET	EXT CITY MALL	EXT STREET	EXT STREET	INT BOARD ROOM / 1ST DAY	INT CORRIDOR (ESTABLISH)	INT CORRIDOR	INT CORRIDOR 12	INT CORRIDOR	INT COCKPIT	INT COCKPIT	INT COCKPIT	INT COCKPIT	INT COCKPIT	INT CORRIDOR	INT TALK SHOW

Character	Artist	No.	49	47	46	48	47A	2	59	87	66	5	18	41	52	81	10	43
ANNIE	CINDY WILLIAMS	1																
JOHN	BRUCE KIMMEL	2																2
JAMESON	LESLIE NIELSEN	3										3	3	3	3			
RODZINSKI		4										4	4	4				
DR. STARK	PATRICK MACNEE	5																
CREATURE		6								6	6							
MAX (V.O.)	BRODERICK CRAWFORD	7																
OLD MAN	PAUL BRINEGAR	8	8	8	8	8	8											
LINDA		9																9
GRACE		10																10
MARGIE	CAROL ANN WILLIAMS	11																11
BOARD MEMBER	KEN TOBEY	12					12											
PUNK		13		13														
HOOD #1		14	14															
#2		15	15															
#3		16	16															
#4	RON BURKE	17	17															
PERSON	MARK HAMMILL	18																
NARRATOR (V.O.)		19	19vo	19vo	19vo	19vo												
NEWS ANNOUNCER (V.O.)		20																
BODY TRANS.		21																21
ATMOSPHERE – BITS		22				1	4											
– GENERAL		23	12	12	12													
DRIVER		24		X														
ADD'L CAMERA		25																
VIDEO PLAYBCK		26													X			
CART/CARS		27	X		X	X												
CRANE		28	X		X													
PLAYBACK		29																
FX: VERTIGO		30																
SHUTTLE (MINIATURE)		31																
COMPUTER		32																
COCKPIT LIGHTS		33										33	33			33		
A) BLENBER B) 2001		34																
A) DISCO LGTS B) FLYING		35																
A) PLANET B) TERRAIN		36																
A) WIRES B) MATTE		37																
		38																
		39																
		40																
Notes			CUTS OFF WOODS	CANING A PUNK	OLD MAN ARRIVES	CHECKS OUT ANOTHER PUNK	OLD MAN ARGUES	ESTABLISHING	REESTABLISH	MORE BLOCKING 30A	CREACH. EATS	ESTABLISH CO-PILOTS	REESTABLISH	JAMESON & ROD. TRADE JIBES	JAMESON PUKES	REESTABLISH	MOP BALLET	INTRO THE BODY TRANSPLANT

Scene	Pages	Sc.	Set	Cast	Other	Description
63	1 4	73B PT 73C	INT TALK SHOW	9, 10, 11		HAPPY NEWS AGAIN
			2ND DAY			
12	1 6	12	INT COCKPIT	1, 3	33	ANNIE TALKS TO JAMESON
8	3 2	8	INT ANNIE'S OFFICE	1, 4		ROD. MAKES A PLAY
19	1/	20	INT ANNIE'S OFFICE	1		ESTABLISH
50	2 0	57	INT ANNIE'S OFFICE	1, 5		STARKS IS FEARFUL
83	1 3	99	INT ANNIE'S OFFICE	1, 2		FINDING MUSIC
			3RD DAY			
67	1 6	77	INT CORRIDOR 12	1, 2, 3, 4		CAPTURING THE CREATURE
68	2 2	79	INT OBSERVATION ROOM	1, 2, 3, 4, 5, [6]		OBSERVING CREACH.
69	5 3	80	INT OBSERVATION ROOM	1, 2, 3, 4, 5, 6	X, X	IT SINGS & EATS! 57A
72	3/	83	INT OBSERVATION ROOM	1, 2, 3, 4		IT'S ESCAPED
			4TH DAY			
			5TH DAY			
80	1/	95	INT MAIN CONTROL ROOM			REESTABLISH
4	4/	4	INT MAIN CONTROL RM.	1, 2	32	ESTABLISH ANNIE AND JOHN
17	1/	18	INT MAIN CONTROL RM.	5		REESTABLISH
51	2 1	59	INT MAIN CONTROL ROOM	1, 2, 3, 4, 5		CAUCUS ABOUT CREATURE
56	2 3	67	INT MAIN CONTROL ROOM	1, 2, 3, 4, 5		CHECK-OUT THE NOISE
			6TH DAY			
26	1 2	27, 29 PT 31, 34	INT SHUTTLE	1, 2, 3, 4, 5		ROUND-TRIP TO PLANET
53	1/	63	INT RODZINSKI'S ROOM	4		ROD SLEEPS
57	7 0	68	INT LONG CORRIDOR	1, 2, 3, 4, 5, [6]		ENTER THE CREATURE
			7TH DAY			
			8TH DAY			
82	1/	97	INT REC ROOM			REESTABLISH
39	1 0	41	INT REC ROOM	2		JOHN PLAYS WITH HIMSELF
101	1/	23B	INT REC ROOM	1, 2, 3, 4, 5		WINDEXING.
24	2 2	25	INT REC ROOM	1, 2, 3, 4, 5		A TOAST!
64	3 3	75	INT REC ROOM	1, 2, 3, 4, 5, [6]		DISCUSS CREACH.
			9TH DAY			
15	6/	15	INT BACKSTAGE	1, 7	32	ANNIE CHANGES

Production strip board / cross-plot chart.

	INT REC ROOM	INT REC ROOM	INT REC ROOM	INT ENGINE ROOM	INT CORRIDOR (T)	INT CORRIDOR (T)	INT SOLARIUM	INT MUSIC LIBRARY	INT MUSIC LIBRARY	INT NEW CRAFT	EXT PLANET	INT COMP. ROOM	INT COMP. ROOM	INT COMP. ROOM	INT COMP. ROOM	INT COMP. ROOM	INT COMP. ROOM	INT COMP. ROOM	INT ANOTHER CORRIDOR	INT CORRIDOR	INT CORRIDOR	INT CORRIDOR 3
Scene #	14	42	44	55	20	70	62	84	86	98	30	3	21	11	54	88	65	73	60	74	76	78
Pages	6¾	2/	4⁴	1/	1/	2⁰	1⁴	1²	1/	1²	5⁴	2/	6/	2/	3/	1⁶	1⁴	1³	1/	1/	2/	6/
Scene #	14,148 16,16A	45 PT	48	66	21	81 (73,75A,75B PT)	—	100,102	104	115,116	32,33	94 (3,23PT)	22,23PT	11	64	105,76PT	84	—	71,98PT	86	88	90
Cast	1	1	1			1	1	1								1	1	1				
Cast	2	2	2	2	2	2		2							2	2	2	2				
Cast	3	3	3	3	3											3	3		3	3	3	
Cast	4	4	4		4	4										4	4		4	4	4	
Cast	5	5	5									5	5			5						
Cast						6			6	6												6
Cast														7	7	7	7					
X	X						X									X						
X	NIKE X							X	X													
32												32	32	32	32	32	32	32				

18 (under INT NEW CRAFT)

Descriptions:
- SHOWTIME!
- ANNIE WATCHES NEWS (34A, 35A)
- SYNTHETIC DINNER
- JOHN QUIVERS (32B)
- TRASH
- EULOGIZE STARK
- ANNIE AND ROD MEET THE CREATURE
- FINISH REHEARSING
- CREATURE HITS BUTTON
- NEW ENCOUNTER
- PLANET / RUINS (35B, 36B)
- ESTABLISHING
- STARK PLOTS
- STARK COMPUTES
- MAX TELLS JOHN
- CONFRONTATION
- CREACH. EATS CAMERA
- SPLIT UP TO LOOK
- REESTABLISH
- CREEPING DOWN CORRIDOR
- TRACKING CREACH
- CREACH ATTACKS

Day markers: 10TH DAY, 11TH DAY, 12TH DAY, 13TH DAY, 14TH DAY, 15TH DAY, MEMORIAL DAY — HOLIDAY, 16TH DAY.

PICK-UPS AS NEEDED

Production Strip Board — Scene Breakdown

Scene	78A	33	35	36	75	77	78/80		85	89	90	91		92	93	94			INT CORRIDOR	
Pages	2/	10/	4/	1/	7/	14/	6/		1/	12	1/	3/		1⅛	32	1/			7	
	91	37,40,43,45,62	58	65	87	89/91	78/54		101	106	107	108		109	111	112			7	
Set	INT CORRIDOR 3	INT CORRIDOR	INT CORRIDOR (BY VAULT)	INT CORRIDOR (BY VAULT)	INT OTHER CORRIDOR 13	INT OTHER CORRIDOR 14	INT SCREENING ROOM	18th DAY	INT CORRIDOR	INT CORRIDOR 14	INT OTHER CORRIDOR 13	INT ANOTHER CORRIDOR	19th DAY	INT AIRLOCK AREA	INT AIRLOCK AREA	INT CORRIDOR	20th DAY / 21st DAY		INT CORRIDOR	22nd DAY

17th DAY

Cast / action:

Action	78A	33	35	36	75	77	78/80	85	89	90	91	92	93	94
FIND REMAINS	1		1	1	1	1	1		1	1	1	1	1	1
STARK ENTERS VAULT	2				2	2	2		2	2	2	2	2	2
CREATURE SCREAMS							3							
ANNIE CHECKS OUT VAULT							4							
TRACKING CREACH		5	5											
DO THEY WANT TO FIND HIM								6	6				6	
AT THE MOVIES							?X							
LOOKING TO EAT														
RUNNING														
STILL RUNNING														
LOST HIM.														
SETTING THE TRAP												X	X	
SONG & DANCE.													X	
ANNIE CARRIES JOHN														

34B

night lighting, page-count, and scene number(s).[14] The other significant line in the top portion of the header is the script date entry, which
should be updated to indicate whether the most recent revisions have
been taken into account. In theory, all the lines below are available
for designating the characters, i.e., all the speaking parts. In the case
of *The Creature Wasn't Nice,* which has only twenty such parts,
there are a number of lines left over. In practice, even with forty or
more characters entries, most board preparers prefer to reserve some
of these lines for other information.[15] In the illustration, two lines
are used for atmosphere. The numbers in the boxes indicate how many
people will be used for *Bits* who will figure prominently and for
general background. The remaining lines indicate various pieces of
supplementary equipment and special effects.

Individual production managers and assistant directors will cus-
tomize their production boards to reflect both the needs of a particular
production and the requirements which they personally consider most
significant. It is not uncommon for both the production manager and
first assistant director to prepare boards, although it is the formal job
function of only the first assistant. The discrepancies between boards
prepared independently underscore the wide range of individual
methods. In the case of *The Creature Wasn't Nice,* there was only one
production board which the production manager and assistant director
prepared in collaboration. There are some interesting idiosyncrasies.
For example, there are colored boxes (which, unfortunately, in a
black-and-white reproduction appear as various shades of gray) for
all the strips that designate action in a spaceship corridor. The script
refers to several levels and kinds of corridors within the spaceship,
but only one major corridor with two wings was actually constructed
on a sound stage. It was decided early in preproduction that the
corridors would be redressed by changing certain wall sections and
hanging fixtures. The production designer devised a method of accen-
tuating the difference between levels by using colored signs and

---

[14] Since most of *The Creature Wasn't Nice* is located in the perpetual
"day" of a spaceship interior, most of these boxes are blank. An alternative
to the "D" or "N" entry is the use of colored strips which will be discussed
in detail later in the text.

[15] Lines may be economized by doubling over. For example, the board
preparer may place several characters on line 20 by numbering them 20A,
20B, 20C, etc.

decorative wall strips. Three fictional levels were indicated by the colors blue, green, and orange. The board preparers used the indications in the script and notes from the director to determine the appropriate color for each scene. Colored pens quickly provided an unmistakable reference on each board strip. This simple procedure became invaluable, as it was used numerous times on the set by the director and first assistant to verify quickly whether the large percentage of scenes situated in corridors were properly color-coded.

There are two sizes of board strips in current use: 15 inches and 18¼ inches high. The widths vary from 3/16 to 5/16 inches. Many board preparers use colored strips for quick identification of lighting and location. There is no standard code, but the four most common are: white to indicate interior day, yellow to indicate exterior day, blue to indicate exterior night, and green to indicate interior night.[16] Various kinds of black strips may serve as dividers and may have white areas for marking the shooting day. The boards themselves have no standard size. Older varieties consist of two wide, wooden panels hinged at one edge. More recently, several suppliers have been selling lightweight boards of vinyl-covered cardboard. Most of these feature a series of two to twelve folding panels, each ten inches wide and capable of accommodating thirty strips.

Each strip, like the breakdown sheet from which it was derived, begins with a discrete unit. These may be master scenes which run for several pages or an establishing shot that barely qualifies as an eighth of a page. The most fundamental concept remains that of continuous action from the same camera angle. The board preparer may well be aware that the director plans for coverage of a given master with dozens of supplementary angles. The purpose of the production board, however, is to continue the process of the breakdown sheet in extracting and encapsulating the action of the script scenes, i.e., the narrative content and not the proposed visual treatment. Accordingly, the board preparer may wish to condense and reorganize some of the breakdown sheet information. For example, scene 49, which has already been discussed, takes place in the screening room.

---

[16] As with the script page color codes, methods differ. The Universal Production Guide lists that studio's strip codes as: white for stage, yellow for backlot, light green for local location, dark green for distant location, blue for blue screen. The distinction between day and night is made solely by using "D" and "N"—which is easier for a call sheet preparer to misread or overlook.

In working with the breakdown pages and script, the board preparers noted another scene which occurred in the same set:

                                                         CUT BACK TO:
54.   INT. SCREENING ROOM   54.

    They continue watching. Rodzinski changes seats, so that he is again sitting next to Annie.

                RODZINSKI
             Hi, baby.

    Annie gets up and changes seats.

                                                         (CONTINUED)

As the excerpt reveals, scene 54 may be considered part of a continuous action beginning with scene 49 and interrupted by cutaways to the screen. Although such an interruption may suggest separate treatment of scenes 49 and 54 on the breakdown sheets, it is quite reasonable to combine them on one board strip. The result is shown on page 49.

The reader may note that the board preparers have indicated a question regarding the video playback. This carries over from the notes made by the production manager on the margin of page 39 and carries over onto the breakdown sheets. Conversations between the director and first assistant before the board preparation have resolved that no special effects will involve "Max," the computer, and that the prevue will not be projected but may be seen on a television screen. (Ultimately, after the scenes which constitute the prevue had been filmed and viewed in dailies, the director decided they would not be tied in to the actors in the screening room, and no video playback was required.) The reader may also notice that the effect of dimming the lights is not coded onto the strip, which again indicates a conscious choice by the board preparers. The production manager had determined after breaking down the script, but before the board preparation, that several dimmer panels would be part of the stage electrical equipment package and no additional equipment would be needed for a simple dimming effect. In keeping with the concept of avoiding unnecessary clutter in strip data, the board preparers decided that notation of the lighting effect on the breakdown sheets and subsequent shooting schedule would be sufficient.

45	Breakdown sheets 45 and 51
51	
3/	6/8 page (sc. 49, 2/8 + sc. 54, 4/8)
49 54	Script scenes 49 and 54
INT SCREENING ROOM	The setting is INT. SCREENING ROOM
1	Characters
2	1. Annie
3	2. John
4	3. Jameson
	4. Rodzinski
~~	(No atmosphere, vehicles, etc., in these scenes)
?X	"X" in box #26 indicates possible use of the item listed in Header line #26: a video playback machine
AT THE MOVIES	Brief description of action: AT THE MOVIES

The next breakdown sheet illustrated was for scene 50. It is one of the few day exteriors in the shooting script and was transposed onto a yellow strip. The board preparers examined other breakdown pages for "EXT. STREET" but determined from script and director indications that these were clearly discontinuous action and different setups. Accordingly, the strip for scene 50 was drawn as follows:

Breakdown sheet 46
A Day scene (also indicated by yellow strip)
4/8 page in length

Scene 50

The setting is EXT. STREET

Characters:
8. Old Man

19. Narrator. The subscript "vo" indicates "voice-over." [This is a reference to a narration to be recorded in preproduction and to be taken into account in timing the action.]
12 persons will be used as "General Atmos." Confirming the need for a driver for the Modernistic Car noted with a question mark on the breakdown sheet

The
Modernistic
Car

A camera crane may be required

Brief description of action: OLD MAN ARRIVES

The reader may notice several differences between the breakdown sheet and strip information for scene 50. The location, prop, and communication requirements do not figure in the strip, as they will be adequately served by notation on the shooting schedule. After discussion with the director, the possible effect of tires smoking is likely to be deleted and is also not transposed. By the time of board preparation, it had been determined that the actor's wig would be taken from the wig box of the hairstylist hired for the production. As with the dimmer in scene 49, the board preparers decided not to clutter the strip with an unnecessary note to this effect. On the other hand, what may seem to be clutter, i.e., the listing of "19_{vo}" to indicate a voice-over narration which the board preparers know will have already been recorded, is included on the strip in the interests of clarity. The narrator figures prominently in the script, and there is no indication on those pages that the narration will be strictly voice-over. By noting this on the breakdown sheet, board, and later shooting schedule and call sheet, the production manager and assistant director are providing a reminder for any cast or crew who might be confused by the script's indication that neither the narrator nor his voice will be present for the location filming. The operative method in the preparation and updating of the production board should be one of expedient and positive annotation. This means that the board preparer, whether production manager or first assistant, must reanalyze the raw data of the script and the refined data of the breakdown sheet to reduce them further in both a logical and economical fashion. Although this process is essentially subjective, the underlying assumptions are commonly held by most industry professionals. The final illustration is scene 50A:

Again the emphasis is consistently on clarity and economy. The strip should contain only a clearly encoded representation of the content and basic physical requirements of the scene to be filmed.

SCHEDULING

Once the entire script has been broken down and transposed to strips, the first assistant in conjunction with both director and production manager is responsible for ordering the strips into a sequence of shooting days. *The Creature Wasn't Nice* is represented by slightly more than one hundred strips, which fall within the average range

47	Breakdown sheet 47
D	A Day scene
4/	4/8 page in length
50A	Scene 50A
EXT CITY MALL	The setting is EXT. CITY MALL
	Characters:
8	8. Old Man
13	13. Punk
19 vo	19. Narrator—vo only
12	12 persons to work as General Atmosphere
?X	Possible camera crane
CANING A PUNK	Brief description: CANING A PUNK

for features. The twenty-four shooting days allocated for production were less than most feature productions. However, the budget for *The Creature Wasn't Nice* was much closer to that of a typical movie-of-the-week, which is normally shot in sixteen to twenty days.

The basic logistical aim of board preparation is to arrange the finished strips into groups designating the content and sequence of the shooting days. A gifted few may be able to accomplish this by organizing the strips as they are lettered. Most board preparers require intermediate stages. Throughout this discussion, the reader may find it informative to refer back to the three complete boards which serve as illustrations and which represent three phases of the production process. The board already reproduced (Board #2) was the final pre-production arrangement for *The Creature Wasn't Nice*. The next example (Board #1) is an antecedent arrangement reflecting the first rough grouping of the scene strips. The last example (Board #3) will be of the production board at the end of actual shooting which retains the alterations and rearrangements of the strips made during the course of filming.

A common method for organizing the board is situational reduction. The strips are clustered according to common elements then segregated according to particular elements, from large clusters to small, from general to specific. The broadest divisions might be between distant and local locations or between exterior and interior scenes. A large subgroup such as exteriors may then be separated into day and night.[17] The usual end result of these initial divisions is, as illustrated, a collation of strips into units or clusters distinguished by setting. In the case of *The Creature Wasn't Nice*, this process yields two dozen discrete units of one to seventeen strips isolated according to set. (The four INT. CORRIDOR groups are actually divided according to the color code discussed earlier.) Within groups, the arrangement is in rough script continuity, as shooting sets in continuity is usually preferred unless other considerations indicate against it. Occasionally, director and cast may insist on working in continuity for the sake of performances.

Continuity provides a primary alignment to which other factors may be applied. One of the keys is the concept of "pages per day." Simply put, this is the average number of script pages which must be filmed each day in order to finish within the allotted time. In the case of *The Creature Wasn't Nice*, there were 94 6/8 pages to be filmed in 24 days or an average of four pages per day (94 6/8 divided

---

[17] This discounts such techniques as day-for-night photography. Night interiors, of course, are simply a matter of adjusting the lighting whether on a soundstage or practical set.

Production Board #1

Title "The Creature Wasn't Nice"
Director Bruce Kimmel
Producer Mark Haggard
Asst. Dir.

Script Dated 2/24/81

			EXT CITY MALL	EXT STREET	EXT STREET	EXT STREET	INT BOARD ROOM	INT TALK SHOW	INT TALK SHOW	INT SCREENING ROOM	INT SOLARIUM	INT ENGINE ROOM	INT MUSIC LIBRARY	INT MUSIC LIBRARY	INT COCKPIT	INT COCKPIT
Date BREAKDOWN PAGE			47	46	48	49	47A	43	63	47/50	62	55	84	86	5	12
Day or Nite			D	D	D	D	D									
Period PAGES			4/	4/	1/	7/	6/	7/	1¼	6/	1¼	1/	1⅜	1/	1⅛	1⅝
Sequence											73					
Prod. No. SCENE #			50A	50	52	53	51	45 PT	73B PT 73C	49/54	62 75A 75B PT	66	100 102	104	5	12
Character	Artist	No.														
ANNIE		1								1	1		1			1
JOHN		2								2		2	2			
JAMESON		3								3					3	3
RODZINSKI		4								4	4				4	
DR. STARK		5														
CREATURE		6									6			6		
MAX (V.O.)		7														
OLD MAN		8	8	8	8	8	8									
LINDA		9						9	9							
GRACE		10						10	10							
MARGIE		11						11	11							
BOARD MEMBER		12					12									
PUNK		13	13													
HOOD #1		14				14										
#2		15				15										
#3		16				16										
#4		17				17										
PERSON		18														
NARRATOR (V.O.)		19	19ᵥₐ	19ᵥₒ	19ᵥₒ	19ᵥₒ										
NEWS ANNOUNCER (V.O.)		20														
BODY TRANS.		21						21								
ATMOSPHERE – BITS		22			1		4									
– GENERAL		23	12	12		12										
DRIVER		24	X													
ADD'L CAMERA		25														
VIDEO PLAYBCK		26								?X	X					
CART/CARS		27		X	X	X										
CRANE		28	?X	X												
PLAYBACK		29											X	X		
FX: VERTIGO		30														
SHUTTLE (MINIATURE)		31														
COMPUTER		32														
COCKPIT LIGHTS		33													33	33
A) BLENDER B) 2001		34														
A) DISCO LGTS B) FLYING		35														
A) PLANET B) TERRAIN		36														
A) WIRES B) MATTE		37														
		38														
		39														
		40														

Column notes (handwritten, bottom):
- COMING A PUNK
- OLD MAN ARRIVES
- CHECKS OUT ANOTHER PUNK
- CUTS OFF HOODS
- OLD MAN ARGUES
- INTRO THE BODY TRANSPLANT
- HAPPY WEELS AGAIN
- AT THE MOVIES
- ANNIE AND ROD MEET THE CREATURE
- JOHN QUIVERS
- FINISH REHEARSING
- CREATURE HITS BUTTON
- ESTABLISH CO-PILOTS
- ANNIE TALKS TO JAMESON

52	81	41	18	8	19	50	83	80	4	17	51	56	26	68	69	72	53	15	14	101	24	39	42	44	64
1/	1/	1/	1/	32	1/	20	13	1/	4/	1/	21	23	12 / 27	22	53	3/	1/	63	63	1/	22	12	2/	44	33
62	96	43	19	8	20	57	99	95	4	18	59	67	24PT 31 34	79	80	83	63	15	14 148 16 16A	23B	25	41	45 PT	48	75
INT COCKPIT	INT COCKPIT	INT COCKPIT	INT COCKPIT	INT ANNIE'S OFFICE	INT ANNIE'S OFFICE	INT ANNIE'S OFFICE	INT ANNIE'S OFFICE	INT MAIN CONTROL ROOM	INT MAIN CONTROL RM.	INT MAIN CONTROL RM.	INT MAIN CONTROL ROOM	INT MAIN CONTROL ROOM	INT SHUTTLE	INT OBSERVATION ROOM	INT OBSERVATION ROOM	INT OBSERVATION ROOM	INT RODZINSKI'S ROOM	INT BACKSTAGE	INT REC ROOM	INT REC ROOM	INT REC ROOM	INT REC ROOM	INT REC ROOM	INT REC ROOM	INT REC ROOM

Cast numbers:

				1	1	1			1		1	1	1	1	1	1		1	1	1	1			1	1
							2		2		2	2	2	2	2	2			2	2	2	2		2	2
3		3	3								3	3	3	3	3	3			3	3	3			3	3
		4	4	4							4	4	4	4	4	4	4		4	4	4			4	4
					5					5	5	5	5	5	5				5	5	5			5	5
														6	6										6
																		7							

X marks row: 52 → X; OBSERVATION ROOM (68) → X; BACKSTAGE (15) → X; REC ROOM (42) → X

NIKE X — REC ROOM (14); OBSERVATION ROOM (68) → X

32 — (MAIN CONTROL 80); 32 — (BACKSTAGE 15)

33 — (COCKPIT 81); 33 — (COCKPIT 18)

34A 35A — (REC ROOM 14)

Scene descriptions:
- JAMESON POWERS
- REESTABLISH
- JAMESON & ROD. TARDE TUBES
- REESTABLISH
- ROD. MAKES A PLAY
- ESTABLISH
- STARKS IS FEARFUL
- FINDING MUSIC
- REESTABLISH
- ESTABLISH ANNIE AND JOHN
- REESTABLISH
- CAUCUS ABOUT CREATURE
- CHECK-OUT THE NOISE
- ROUND-TRIP TO PLANET
- OBSERVING CREACH.
- 37A IT SINGS / EATS!
- 37B ESCAPED
- ROD SLEEPS
- ANNIE CHANGES
- SHOWTIME!
- UNWIDEXING.
- A TOAST!
- JOHN PLAYS WITH HIMSELF
- ANNIE WATCHES NEWS
- SYNTHETIC DINNER
- DISCUSS CREACH.

Scene	Pages	Script page	Set	Cast	Other	Description
82	1/	97	INT REC ROOM			REESTABLISH
3	2/	3, 94	INT COMPUTER ROOM		32	ESTABLISHING
21	6/	22, 23PT	INT COMPUTER ROOM	5	32	STARK PLOTS
11	2/	11	INT COMPUTER ROOM	5	32	STARK COMPUTES
54	3/	64	INT COMPUTER ROOM	2, 7	32	MAX TELLS JOHN
88	16	105	INT COMPUTER ROOM	1, 2, 7	32	CONFRONTATION
65	14	76PT	INT COMPUTER ROOM	1, 2, 3, 4, 5, 7	X, 32	CREACH. EATS CAMERA
73	13	84	INT COMPUTER ROOM	1, 2, 3, 4, 7	32	SPLIT UP TO LOOK
30	54	32, 33	EXT. PLANET	1, 2, 3, 4, 5	X, 35B, 36B	PLANET HIJINKS
93	32	111	INT AIRLOCK AREA	1, 2, 6	X, X	SONG & DANCE.
92	11	109	INT AIRLOCK AREA	1, 2	X	SETTING THE TRAP.
20	1/	21	INT CORRIDOR (T)	2, 3		TRASH
70	20	81	INT CORRIDOR (T)	1, 2, 3, 4		EULOGIZE STARK
87	1/	103	INT CORRIDOR	6		MORE LOOKING
2	1/	2	INT CORRIDOR (ESTABLISH)			ESTABLISHING
85	1/	101	INT CORRIDOR	6		LOOKING TO EAT
59	2/	70, 98PT	INT CORRIDOR			REESTABLISH
10	2/	10	INT CORRIDOR	2		MOP BALLET
66	1/	76PT, 98PT	INT CORRIDOR 12	6		CREACH. EATS
67	16	77	INT CORRIDOR 12	1, 2, 3, 4, 5, 6		CAPTURING THE CREATURE
33	10/	37, 40, 44, 47, 56, 60	INT CORRIDOR	5		STARK ENTERS VAULT
35	4/	58	INT CORRIDOR (BY VAULT)	1, 5		CREATURE SCREAMS
36	1/	65	INT CORRIDOR (BY VAULT)	1		ANNIE CHECKS OUT VAULT
57	70	68	INT LONG CORRIDOR	1, 2, 3, 4, 5, 6		ENTER THE CREATURE
60	1/	71, 98PT	INT ANOTHER CORRIDOR			REESTABLISH
91	3/	108	INT ANOTHER CORRIDOR	1, 2		LOST HIM.

Production strip board / scene breakdown sheet

Top No.	(/)	Bottom No.	Location	Description	Marked cells
74	1/	86	INT CORRIDOR	CREEPING DOWN CORRIDOR	3, 4
76	2/	88	INT CORRIDOR	TRACKING CREACH	1, 2, 3, 4
94	1/	112	INT CORRIDOR	ALINE CARRIES JOHN	1, 2
175	7/	87	INT OTHER CORRIDOR 13	TRACKING CREACH	1, 2
90	1/	107	INT OTHER CORRIDOR 13	STILL RUNNING.	1, 2
77	14/	89/9/7	INT OTHER CORRIDOR 14	DO THEY WANT TO FIND HIM	1, 2
89	12	106	INT CORRIDOR 14	RUNNING	1, 2, 3(vo), 4(vo)
79A	6/	91A	INT TWO CORRIDORS	FIND GUARDIANS HURRYING	1, 2, 6
78A	2/	91	INT CORRIDOR 3	FIND REMAINS	
78	6/	90	INT CORRIDOR 3	CREACH ATTACKS	3, 4, 6
7	2/	7	INT CORRIDOR	ZOO WALK (34B)	2
98	10	115, 116	INT NEW CRAFT	NEW ENCOUNTER	6, 18
			Spec. Effects in Post-Prod.		
1	16	1	EXT SPACE	VERTIGO RUN-BY	3 vo, 4 vo (4)
13	2/	13	EXT SPACE	SPACEWALK BY POD.	30
16	1/	17	EXT SPACE	RUN-BY	30
23	1/	24	EXT SPACE	HEADING FOR PLANET (36A)	30
25	1/	26	EXT SPACE	RUN-BY	30
28	1/	28	EXT SPACE	SHUTTLE DISENGAGES	30, 31
27	1/	29 PT	EXT PLANET	HEADING FOR SURFACE	31
29	1/	30	EXT PLANET	SHUTTLE LANDS (36A)(36B)	31
31	1/	35	EXT PLANET	SHUTTLE TAKES OFF (36B)	30, 31
32	1/	96	EXT SPACE	RETURNING TO SHIP	30
40	7/	46, 55, 61, 74, 78, 83, 93	EXT SPACE	STATIC RUN-BYS	1 vo, 2 vo, 7 vo, 30
96	4/	114	EXT SPACE	VERTIGO HEADS OFF	
99	1/	117	EXT SPACE	END TITLES. STARS.	

by 24 = 3.95). As the shooting order is determined, this average page-count serves as a rough minimum of work which must be accomplished each day.

Once the strips have been grouped by set, the production manager and first assistant must confront all the interrelating production elements and arrive at the best working sequence for the entire production board. The next step is to attempt to isolate one or more specific items in each group that may dominate the other factors and suggest a logical order of filming. The first panel of sample Board #1 is made up of short scenes which span fifteen different settings. The EXT. STREET scenes, which appear darker because they are on yellow strips, are the only exterior locations. The EXT. PLANET scenes were actually shot on a sound stage; they appear darker because they are on a green strip signifying that they will be shot on a different soundstage from the other studio work. The details of these isolated strips are as follows:

- 1 2/8 pages of EXT. STREET—locations representing a modernistic city. No principal actors.
- 6/8 page of INT. BOARD ROOM—no principal actors. This may be shot on location or on stage.
- 5 4/8 pages of EXT. PLANET—To be shot on Stage #8. All principal actors.
- 2/8 page of INT. CORRIDOR—A special effect rig in which the actor will walk on the walls and ceiling.
- 2/8 page EXT. SPACE—To be shot on Stage #11. A special effect to simulate floating in space.
- 2 3/8 pages of INT. TALK SHOW—no principal actors. May be shot on stage or location.

Except for the EXT. PLANET, none of the setting groups in the first panel are long enough to satisfy the four-page average day. The board preparer must therefore anticipate that they will be melded with other work to form complete days.

At this point in board preparation, the production manager and first assistant were already aware that all of the remaining strips representing various spaceship interiors would be shot on the same soundstage (#11). Not having to consider numerous stage moves simplifies the task of scheduling. The board preparers continued by considering the various scenes occurring in the same set. For example, the REC. ROOM group consists of nine strips representing nine master scenes. Their total page count is 18 3/8 pages which, divided by the day average, implies roughly four days of work. These strips contain the following information:

Scene Numbers	Page-count	Cast	Action	Production Requirements
14, 14B 16, 16A	6 3/8	1,2,3,4,5	Showtime!	crane, additional camera, playback, disco lights, exploding blender
25	2 —	1,2,3,4,5	A toast	— 0 —
41	1	2	John plays himself	— 0 —
75	3 3/8	1,2,3,4,5,6	Discuss Creach	— 0 —
97	1/8	— 0 —	Establishing shot	— 0 —
23B	1/8	1,2,3,4,5	Windexing	harness
45pt	2/8	1	Annie watches news	video playback
48	4 4/8	1,2,3,4,5	Synthetic dinner	— 0 —
113	5/8	1,2,6	The kiss	FX table
	18 3/8			

The longest master scene is 6 3/8 pages and likely to be more than a day's work. The scripted action, which describes a talent show put on by the spaceship's crew including a monologue, a cooking lesson, and a song-and-dance routine, is complex and likely to require more time than the average. Additionally, the director's request for a second camera, a stage crane, and disco lights promise technical complications on top of the script requirement of sound playback for the song. Finally, the director has indicated a desire to film lengthy reaction shots of the crew members who were not performers in the talent show. All this suggests two difficult days of work. More in consideration of the complex production requirements than of continuity, the board preparer's instincts should strongly urge shooting these scenes first. The rationale is that, should any problems arise and more than two days be required for the 6 3/8 pages, there would still be a possibility of making up lost time in the remaining REC. ROOM scenes. However, the director preferred to film the musical number as late in the schedule as possible in order to allow the actress and choreographer more time to rehearse the routine.

Despite these conditions, the board preparer may still schedule all the REC. ROOM scenes in four days. A compromise may be based on the following analysis: divide the remaining scenes which contain few if any technical complications as evenly as possible and schedule the halves for one day each before and after the talent show. The result is illustrated in days eight through eleven of Board #2.

The last level of scheduling is the work within each day, and it relies on the same sort of logical reduction. Day eight, for example, consists of four master scenes. Scene 97 begins the day because it is an establishing shot with no cast requirements. This means it will not be delayed by any wardrobe or makeup problems. Scene 41 is next for the same reason; it involves only one character. The choice between scheduling scene 25 or scene 75 to follow is more difficult. Both scenes involve all five principals. The fact that the creature (#6) works only in scene 75 is of little consequence in terms of preparation, since the creature is a man in a latex suit who takes only a few minutes to get ready. Scene 75 is longer and slightly more complicated in narrative action. Based on this superficial comparison, many production managers and assistant directors would suggest that scene 75 be scheduled earlier, on the principle that the more complicated work should be tackled first. There are two reasons for this. First, if there are any problems getting started that cost time, the chances of making it up are better if the day ends with less complicated scenes. If the more difficult scene is kept for last and problems do arise, there is a greater chance that overtime will be required to complete the day's work. Overtime means not only cost overruns but also, because cast and crew must be given minimum turnaround time between workdays, a potential delay in starting the next day's work. As sound as these reasons are, a review of the content of scene 75 reveals an overriding reason for scheduling it at day's end. The storyline calls for the creature to burst on the crew members who, in turn, overturn furniture and create chaos as they attempt to flee. There is considerable likelihood that the set may be damaged when the end of scene 75 is filmed. Since it would be unwise to expose the day's schedule to the risk of having to wait for repairs, the board preparers determined that the conclusion of scene 75 should be the last planned setup.

A similar problem affects the scheduling of the INT. OBSERVATION ROOM (days four and five). Two days are allowed for filming the capture and observation of the creature, who sings and dances, by the crew. Scene 83, however, while only 3/8 page in length, has been scheduled for a later day. This is because scene 83 calls for the glass walls of the observation chamber to have been shattered. If scene 83 were to be filmed on the same day as the creature's song and dance—a difficult scene involving a second camera, playback, and special effects—the set would have to be destroyed before the day's filming had been processed and viewed. Whenever possible, most production managers and assistant directors will schedule so that a set need not be destroyed until after *dailies* have been seen, and it is certain no retakes are needed. Because the potential for camera or laboratory damage to the film always exists and because replacing the glass for retakes of earlier scenes would have been very expensive and inconvenient, the producer viewed the rushes from day five and approved them before scene 83 was shot on day six.

ORGANIZING PRINCIPLES

The procedure for organizing the overall production schedule is much the same as for the strips—systematic reduction from largest situation to smallest, from general to specific, from complex to straightforward. As has been mentioned with regard to each day's work, industry practice often deems it preferable to film the most difficult scenes of the entire motion picture as early in the schedule as possible. The rationale is the same. If problems arise early, there is still time to readjust the schedule to accommodate them, as the remaining days of work may serve as a buffer against overruns of time and money. Obviously, placing a difficult sequence at the end of filming precludes this advantage.

Since shooting on a practical site is generally held to be more difficult than stage work, local location days are often placed early in the schedule. This is not to imply that all such days should be clustered together at the beginning of shooting. Location work can be more time-consuming and arduous because of the logistics of moving crew and equipment and the added chances of technical breakdown or poor weather. On the other hand, alternating location and stage days may be useful in affording a production company the opportunity to regroup in the relative security of a soundstage before going on the road again. Moreover, in episodic television, where studio operations are usually restricted to one or two home stages, intervening location days may be necessary to give the art director time to reconstruct and/or redress sets.

The employment of actors and the rental of ancillary equipment from second cameras and cranes to wind machines and water wagons are also important factors. Between commencing and ending work, actors must be paid for hold days, even if not on call; and it is both time-consuming and unwieldly to take equipment repeatedly on and off rental. Ideally, all the scenes involving a given actor or a piece of expensive apparatus should be grouped together. Practically, this is seldom feasible. All too often, rescheduling to improve the *carry* situation on one person or item has a counterproductive effect on another person or item. Even when applied, such tactics should never simply be a question of striving for the least cost. What production needs most is the least inconvenience. Added cost which brings added convenience is probably cheaper in the long run.

All these principles were applied to *The Creature Wasn't Nice.* Their influence is reflected in the preproduction disposition of Board #2. For instance, actor availability imposed restrictions of the characters of Annie (#1) and Dr. Stark (#5). Cindy Williams had been cast as Annie and was available under her picture deal for only twenty shooting days. As a result, the board shows Annie starting work on day three and finishing on day twenty-two. Patrick MacNee, who portrayed Stark, was not a resident of Los Angeles and was to be paid a cash living allowance for each workday. The fact that Dr. Stark is the first crew member to be eaten by the creature facilitated grouping the scenes in a way that held his character's workdays to eleven out of twenty-four shooting days. Normally, such *picture deal* performers may be scheduled without too much concern over their hold days. In fact, when production is protracted, many run-of-the-picture actors welcome additional days of rest. Day players are a more significant consideration. As the term implies, such actors are paid a predetermined salary for each day, whether it be a work or a hold day.[18] For example, a day player might be set to work days two and three of a given production but if a problem arises which postpones day three's scenes until day five, the actor must be paid two additional days for the intervening time. Fortunately for the board preparers on *The Creature Wasn't Nice,* the script called for relatively few day

---

[18] The daily rate is only cost efficient for an actor who will work three days or less in features or two days or less in television. The SAG contract stipulates a current scale weekly rate that is less than four times daily scale. In television, there is a separate rate for a three-day player, which is only slightly more than twice the daily rate. Clearly, if a feature actor is scheduled to work four consecutive days and will be paid scale, it is less expensive to pay for a full week.

players, and these were easily restricted to the first two days of shooting.

The advantages to beginning the filming of *The Creature Wasn't Nice* with a location day were multiform. Because only one location was required by the script, the cost of additional personnel and equipment was minimal. The advantage of being able to set all these one-day needs in preproduction outweighed the slight possibility of saving money by prepping or wrapping the location rentals after the shooting company was already at work on stage. As has been suggested, the increased technical and logistical aspects of location work bring with them increased chances of problems and delays. The planned first day of *The Creature Wasn't Nice* ended with INT. BOARD ROOM. This could easily have been done on stage and might have been less expensive then dressing a practical room on location. This was outweighed by the reduced cost of permitting all the scenes involving the old man—the highest-paid day player in the picture—to be shot in a single day. As it turned out, a generator problem (not evident at the time of filming) rendered all the INT. BOARD ROOM scenes useless. The fiscal impact of this development was mitigated in two days. There was an insurance claim which will be discussed in greater detail later. More significantly, there was an anticipation of first-day difficulties built into the schedule. The board preparers expected that the first day on location would be long, strenuous, and fraught with potential problems. Accordingly, the second shooting day and first stage day was kept free of any demanding scenes. This was to permit the crew time to wrap equipment needed only for location work while orienting themselves to shooting on stage. As the disposition of strips in the board at the end of production (Board #3) reveals, anticipating problems allowed the INT. BOARD ROOM to be immediately rescheduled and reshot at the end of day two on an alternate set erected on stage.

Perhaps the most uncommon scheduling challenge on *The Creature Wasn't Nice* was the many sets which were to represent the interiors of the spaceship. Budgetary restraints dictated at an early stage that all the sets (except as already mentioned the EXT. PLANET) should be constructed on a single, large soundstage. Accordingly, three areas of the stage were marked off for construction. As the reader may have noted, there are considerably more than three sets designated on the production boards. The plan was that as sequences were completed, the finished sets would be converted into others. Obviously, sufficient time would have to be allowed for the

Production Board #3

Title " The Creature Wasn't Nice "

Director BRUCE KIMMEL
Producer MARK HAGGARD
Asst. Dir.

Script Dated 2/24/81

Breakdown Page	49	47	46	48	43	63	2	66	85	100	10	47A	81	8	83	19
Day or Nite	D	D	D	D								D				
Pages	7/	4/	4/	1/	7/	1⅘	1/	1/	1/	4/	2/	6/	1/	32	12	1/
Scene #	53	50A	50	52	45 PT	73B PT 73C	2	76PT 78PT 110	101	23A	10	51	96	8	99	20
Location	EXT STREET	EXT CITY MALL	EXT STREET	EXT STREET	INT TALK SHOW	INT TALK SHOW	INT CORRIDOR (ESTABLISH)	INT CORRIDOR 12	INT CORRIDOR 12	INT CORRIDORS	INT CORRIDOR	INT BOARD ROOM	INT COCKPIT	INT ANNIE'S OFFICE	INT ANNIE'S OFFICE	INT ANNIE'S OFFICE

(1ST DAY divider before INT TALK SHOW · 2ND DAY divider before INT COCKPIT)

Character	Artist	No.	53	50A	50	52	45	73B	2	76	101	23A	10	51	96	8	99	20
ANNIE	Cindy Williams	1														1	1	1
JOHN	Bruce Kimmel	2									2	2					2	
JAMESON	Leslie Nielsen	3																
RODZINSKI	Gerrit Graham	4														4		
DR. STARK	Patrick MacNee	5																
CREATURE	Ron Kurowski	6								6	6							
MAX (V.O.)	Broderick Crawford	7																
OLD MAN	Paul Brinegar	8	8	8	8	8								8				
LINDA	Margaret Willock	9					9	9										
GRACE	Sheri Eichen	10					10	10										
MARGIE	Carol Ann Williams	11					11	11										
BOARD MEMBER	Ken Tobey	12												12				
PUNK	Alan Abelew	13		13														
HOOD #1	Bob Carpenter	14	14															
#2	Jed Mills	15	15															
#3	Peter DuPre	16	16															
#4	Ron Burke	17	17															
PERSON	Mark Hammill	18																
NARRATOR (V.O.)		19	19vo	19va	19vo	19vu												
NEWS ANNOUNCER (V.O.)		20																
BODY TRANS.		21					21											
ATMOSPHERE – BITS		22				1								4				
– GENERAL		23	12	12	12													
DRIVER		24			X													
ADD'L CAMERA		25																
VIDEO PLAYBCK		26																
CART / CARS		27	X		X	X												
CRANE		28		?X	X													
PLAYBACK		29																
FX: VERTIGO		30																
SHUTTLE (MINIATURE)		31																
COMPUTER		32																
COCKPIT LIGHTS		33													33			
A) BLENDER B) 2001		34																
A) DISCO LGTS B) FLYING		35																
A) PLANET B) TERRAIN		36																
A) WIRES B) MATTE		37																
		38																
		39																
		40																

Scene descriptions (per column):
CUTS OFF HOODS · CANING A PUNK · OLD MAN ARRIVES · CHECKS OUT ANOTHER PUNK · INTRO THE BODY TRANSPLANT · HAPPY NEWS AGAIN · ESTABLISHING · CREACH. EATS · LOOKING TO EAT · — · JOHN LOST · MOP BALLET / OLD MAN ARGUES · REESTABLISH · ROD. MAKES A PLAY · FINDING MUSIC · ESTABLISH

This is a film production strip board / scheduling sheet.

Scene / Location	Top No. 1	Top No. 2	Top No. 3	Character Nos.	Scene Description
INT ANNIE'S OFFICE	50A	20	57	1, 5	STARK'S IS FEARFUL
INT MAIN CONTROL ROOM	80	11	95	2	REESTABLISH
3RD DAY					
INT COCKPIT	5	14	5	1, 3, 4 / 33	ESTABLISH CO-PILOTS
INT COCKPIT	12	16	12	3, 4 / 33	MIKE TALKS TO JAMESON
INT COCKPIT	41	11	43	3, 4	JAMESON & ROD. TUBES
INT COCKPIT	18	11	19	3	
INT COCKPIT	52	11	62	3 / 33	REESTABLISH
INT CORRIDOR 12	67	16	77	1, 2, 3, 4	JAMESON PANICS / CAPTURING THE CREATURE
4TH DAY / 5TH DAY					END OF WEEK #1 ~ SAT. 5/9 AND SUN. 5/10/81
INT OBSERVATION ROOM	68	22	79	1, 2, 3, 4, 5, 6	OBSERVING CREACH.
INT OBSERVATION ROOM	69	53	80	1, 2, 3, 4, 5, 6	17 STARES / EATS! 37A
6TH DAY					
INT CORRIDOR	59	21	70 (98PT)	1, 3, 4, 6	REESTABLISH
INT SOLARIUM	62	14	73 / 75A / 75B	2, 4, 6	ANNIE AND ROD MEET THE CREATURE
INT CORRIDOR	87	11	103	2, 3, 4	MORE BLOCKING
INT OBSERVATION ROOM	72	31	83	1, 2, 3, 4, 6	17'S ESCAPED
INT LONG CORRIDOR	57	70	68	1, 2, 3, 4	ENTER THE CREATURE
INT SHUTTLE	26	12	27 / 24PT / 31 / 34	5	ROUND-TRIP TO PLANET
7TH DAY / 8TH DAY					D° Radzinski to McHugh
INT REC ROOM	39	12	41	1, 2	JOHN PLAYS WITH HIMSELF
INT REC ROOM	82	11	97	1, 2, 3	REESTABLISH
INT REC ROOM	101	11	238	1, 2, 3	WALD-EXING
INT REC ROOM	24	22	25	1, 2, 3	A TOAST!
INT REC ROOM	64	33	75PT	1, 4, 5, 6	DISCUSS C-REACH
INT REC ROOM	42	21	45		ANNIE WATCHES NEWS
INT REC ROOM	44	144	48	1, 2, 3, 4, 5	SYNTHETIC DINNER
9TH DAY / 10TH DAY					END OF WEEK #2 ~ SAT 5/17 AND SUN 5/17/81

NEED VIDEO INSERTS — W/O CHAR #1

Sheet	Pages	Scenes	Set	1	2	3	4	5	6	7	Notes / X	Extras	Other	Description
20	1/	21	INT CORRIDOR		2	3								TRASH
102	2/	73D	INT CORRIDOR			3			6					CREACH PIT STOP
84	1 3/	100, 102	INT MUSIC LIBRARY	1	2						102 complete 5/12. Need insert hands w/cassette for 100; X			FINISH REHEARSING
15	6/	15	INT BACKSTAGE	1						7		32		ANNIE CHANGES
14	6 3/	14, 14B, 16, 16A	INT REC ROOM	1	2	3	4	5			X; NIKE X		34A 35A	SHOWTIME!
			11TH DAY											
			12TH DAY											
53	1/	63	INT RODZINSKI'S ROOM				4							ROO SLEEPS
70	2 0/	81	INT CORRIDOR	1	2	3	4							EULOGIZE STARK
49/50	6/	49 54	INT SCREENING ROOM	1	2	3	4				?X			AT THE MOVIES
51	2 1/	59	INT MAIN CONTROL ROOM	1	2	3	4	5						CAUCUS ABOUT CREATURE
			13TH DAY											
86	1/	104	INT MUSIC LIBRARY						6		X			CREATURE HITS BUTTON
4	4/	4	INT MAIN CONTROL RM.	1	2							32		ESTABLISH ANNIE AND JOHN
56	2 3/	67	INT MAIN CONTROL ROOM	1	2	3	4	5						CHECK-OUT THE NOISE
54	3/	64	INT COMPUTER ROOM		2					7		32		MAX TELLS JOHN
88	1 6/	105	INT COMPUTER ROOM	1	2					7		32		CONFRONTATION
			14TH DAY											
11	2/	11	INT COMPUTER ROOM					5				32		STARK COMPUTES
21	6/	22, 23PT	INT COMPUTER ROOM					5				32		STARK PLOTS
17	1/	18	INT MAIN CONTROL RM.					5						REESTABLISH
3	2/	3, 94	INT COMPUTER ROOM									32		ESTABLISHING
73	1 3/	84	INT COMPUTER ROOM	1	2	3	4			7		32		SPLIT UP TO LOOK
65	1 4/	76PT	INT COMPUTER ROOM	1	2	3	4	5		7	X	32		CREACH. EATS CAMERA
			15TH DAY											
			END OF WEEK #3 ~ SAT 5/23 AND SUN 5/24/81											
			MEMORIAL DAY ~ HOLIDAY								PICK-UPS AS NEEDED			
30	5 4/	32, 33	EXT. PLANET	1	2	3	4	5			X	31	35B 36B	PLANET HIJINKS
			16TH DAY											
			17TH DAY											
60	1/	71, 98PT	INT ANOTHER CORRIDOR											REESTABLISH

Production Strip Board

Scene	Pages	Alt	Set	Cast / Notes	Description
74	1/	86	INT CORRIDOR	3, 4	CREEPING DOWN CORRIDOR
76	2/	88	INT CORRIDOR	3, 4	TRACKING CREACH
75	7/	87	INT OTHER CORRIDOR 13	1, 2	TRACKING CREACH
77	14/	89'/97'	INT OTHER CORRIDOR 14	1, 2	DO THEY WANT TO FIND HIM
78A	2/	91B	INT CORRIDOR 3	1, 2	FIND REMAINS
92Λ	1/	110	INT CORRIDOR	1, 2, 6	CREATURE SCREAMS

18TH DAY

Scene	Pages	Alt	Set	Cast / Notes	Description
89	12/	106	INT CORRIDOR 14	1, 2, 6	RUNNING
90	1/	107	INT OTHER CORRIDOR 13	1, 2	STILL RUNNING.
91	3/	108	INT ANOTHER CORRIDOR	1, 2	LOST HIM.
33	10/4	37,40 / 44,47,56,60	INT CORRIDOR	5	STARK ENTERS VAULT
35	4/	58	INT CORRIDOR (BY VAULT)	5	CREATURE SCREAMS
36	1/	65	INT CORRIDOR (BY VAULT)	1, 2	ANNIE CHECKS OUT VAULT
94	1/	112	INT CORRIDOR	1, 2, 6	ANNIE CURSES JOHN

19TH DAY

END OF WEEK #4 — SAT 5/30 AND SUN 6/1/81

Scene	Pages	Alt	Set	Cast / Notes	Description
13	2/	13	EXT SPACE	4, ZEUS X	SPACEWALK BY ROD.
55	1/	66	INT ENGINE ROOM	2, 3, 4, 6	JOHN QUARTERS
78	6/	90	INT CORRIDOR 3	X, X	CREACH ATTACKS
92	1'/	109	INT AIRLOCK AREA	1, 2, 6, X	SETTING THE TRAP
93	32	111	INT AIRLOCK AREA	1, 2, 6, X	SONG & DANCE.

20TH DAY
21ST DAY

Scene	Pages	Alt	Set	Cast / Notes	Description
'7	2/	7	INT CORRIDOR	2, 18, 34B	20? WALK
98	12	115,116	INT NEW CRAFT	2, 6	NEW ENCOUNTER

22ND DAY

COMPLETION OF PRINCIPAL PHOTOGRAPHY

art director, set decorator, and construction crew to transform the sets. The REC. ROOM, for example, was to be reconstructed in the MAIN COMPUTER ROOM. The COCKPIT became the SHUTTLE. The MUSIC LIBRARY was also the SOLARIUM and RODZINSKI'S ROOM. Clearly, these could not be scheduled to be used on the same day and it was preferable to allow more time than merely overnight to make the necessary changes. Several other portions of sets were designed to do double or triple duty. As discussed earlier, the single CORRIDOR was to have maximum flexibility with wild walls and colored panels. The implicit restrictions of this proposed use of the sets became the major factor in scheduling the stage work. Ordinarily, if a certain actor worked in only one or two scenes on a major set, an attempt might be made to group those scenes with that actor's work on another set. In this instance, priority had to be given to finishing sets over limiting actor workdays. Actors had to remain available until all the work in each set to be changed over was completed. When possible, completion of work on one of these sets was followed by corridor scenes and then a return to the reconstructed set. The interval of working in the corridor permitted the art director, set director, and construction crew a bit more time for set transformation. Most of the sets had to be *struck,* or dismantled, as soon as the scripted work in them was finished. It was seldom feasible to wait for dailies before striking, as this would have delayed transformation. The only exception, already mentioned, was scene 83. In all other instances, the sets could have been reconstituted if the dailies were not approved by the director and producer.

A final element in scheduling *The Creature Wasn't Nice* was playback. Audio playback for the musical numbers meant that actors would synchronize their singing and dancing on film to previously recorded track. These scenes were treated as semidetached units. The music was prerecorded at a sound studio as early as possible before filming began, so that there would be added time to rehearse. There were also several scenes which involved video playback in which a principal would be filmed reacting to a television monitor. For example, the talk show scenes are watched by Annie in the REC. ROOM. The creature is observed on television by the other actors in the MAIN CONTROL ROOM. The material to be played back had to be filmed a sufficient number of days prior to being needed to tie-in with the principals to allow time for them to be processed, printed, edited, and transferred to videotape.

PROBLEM SOLVING

The reader may have noticed from Board #2 that it was decided to lay out the strips representing principal photography in fewer than the twenty-four shooting days allowed by the budget.[19] This was accomplished by packing certain days with extra work wherever there was a reasonable chance that the extra work could be done. This created a sort of built-in time contingency, which is not standard industry procedure but has certain advantages. Most notably, if problems arise on an artificially tight schedule, there would still be extra days available and the production as a whole could still avoid overruns. Ultimately, *The Creature Wasn't Nice* was completed not according to the shorter schedule but two days ahead of it. Ironically, part of the peril of being off schedule, whether ahead or behind, is that it upsets the work plan. Altering the work plan even if it means picking up days may, in the short run, entail added costs. In this case, because the production manager and assistant directors had kept the crew apprised that work was ahead of schedule, the art director was able to oversee the completion of the planet exteriors two days early. However, it cost weekend overtime and two extra rental days to prepare stage 8 in time. This is not to imply that such expenses offset the long-term benefits of being ahead on the work. Had production been behind, the crew was alerted that work on the scheduled holiday might be needed; it was not. Moreover, the director was able to use one of the two days not used for principal photography to bring a special rig on stage and employ the full crew in what had been planned as a post-production special effect.

All these scheduling considerations are an integral part of the first stage of problem solving by the production manager and assistant directors. The preproduction consultations and conferences with director, producer, and various crew members are the chief corollaries to the assembly of the production board. With these in mind, the completed board becomes an analytical tool with which to pry apart whatever potential problems remain evident but unresolvable. As was

[19] The reader should disregard the strips reproduced at the right edge of the board. These EXT. SPACE strips, which are blue on the original, represent shots of miniatures of a spaceship and shuttlecraft which were photographed by a special effects firm under a subcontract. They were included on the board merely for reference but were not part of the on-production work.

suggested in Part I, the members of the full director's team must be able to isolate not just their own production concerns but also problems that affect the creative personnel. These above-the-line matters require the attention of the director or producer for a final resolution. But only by recommending solutions and alternatives to the individual(s) who properly controls this final decision can the production manager and assistant directors insure that such a decision is fully informed. Whether the UPM or assistant directors are conferring with the director on a creative question or over budgetary issues with the producer, they cannot be passive participants and expect to fulfill their own job functions. The most common of problems, such as a script that appears too difficult to be filmed in the allotted days, may defy straightforward solutions. In such circumstances, whatever the production manager and assistant directors may recommend, they must prepare alternatives. If the director or producer decides to increase the shooting days and raise cost or to revise the script and reduce the work or to disregard the problem and simply pack the schedule with more work than seems feasible—whatever the decision, the production manager and assistant directors have a line responsibility to implement it. Another common problem already described is actors' workdays. In an extreme example, an important star may insist that all of his or her scenes be shot on specific dates between specific hours with the soundstage thermostat set at a specific temperature. The director and producer are the ones who must weigh if a particular star's value is worth all this trouble. If it is, the bottom line is that the production manager and assistant directors must make the necessary accommodations.

The problems of filmmaking, like those of any manufacturing process, are bound up in all sorts of artificial constructions. To attack this artifice directly is to threaten the process itself. Effective problem solving centers not around counterthrusts but on alternative measures. The production board evolved as a cluster of flexible components so that it might help to visualize alternatives; but the production managers and assistant directors must have a flexible frame of mind to make effective use of it. Change is a ground rule of film production. As a result, no schedule can be absolute. Even the perfect plan is vulnerable and difficulties call for resolution not recrimination.

The process of resolution is not just a matter of organizing priorities but also of eliminating superfluous or distracting elements. As has been suggested, the ability to recognize quickly those elements which are problematic is a significant skill for both production manager and assistant directors. The same logical procedure which was the basis for breaking down a script may also be used to break down problems. Some people call this thinking on your feet. It is more accurately thinking on the run or simply being alert. If there is a moment on the set when the assistant directors are not alert to what is happening, what may happen, and what should happen, a likely consequence is that work time will be lost. Keeping alternatives in mind does not imply a need for anxiety. If anything, awareness of pitfalls makes missteps less likely. Such awareness is enhanced by experience, but it begins with a skill that may be acquired and developed by anyone. It is cognitive, not intuitive.

THE DAY-OUT-OF-DAYS

The day-out-of-days form is a chart of workdays for all cast from run of the picture actors to day players.[20] This information is of critical importance to the producer(s) and the casting agency or department in booking actors[21] and making deals for their services. The production manager must maintain a liaison with the casting office regarding

[20] Leading actors who are on run-of-the-picture deals may nonetheless have restrictions on the amount and/or types of days worked. The production manager and assistant directors must be informed if there are any penalty provisions for excess days.

[21] It may be useful to distinguish between *actors* and *extra players*. Actors are performers who portray a specific character by using body movements, facial gestures, and, most significantly, meaningful sounds, usually words of dialogue. There are performers in commercials and stuntpeople in general who do not speak lines or make sounds; they are considered actors by virtue of interacting with advertised products or doubling others. Extra players are persons visible in the background or general atmosphere of a scene. They do not speak lines of dialogue. An extra who performs a pantomime action significant to the story line is called a *silent bit*. Under union conditions, silent bits are paid a higher rate. There are other union categorizations which may earn additional pay, including a *photo double*, a person who doubles an actor but not because of hazardous or stunt conditions.

The Screen Actors Guild and Screen Extras Guild have negotiated contracts to set minimum conditions and pay rates for actors and extra players, respectively. Production companies who are signatory to these agreements must abide by their terms. The majority of motion pictures produced use SAG members under signatory status. An increasingly large number of independent film and television productions—including *The Creature Wasn't Nice*—do not employ SEG members.

DAY – OUT – OF – DAYS

W=work
H= hold
T=total
SW=Start Work
WF=Work Finish

TITLE: THE CREATURE WASN'T NICE   PRODUCER: MARK HAGGARD

PROD. NUMBER 002x   DIRECTOR: BRUCE KIMMEL

DATES: May 4 thru June 5, 1981   ASS'T DIR.: PATRICK REGAN

PP 203

CHARACTER	ACTOR	MAY 4 / 1	5 / 2	6 / 3	7 / 4	8 / 5	11 / 6	12 / 7	13 / 8	14 / 9	15 / 10	18 / 11	19 / 12	20 / 13	21 / 14	22 / 15	25 / 16	26 / 17	27 / 18	28 / 19	29 / 20	W	H	T
1. ANNIE	C.WILLIAMS			SW	W	W	W	W	W	W	W	W	W	W	W	W	H	W	W	W	W			
2. JOHN	B.KIMMEL		SW	W	W	W	W	W	W	W	W	W	W	W	W	W	H	W	W	W	W			
3. JAMESON	L.NIELSON		SW	W	W	W	W	W	W	W	W	W	W	W	W	W	H	W	W	W	W			
4. RODZINSKI	G.GRAHAM		SW	W	W	W	W	W	W	W	W	W	W	W	W	W	H	W	W	W	W			
5. STARK	P. MACNEE			SW	W	W	W	W	W	W	W	H	W	W	W	W	H	W	W	W	W			
6. CREATURE	R.KUROSKI		SW	W	W	W	W	W	W	W	H	H	H	H	W	W	H	W	W	W	H			
8. OLD MAN	P.BRINEGAR	SWF																				1	0	1
9. LINDA	S.EICHEN			SWF																		1	0	1
10. GRACE	CA.WILLIAMS			SWF																		1	0	1
11. MARJ	M. WILLOCK			SWF																		1	0	1
12. BOARDMAN	K.TOBEY	SWF																				1	0	1
13. PUNK	A.ABELEW	SWF																				1	0	1
14. HOOD #1	B.CARPENTER	SWF																				1	0	1
15. HOOD #2	J.MILLS	SWF																				1	0	1
16. HOOD #3	P. DU PRE	SWF																				1	0	1
17. HOOD #4	R. BURKE	SWF																						
																-HOLIDAY-								
7. MAX	B.CRAWFORD	--------PRE-PRODUCTION, ONE DAY ONLY--------																				1	0	1
18. NARRATOR	A.GILMORE	--------PRE-PRODUCTION, ONE DAY ONLY--------																				1	0	1
19. NEWS – ANNOUNCER	P. REGAN	--------PRE-PRODUCTION, ONE DAY ONLY--------																				1	0	1

CONTINUED

CHARACTER	ACTOR	JUNE 21	22	3 / 23	4 / 24	5 / 25	W	H	T
1. ANNIE	C.WILLIAMS	W	W	WF			20	1	21
2. JOHN	B.KIMMEL	W	W	W	W	WF	23	1	24
3. JAMESON	L.NIELSON	WF					19	1	20
4. RODZINSKI	G.GRAHAM	WF					19	1	20
5. STARK	P. MACNEE	WF					18	2	20
6. CREATURE	R.KUROSKI	H	W	W	W	WF	19	6	25

budget. The first assistant director may also work directly with casting regarding schedule. The encumbrances which an actor's deal may place upon a schedule have already been illustrated. The key to minimizing the disruptive effect of casting conditions is good communication between the casting authorities and the production manager and assistant directors.

The sample form is that used on *The Creature Wasn't Nice*. As may be seen, the left columns provide space for a listing of characters and the actors who portray them. The crosshatched area is used to indicate the scheduled status of an actor according to shooting day and date. The key in the upper right explains the letter codes. On the far right are the number of work days, hold days, and total days, the latter also representing days to be paid.

The day-out-of-days form usually serves as the top-sheet of the shooting schedule, which will be discussed next. Although its primary function is as a reference for the production manager, assistant directors, and casting office, it may be useful to others. Cast members, quite obviously, may wish to discover their probable hold days. Probable because, like all production forms, the day-out-of-days is subject to revision at a moment's notice. Hold days may also be a guide to staff or crew whose purposes are other than filming, such as costumers who need actors for fittings; associate producers who need them for looping; and publicists arranging press interviews.

THE SHOOTING SCHEDULE

The typed shooting schedule reproduces the sequence of work from the production board and the breakdown sheet information in a condensed form which may be distributed to the entire cast and crew. This schedule is easily appended to the script and provides a detailed outline of the day-to-day production plan.

The shooting schedule page for the first day of *The Creature Wasn't Nice* is illustrated. Information is arranged in blocks, each of which represents data from a breakdown page. The details of props, costumes, cars, stand-ins, and the like, which may not have been included on the board strips, are listed in the typed shooting schedule. There is day and date information in the left-hand margin: the sequential day of shooting, day of the week, date, and day's page-count. Sequence and page-count are repeated at the end of each day's blocks;

PROD. NO. 002X   April 23, 1981
DATE

DIRECTOR Bruce Kimmel   UNIT MANAGER Alain Silver   ASST. DIR. Patrick Regan

DAY AND DATE	SET OR LOCATION SCENE NUMBERS	WHERE LOCATED	CAST WORKING
1st DAY MONDAY MAY 4, 1981 TOTAL PAGES: 2 6/8 pages	sc. 50A 4/8 pg EXT. CITY MALL OLD MAN WASTES YOUNG PUNK. PROPS: cane, title card CARS: future car(s)	Cypress	8. Old Man 13. Young Punk 19. Narrator (V.O.)
	sc. 50 4/8 pg. EXT. STREET OLD MAN ARRIVES. PROPS: cane CARS: Modern car	Cypress	8. Old Man 19. Narrator (V.O.)
	sc. 52 1/8 pg. EXT. STREET OLD MAN PURSUES PUNK. PROPS: cane CARS: N.D. cars ATMOS: Punk #2	Cypress	8. Old Man 19. Narrator
	sc. 53 7/8 pg. EXT. STREET OLD MAN RUNS OFF HOODS. PROPS: cane, title card CARS: mechanical car, sleek cars, N.D. cars SP FX M.U.: blood spurt ATMOS: pedestrians	Cypress	8. Old Man 14. Hood #1 15. Hood #2 16. Hood #3 17. Hood #4 19. Narrator (V.O.)
	sc. 51 6/8 pg. INT. POLICE BOARD ROOM OLD MAN VS. THE BOARD PROPS: badge, cane ATMOS: 4 board members		8. Old Man 12. Board Member
	END OF DAY 1		TOTAL PAGES: 2 6/8

in this instance, at the bottom of the page. The reader may compare this page with the same scenes covered in the previous samples of the script page, the breakdown sheets, and the production board strips. It should be clear at this point that the various kinds of production paperwork provide the same information in different forms for different purposes (see Appendix III for a comparative chart of production forms). The purpose of the shooting schedule is revealed in its name. It should be concise but complete as the staff and crew may occasionally refer to it rather than the script during actual production to anticipate departmental requirements. Although the shooting schedule may help to recall quickly key details of a scene, it is not intended as a substitute for the script. Crew members, as well as the production manager and assistant directors, should always review the script in conjunction with the shooting schedule to verify all information, particularly when preparing the next day's work.

The shooting schedule is usually typed by the production coordinator or secretary directly from the breakdown sheets. Once the board is finalized, the production manager or first assistant uses the breakdown page number key on each strip to conform the pages to the strip sequence. The day's pages are clipped together with a top-sheet giving date, page-count, etc. At the end of the schedule, the daily page totals are tallied to establish a grand total for the entire script. Depending on revisions or the presence of inserts, stock footage, and the like, this figure may or may not conform to the total suggested by the final page of the shooting script.

DEAL MAKING

Deal making prior to production is not the exclusive province of producers and agents. Although the deal memos for the below-the-line personnel may be less complicated than that of a director or star, they are subject to the same sort of negotiation. Except for composers, cinematographers, an occasional production designer or editor (and even a few production managers), none of the staff or crew is likely to have a deal-making representative. Department heads may often negotiate for their subordinates as well as themselves; but theoretically, each craftperson offered employment may negotiate the terms of that employment directly with the production manager.

Beyond the considerations of applicable union minimum wages, there are several concepts in common use in the film industry. From the production manager's viewpoint the most that can be offered is not just a question of salary but also includes working conditions and opportunity for advancement. Money remains a good starting point, however; and the production manager should not begin negotiations without a sense of the extent to which money will restrict his or her flexibility. Even if the total budget figure is a tight one, the production manager may have anticipated shifting money within or between categories without liability. Thus, making a better deal than expected on rentals or laboratory costs may allow the company to hire a more experienced and higher priced cameraman or editor.[22] The reverse situation is less comfortable but equally common: the crew deals have gone over budget and must be offset by cutting back on equipment and expendables. This sort of trade-off may, in fact, enter directly into negotiations, since many technicians own their own equipment. A production mixer, for example, may be willing to work for less than top rate in exchange for receiving equipment rental revenue. Many department heads prefer a box rental or a car allowance (cash payment), to overscale salaries.[23]

If the balance of salary, rentals, and allowances, which the production manager can offer within the budget, proves inadequate, there may be alternative values available. On *The Creature Wasn't Nice*, good working conditions were a part of numerous crew deals. Department heads whose credits placed them at the top of wage demands, but who had just finished a production involving long, sometimes inclement days and nights on location, agreed to work for less money on the promise of short hours in the controlled environment of a soundstage. When budgetary limits establish salaries too low to attract experienced persons under any conditions, the production manager's last enticement is opportunity. Most production departments have a hierarchy of on-set functions, and many technicians would prize a chance to move up. Thus, while very few IATSE first camera-

[22] Of course, this kind of trading off between accounting categories may have undesirable consequences. A higher priced cameraman may require a higher priced camera crew, gaffer, and key grip to assist him. Or, worse yet, the cameraman may find the economy camera package which made his employment possible below his standards and unacceptable to his use.

[23] There should be no evading that cash payments in excess of $750.00 must be reported to the Internal Revenue Service on Form 1099.

men (directors of photography) will work for union scale, some experienced second cameramen (camera operators) would gladly do so if given an opportunity to advance in category.

If there is any rule for deal-making it is simply this: do not misrepresent. To promise working conditions or a screen credit that cannot be delivered is a sure way to destroy good working relationships and build a poor reputation. Few technicians have the leverage of major actors and directors to demand *pay or play* provisions or the escrowing of funds to guarantee performance of their deal. In the minds of those in the film industry, the deal memo, no matter how it is worded or certified, is a binding contract. Once set, good faith forbids willful violation by either party.[24]

The deal-making procedures for rentals, purchases, or location sites are substantially the same as for personnel. Again, when budgeted amounts fall short of satisfying production needs, alternatives must be sought. Rental packages may occasionally be restructured to be more economical, and unused expendables, returned for partial refunds. In the case of props, set dressing, and even locations, many suppliers will provide goods and services at little or no cost in exchange for the promotional consideration of receiving an acknowledgment in the credits or simply being seen in the film.

THE PRODUCTION MEETING

The last phase of preproduction begins with the production meeting. This meeting occurs after all the production elements of script, actors, crew, locations, and schedule have been or are close to being finalized. The first day of shooting is usually a week or less away.

The production meeting is most often the first opportunity for

[24] The assistant directors on the set are also responsible for certain negotiations. These involve potential adjustments to basic salary. For example, a stuntman performing a fall will expect an adjustment to his scale salary commensurate with the risk of injury. Crew members may also request adjustments for working under hazardous conditions. Basic rate extras will request adjustments when they believe they have performed silent bits. Usually, the first assistant director, who will have witnessed the scene which involved the stunt, hazard, or silent bit, will negotiate the amount of the adjustment which he or she believes is reasonable, if any. In a case where agreement cannot be reached, the matter may be submitted to the appropriate guild or union for arbitration.

the various department heads and assistants to meet altogether with producer, director, production manager, assistant directors, and other staff. The purpose of the meeting is for the entire crew to review all the preproduction arrangements and the director's production concepts. The department heads have more than likely already consulted individually with the director, and they may have had several discussions with the production manager about the script and their departmental needs. But the production meeting is the first and probably only chance for all to participate in an open discussion of the picture. The meeting for feature films and long-form television is held approximately a week before the first day of shooting. Episodic television, which is shot back-to-back, that is, without an off-day between episodes, may not have the benefit of a meeting until a day or two before an upcoming episode. On some series, the production meeting may take place during lunch hour on the day before work on the next episode begins.

The production meeting is typically led by the production manager or the first assistant, one of whom reads aloud the descriptive portions of the script in continuity, summarizes the dialogue, and indicates on what day each master scene is set to be filmed. The assembled group follows along in their own copies of the script and shooting schedule. As a portion of the script that concerns a particular department head is read, that individual may ask a question or make a comment. The production manager or first assistant director answers the question, if possible or defers to the director for a remark. The reading of sample page 39 from *The Creature Wasn't Nice* at a production meeting might proceed in this manner:

"Scene 49. Interior Screening Room. This set will be constructed from the sidewalls of Annie's office and the REC. ROOM and is set for the 12th day of shooting. 'Annie, John, Jameson, Rodzinski enter and sit in the comfortable, modernistic chairs.' These are new vinyl-covered chairs, not the wooden ones from the talent show or the red plastic from the dining table. 'Rod tries to sit next to Annie but she moves, etc. The lights dim, there's a prevue of coming attractions.' This will be the 'Dirty Harry' sequence but there is no tie-in with the screen." The reader may check for a nod of acknowledgment from the gaffer or chief electrician at the note that the lights dim. A similar nod of confirmation comes from the director regarding the absence of any tie-in. At this point the set decorator may wish to verify that the director still does not need to have one of the MAX computer terminals present in the set. After all the questions are answered the reader goes on to the next scene:

"Scene 50. Exterior City Street. Day. This is to be shot Day One on location at Cypress Junior College. The company will drive-to. 'A modernistic car screeches around a corner.' This will be either a Lotus or Pantera depending on availability. The location manager is making the deal and will pick it up Sunday and drive it to the location. The narrator is voice-over only, which has already been recorded and will not be needed for playback when we shoot." The mention of playback gets the attention of the sound mixer, who may ask the director about the use of radio mikes on location. And so on.

The production meeting may last for half an hour or half a day or more, depending on the complexities of the script and the stamina of the readers. (The production meeting for *The Creature Wasn't Nice* took three hours.) The atmosphere should be that of an open forum but those present should keep their remarks brief and pertinent. Any question that cannot be quickly resolved should be tabled for further individual discussion after the general meeting is over.

The production meeting is fundamentally an attempt to synchronize the entire shooting company before production actually begins. From it should emerge the final preproduction alterations and revisions. There may, of course, continue to be script changes even after filming begins. This is particularly true in episodic television where new pages for the afternoon's work may reach the set in the late morning. As has been noted, the function of the production manager and assistant directors is not to question the need for script changes but to incorporate them into the work plan as quickly and smoothly as possible. Major script changes affecting cast, sets, or location may call for a revision of the production paperwork. As with script changes, a new day-out-of-days or new pages for the shooting schedule should be copied on colored paper, in the same code as the script itself. Like the new script pages, new production forms should be labeled "revised" and redated (*see* footnote #11).

DGA AD/UPM DEAL MEMO

UNIT PRODUCTION MANAGER AND ASSISTANT DIRECTOR FILM DEAL MEMORANDUM
This confirms our agreement to employ you on the project described below
as follows:

Name:_____ SS#:_____

Loanout:_____ Tel#:_____

Address_____ ____Unit Production Manager
                                          ____First Assistant Director
_____ ____Second Assistant Director
                                          ____2nd Second Assistant Dir.
                                          ____Additional Second Asst.Dir.
____Principal Photography   ____Technical Coordinator.
____Second Unit
____Both

Salary: $_____ $_____ ____per week ___per day
               (studio)   (location)

Production Fee: $_____ $_____
                    (studio)   (location)

Start Date:_____ Guaranteed Period:_____

Film or Series Tile:_____

Episode Title:_____ Length of Show:_____

Intended Primary Market:

____Theaters   ____Network   ____Syndication   ____Basic Cable

____Discs/Cassettes   ____Pay TV:_____
                                     (service)

Other Terms(e.g.,credit,suspension,per diem etc.):_____

_____

_____

____Studio ____Distant Location ____Both
              ____Check if New York Area Amendment Applies

This Employment is subject to the Provisions of the Directors Guild of
America, Inc. Basic Agreement of 1987.

Accepted and Agreed: Signatory Co:_____

Employee:_____   By:_____

Date:_____   Date:_____

RC301/071487

III

Production

THE CALL SHEET

The call sheet is the planned work for each day of actual shooting. It informs everyone on production of where, when, and how the day's work is planned to be done. The word planned merits emphasis, because the call sheet, like all the production paperwork, is always subject to change. Unlike other forms, the call sheet is the culmination of all the preproduction scheduling and deal-making; the implement by which production itself is initiated. Simply put, the call sheet is the document which officially releases work calls and requisitions equipment. In a studio operation—where the call sheet is processed and distributed via intrastudio delivery—the call sheet is a direct line of communication from the set to the departments. Placing an order for anything from a camera crane to coffee and donuts by writing it on the call sheet should mean that they will arrive at the appointed time and place without any further action. When the production manager and assistant directors are uncertain whether a call sheet will be operative, a common notation is "hold for confirmation." Because it has such impact, a call sheet must allow for all the significant needs of a given day's work to be clearly inscribed, which is not always easy to do on a single, letter-size piece of paper.

There are, in fact, many different formats of call sheet in use but each should allow for the following data to be entered (the numbers are reproduced on the two illustrations for reference):

1. *Basic heading information*
   Picture title, production number, the date, and day of shooting.
   The call time (shooting, crew, or leaving), and location.
   Producer, director, other pertinent staff.

CALL SHEET ILLUSTRATION #1

CALL SHEET

DIR _____

DATE _____

PRODUCER _____

DAY OF SHOOTING

SHOOTING CALL _____

ASSOC PROD. _____

(1) PICT. _____

ART DIRECTOR _____

LOC. _____ PHONE _____

SET #	SET	SCENES	CAST #	PAGES
(2)

CAST #	ACTOR	CHARACTER	MAKE UP	Report	SET	REMARKS
(3)

ATMOSPHERE & STANDINS: _____ REPORT TO: _____

(4)

CREW CALL: _____ (UNLESS NOTED BELOW) REPORT TO: _____

(5)

SCRIPT SUP.	PROPMASTER	GAFFER	
ASST. DIR.	ASST. PROPMAN	BEST BOY	
CAMERAMAN	SET DRESSERS	LAMP OPER.	
OPERATOR		GEN. OPER.	
1ST ASST.	WRANGLERS		
2ND ASST.	LIVESTOCK/WAGONS	KEY GRIP	
EXTRA OPERATOR		2ND GRIP	
EXTRA ASSISTANT	FIRE WARDEN	GRIPS	
STILLMAN	MOTORCYCLE POLICE	DOLLY GRIP	
DIALOGUE COACH	POLICE	CRANE & CREW	
MIXER	MAKE UP MEN	CRAFTSERVICE	
BOOMAN	HAIRDRESSER	GREENSMAN	
RECORDER		PAINTER	
CABLEMAN	WARDROBE MEN	MAKEUP Room	
P.B. & OPER.	WARDROBE WOMEN	School Room	
PHOTO. FXS.		GAL. COFFEE/DZ. DONUTS	
EFFECTS MEN	Prod'n Asst's	LUNCHES Rdy @	
	1ST AID	DINNERS	

SPECIAL INST. — EQUIPT. — REMARKS: TRANSPORTATION:

(6)   (7)

(8) ADVANCE SCHEDULE: _____

(9) Production Manager _____   Asst. Dir. _____

⑤ PRODUCTION :   DATE   W. A.

	NO.	ITEM	TIME	CHARGE	REMARKS
PRODUCTION		EXTRA ASST. DIRECTOR		705-04	
		2ND ASST. DIRECTOR		705-04	
		SCRIPT SUPERVISOR		705-06	
		DIALOGUE COACH		620-05	
CAMERA		CINEMATOGRAPHER		710-01	
		OPERATOR		710-02	
		ASSISTANT		710-03	
		ASSISTANT		710-04	
		CAMERA		710-08	
		EXTRA OPERATOR		710-02	
		EXTRA ASSISTANT		710-04	
		STILL PHOTOGRAPHER		710/920	
SET OPERATIONS		KEY GRIP		725-01	
		2ND GRIP		725-01	
		EXTRA GRIPS		725-02	
		CRANE OPERATOR		725-03	
		CRAB DOLLY GRIP		725-03	
		CRAB DOLLY		725-05	
		BOOM #		725-06	
		CRAFT SERVICE		725-11	
		GREENS PERSON		725-13	
		PAINTER		725-14	
		PLUMBER		725-17	
		PROP. MAKERS		735-04	
		SPEC. EFFECTS PERSON		735-01-02	
		WIND MACH.		735-08	
		WARD. CHECK ROOM		725-23	
		BENCHES FOR PEOPLE		725-25	
		KNOCK DOWN SCH. ROOMS		725-23	
		KNOCK DOWN DR. ROOMS		725-23	
		PORTABLE DR. ROOMS		725-23	
		HOOK-UP DR. ROOMS		725-21	
		SCHOOLROOM TRAILERS		725-24	
		DRESSING RM. TRAILERS		725-24	
SOUND		SOUND MIXER		765-01	
		MIKE OPERATOR		765-02	
		SOUND RECORDER		765-03	
		CABLE PERSON		765-04	
		EXTRA CABLE PERSON		765-04	
		P. A. SYSTEM		765-06	
		PLAYBACK MACH. & OP.		765-07-05	
		SOUND SYSTEM		765	
PROPERTY		PROPERTY PERSON		750-01	
		ASST. PROPERTY PERSON		750-01	
		EXTRA ASST. PROP. PERSON		750-02	
		SET DRESSER		745-01	
		LEAD PERSON		745-02	
		DRAPERY PERSON		725-18	
		SWING GANG PERSONNEL		745-02	
		WARDROBE RACKS		725-25	
		MAKE-UP TABLES		725-25	
		HAIR DRESSING TABLES		725-25	
		ANIMALS		750-06	
		HANDLERS		750-07	
		A.H.A. REPRESENTATIVE		750-07	
		WRANGLERS		750-07	
		WAGONS, ETC.		750-08	
WARDROBE		COSTUMER FOR MALES		755-01	
		COSTUMER FOR FEMALES		755-02	
		EXTRA COST. FOR MALES		755-03	
		EXTRA COST. FOR FEMALES		755-03	

	NO.	ITEM	TIME	CHARGE	REMARKS
MAKE-UP		MAKE-UP PERSON		760-01	
		EXTRA MAKE-UP PERSON		760-02	
		BODY MAKE-UP PERSON		760-03	
		HAIR STYLIST		760-04	
		EXTRA HAIR STYLISTS		760-05	
ELECTRICAL		GAFFER		730-01	
		SECOND ELECTRICIAN		730-01	
		LAMP OPERATOR		730-02	
		WIND MACHINE & OPERATOR		725-22	
		GENERATOR & OPERA.		730	
		AIR COND. & HEAT		725-22	
		OPERATIONS PHONE		725-21	
		PORTABLE TELEPHONE		725-21	
		WIG WAG		725-21	
		WORK LIGHTS		725-21	
POLICE & FIRE		FIRE CONTROL OFFICER		725/775	
		FIRE WARDEN LOC.		775	
		WHISTLE PERSON		725	
		SET SECURITY PERSON		725/775	
		CITY POLICE		775-02	
		STUDIO POLICE		725-15	
		MOTORCYCLE POLICE		775-02	
MISCELLANEOUS		FIRST AID		725/775	
		PROCESS EQUIPMENT		780	
		PROCESS CAMERA PERSON		780-02	
		PROCESS ASST. CAMERA PERSON		780-02	
		PROCESS GRIPS		780-04	
		PROCESS ELECT.		780-04	
		PROJECTION MACHINE		780-08	
		PROJECTIONIST PROCESS		780-03	
		FILM		785-01	
MUSIC		PIANO		810-6	
		SIDELINE ORCHESTRA		810-6	
		SINGERS		810-6	
CATERER		HOT LUNCHES		775/790	
		BOX LUNCHES		775/790	
		DINNERS		775/790	
		GALLONS OF COFFEE		775/790	
		GALLONS:		775/790	
		DOZEN DOUGHNUTS		775/790	
TRANSPORTATION	⑦	STANDBY DRIVER		770/775	
		STANDBY CAR		770/775	
		CAMERA TRUCK		770/775	
		ELECTRIC TRUCK		770/775	
		GENERATOR TRUCK		770/775	
		GRIP TRUCK		770/775	
		PROP. TRUCK		770/775	
		SPEC. EFFECTS TRUCK		770/775	
		SET DRESSING TRUCK		770/775	
		WARDROBE TRUCK/ TRAILER		770/775	
		WATER WAGON		770/775	
		SANITARY UNIT		775	
		TRUCKS		770/775	
		BUSSES:		770/775	
		PICTURE CARS		750-05	

MISC. NOTES _____

CALL SHEET ILLUSTRATION #2

W. A. _____		Day _____
Series _____	(1)	_____ Day out of _____ days
Producer _____	**CALL SHEET**	Reh. or Lv. Call _____
Director _____		Shooting Call _____
Title _____	Prod. No. _____	Location _____

(2) SET # SET	SCENES	CAST	D/N	PAGES	LOCATION

(3) CAST & DAY PLAYERS	PART OF	MAKE-UP/LEAVE	SET CALL	REMARKS

(4) ATMOSPHERE AND STANDINS	(6) SPECIAL INSTRUCTIONS

(8) ADVANCE SHOOTING NOTES

SHOOTING DATE	SET NO.	SET NAME	LOCATION	SCENE NO.

(9) UNIT PROD. MGR. _____ PHONE _____ ASST. DIR. _____ PHONE _____
ART DIR. _____ PHONE _____ SET DEC. _____ PHONE _____
ISSUED BY OPERATIONS: DATE _____ TIME _____ APPROVED _____

CREATURE FEATURES
CALL SHEET

Monday

DATE **May 4th, 1981**

SHOOTING CALL **7:00 AM**

PICT. **"THE CREATURE WASN'T NICE"**

LOC. **Cypress College (714) 826-2220**
9200 Valley View, Cypress

1st DAY OF SHOOTING

Rain or Shine

PHONE **559-0346 office**

DIR **BRUCE KIMMEL**

PRODUCER **MARK HAGGARD**

ASSOC PROD. **ALAIN SILVER & PATRICK REGAN**

ART DIRECTOR **LEE COLE**

SET #	SET	SCENES	CAST #	PAGES
	Ext. Street	53 pt Running shts, 50	8, 14, 15, 16, 17, X (19 vo)	1 3/8
	Ext. City Mall	50 A	8, 13, X	4/8
	Ext. Street	52	8, X	1/8
	Ext. Street	53 to complete	8, 14, 15, 16, 17, X	—
	Int. Police Board	51	8, 12, X	6/8
			Total	2 4/8

CAST #	ACTOR	CHARACTER	MAKE UP	SET	REMARKS
8	Paul Brinegar (NEW)	Old Man (F)	6:30 A	7:00 A	Report to Location
12	Kenneth Tobey	Board Member	11:30 A	12 N	Cypress
13	Alan Abelew	Punk	6:30 A	7:00 A	College
14	Bob Carpenter	Hood #1			9200
15	Jed Mills	Hood #2			Valley View
16	Peter Du Pre	Hood #3			Cypress
17	Ron Burke	Hood #4			(714) 826- 2220
					SEE MAP

ATMOSPHERE & STANDINS: **See Map** REPORT TO: Cypress College, Prk. lot 8, 9200 Valley View

4	Standins	6:30 A	12	Ext. Atmos	6:30 A
			4	Board Members Atmos	12 N

CREW CALL: **6:30 AM** (UNLESS NOTED BELOW) **See Map** REPORT TO: Cypress College, Prk lot 8, 9200 Valley View

1	SCRIPT SUP.			PROPMASTER		1	GAFFER	
2	ASST. DIR.		1	ASST. PROPMAN			BEST BOY	
1	CAMERAMAN		3	SET DRESSERS	Own call	3	LAMP OPER.	
1	OPERATOR						GEN. OPER.	
1	1ST ASST. Load @ Studio	5:15 A		WRANGLERS			KEY GRIP	
1	2ND ASST.			LIVESTOCK/WAGONS		1		
	EXTRA OPERATOR		4	College Security	6:00 A	1	2ND GRIP	
	EXTRA ASSISTANT			FIRE WARDEN			GRIPS	
1	STILLMAN			MOTORCYCLE POLICE		1	DOLLY GRIP	
1	DIALOGUE COACH			POLICE			CRANE & CREW	
1	MIXER			MAKE UP MEN		1	Driver Coord /Craftservice	Load Studio 5:15 A
1	BOOMAN		1	HAIRDRESSER				
	RECORDER						PAINTER	
1	CABLEMAN			WARDROBE MEN			MAKEUP TABLES	
1	P.B. & OPER.		1	WARDROBE WOMEN		3	Drivers	Report Board
1	PHOTO FXS.		2	Production Asst.		X	GAL. COFFEE/DZ. DONUTS	
	EFFECTS MEN			1ST AID		65	LUNCHES Cypress Cafeteria	12:30
1	Dir. Assoc.						DINNERS	

SPECIAL INST. - EQUIPT. - REMARKS:

See Map For directions to Location

TRANSPORTATION:

1	Cam Van	Leave Studio 5:30
1	5-ton Grip/Electric Truck	
1	5-ton set dressing truck	
1	Station Wagon	
1	Crew Cab p.u. truck w/ Car trailer	
1	Motor Home on Location	
1	Equip. Cart	" "

Picture Vehicles: ① lotus car ① Cool Mobile ② Electric Car

ADVANCE SCHEDULE: **5/5/81 Tuesday**

Int. Talk Show Set. Scs. 45 pt, 73 Bpt, 73C   Loc: Laird

Int. Corridors Vertigo Scs 7 (est, 9B, 101, 110, 2, 70, 73 D 23 A, 10   Stage 11

Int. Vertigo Cockpit. Scs 5, 19, 43, 62, 96

Production Manager: Alain Silver / Asst. Dir: Patrick Regan/Elizabeth Ward

2. *Script information*
Set numbers (if any), set description, scene numbers, cast numbers, and page-count.
3. *Cast information*
Cast numbers, actor names, character names, pertinent call times (makeup, wardrobe, set, or shooting).
4. *Atmosphere and stand-in information*
Amount and kind of persons required, their call times and work locations.
5. *Crew information* (on the reverse side of call sheet #2)
Amount and kind of personnel required; amount of some kinds of equipment required.
6. *Special information or remarks*
7. *Transportation information* (on the reverse side of call sheet #2)
8. *Advance schedule information*
The upcoming work (from one to five days ahead).
9. *Production staff information*

Some of this information is repetitive. As each section is to some extent a discrete unit which may be read only by those whom it concerns, some overlap is usually required to insure complete communication. Of the two call sheets illustrated, the two-sided, legal-size format, typical of those used by the major studios, contains considerably more space for data. In fact, the major differences between the single-page call sheet and the front of the studio format are in allocations of space. Of the variant elements in the larger format, most pertain to the peculiar needs of studio production. For example, the top left line labeled "WA" is for entry of a work authorization number. This will serve as a charge number against which all of the daily costs for the particular production will be debited. The "Prod. No." may be from two to ten digits long, and it represents the "on production" account to which all of a feature or television episode's cost will eventually be charged. The crew information on the rear of the studio format call sheet is more detailed than the one-sided form. The sample also has a column in which the studio charge numbers for each person and item have been printed. However, it is likely that fewer than half of the possible crew and equipment requests preprinted on the larger format call sheet will be used. This means that, with a few modifications, the single-page form should prove adequate for most productions (*see* Appendix II for an example of a filled-in studio call sheet). A common operating procedure is for call sheets to be signed or initialed by the production manager before being copied and distributed (*see* completed samples later in this chapter or in Appendix II). The studio format may additionally provide a line for the studio operations office to enter the date and time at which the call sheet is received.

The second assistant director is generally responsible for preparing the call sheet. Since the call sheet for a given day must be distributed to the cast and crew affected on the day before, the call sheet must often be prepared nearly twenty-four hours ahead of the work which it details. For instance, a Wednesday call sheet should be filled in by the second assistant as early as possible on Tuesday morning. Some may even prefer to draft it on Monday night. The call sheet must then be reviewed and approved by both the first assistant and the UPM. In the case of a studio production, it may be presented and discussed by the UPM at a daily production meeting attended by all UPMs, studio department heads, and production supervisors who go over the needs of all current productions. By whatever process, the call sheet is approved and distributed to supporting staff and studio personnel. The primary function of the information is to guide the cast and crew at work with the shooting company. Consequently, sufficient copies of the call sheet must be made and returned to the set. They may be handed out by the second at any time after they are received, but the usual practice is to hold them for final approval by the first assistant and/or the UPM. Should there be problems affecting the next day's work, the call sheet may be revised. This process may take a variety of forms depending on the circumstances and complexity of the material to be revised. If time permits and the call is radically changed, it may be advisable to print a revised call sheet, which should be on a different color paper than the original, especially if the first version of the call sheet has already been distributed. Most often, revisions are made via handwritten notations on the existing copies and/or verbal instructions from the first assistant at the end of the day. If revisions must be made after the company has wrapped for the day, the only alternative is a laborious one: everyone on the cast and crew must be telephoned and informed. In such instances, it may also be useful to prepare a formally revised call sheet for distribution to cast and crew as they arrive the following day. In a studio operation it is important to notify the operations office or the individual departments of calls not issued directly by the second assistant. These may include such items as stage power, dressing rooms, additional crew, other special equipment.

The second assistant director physically prepares the call sheet by consulting the production board and shooting schedule. This implies a final check with the first assistant that the sequence of strips on the production is up to the minute. If no changes are anticipated the second may begin by marking the basic information from date and day of shooting to location and contact phone number(s). Items which do not change, such as the picture title, director, may have already been photocopied onto the blank forms. Weather information may also be included. For instance, the call sheet illustrated from day one of *The Creature Wasn't Nice* has the notation, "Rain or shine." This means that the work call is in effect regardless of weather conditions. Most location days which include exteriors will not be feasible in the case of inclement weather, such as a rainstorm. Consequently, such call sheets may indicate a *cover set,* instructions for alternate work and/or location to be shot if the first plan is canceled due to bad weather.

The most important information on the call sheet is as follows: the sets, scene numbers, cast numbers, and page-count. Much depends on the accuracy of this section. In the illustration, there is evidence of a change from the shooting schedule (*see* the shooting schedule sample on pages 99–105). In the last-minute consultations between the first assistant and the director, it was decided to begin the day with running shots. Running shots are made with the camera moving to follow vehicles, in this case, the old man's cart and the hood's car. These shots were moved up in the order of work when the director chose a site for them that was proximate to the setup for scene 50. This change was first reflected in the board strips (*see* Board #3). To communicate this to cast and crew, the second assistant enters "53 pt (part) Running shots" and notes below "53 to complete" for the remainder of the scene.

Below the work, the cast members are listed according to number, name, character, and call times. A section for remarks is also available and typically may be used to restate reporting instructions. It may also be noted that the characters are new. (As this was the first day of shooting, all cast members were new.) New indicates the first day of work for a particular actor, and, in a studio operation, it means the casting office is responsible for notifying the actors. An "f" is marked after a character name to indicate that it is planned for the actor to finish work on that day.

The significance of the call times cannot be overstressed. As the very name call sheet suggests, the calls themselves are of fundamental

REPORT TO LOCATION
SEE MAP ON BACK

Ratings Game Productions
CALL SHEET

DATE FRIDAY JUNE 22, 1984

SHOOTING CALL 7:30 A CREW, 8:30 A SHOOT

16TH DAY OF SHOOTING

PICT. "THE RATINGS GAME"

NOTE: ORDER MAY CHANGE!!!

DIRECTOR DANNY DeVITO
PRODUCER DAVID JABLIN
ALAIN SILVER
PROD. EXEC. PATRICK REGAN
Assoc. Prod. LEE BIONDI

PAGES	DESCRIPTION	SC. NO.	D/N	LOCATION
				West Coast Bank Bldg 333 S. BEAUDRY AVE.
6/8	INT. MBC LOBBY (1, 26, ATMOS.)	68, 69, 71	D	L.A.
3/8	EXT. MBC BLDG. (ATMOS.)	(x) 13, (x) 67	D	481-9115 / 481-9992
1/8	INT./EXT. ROLLS (8, ATMOS.)	70	D	481-9211
1 3/8	INT. VIC'S OFFICE (1, 3, 7, 11, 48, ATMOS.)	215	D	
1 6/8	INT. PAISAN PROD. OFFICE (1, 2, 6, 7.)	230	D	
2/8	INT. RECEPTION-PAISAN PROD. (58, ATMOS.)	214	D	
1/8	INT. CORRIDOR-"CARSONS REJECTION" (ATMO.)	(x) 79B		
4 5/8				

Advance: EXT. SWEENY HOUSE-D-SCS: 122→124. 162. 233. 234: 1 5/8 Pgs. INT. SWEENY HOUSE-D-SC: 233A, 4/8 Pg., EXT. FRONT YARDS-D-SCS: 125→129, 4/8 Pg., INT. SWEENY HOUSE-N-SCS: 175, 190; 6/8 Pg., EXT. SWEENY HOUSE-N-SCS: 178, 236; 2/8 Pgs., INT. COMPUTRON HOUSEHOLDS-N-SCS: 169→174, 180→184, 211, EXT. NEIGHBORHOODS-N-SCS: 163→167, 4/8 Pgs.; EXT. TELEPHONE POLE-N-SC: 185...

Conditions: R or S Cover Set: —

Cast and Bits	Part Of	Makeup	ON SET	
1. DANNY DEVITO	VIC	W/N AT	WRAP	
2. RHEA PERLMAN	FRANCINE	H	—	—
5. VINCENT SCHIALELLI	SKIP	H	—	—
6. LOUIS GIAMBALVO	GOODY	W/N AT	WRAP	
7. FRED SCIALLA	RICHIE	W/N AT	WRAP	
8. FRANK SIVERO	BRUNO	W/N AT	WRAP	
10. RONNY GRAHAM	CAP'N ANDY	H	—	—
11. MARK L. TAYLOR	KEN	H	—	—
26. JEFFRY LAMPERT	GUARD (NEW-F)	W/N AT	WRAP	
31. RON RIFKIN	DIRECTOR	H	—	—
32. RANDI BROUGH	STACY	H	—	—
33. CANDI BROUGH	TANYA	H	—	—
48. PETER BROCCO	TAILOR (NEW-F)	W/N AT	WRAP	
58. ALICE BEASLEY	RECEPTIONIST	W/N AT	WRAP	
3. GARRIT GRAHAM	PARKER	W/N AT	WRAP	

No.	Extras	Report To	On Set
12	PEDESTRIANS	LOCATION	8A
5	HOLLYWOOD DEAL MAKERS (INCLUDING 1 MAIL BOY)	Having Had Lunch	2P
2	STAND-INS (YASUDA, DiSANTO)		

No.	Crew	CALL
1	Prod. Mgr.	O/C
1	Cameraman	7:30A
1	1st Asst. Dir.	O/C
1	Art Dir.	O/C
2	2nd Asst. Dir.	7A
1	Script Sup.	7:30A
	Prod. Asst.	
1	DGA Trainee	O/C
1	Cam. Oper.	7:30A
2	Cam. Assts.	↓
	Add'l Camera	
1	Mixer	7:30A
1	Sound Crew	↓
	Police	
	Fireman	
2	Makeup	W/N AT WRAP
1	Hairdresser	↓
1	STILL PHOTO	7:30A
3	Costumers	W/N AT WRAP
1	Gaffers	7:30A
3	Electricians	↓
1	Key Grips	↓
2	Grips	↓
3	Prop Crew	O/C
	Special FX	
3	Set Dressers	O/C
	Painter	
1	Craft Serv.	7A
1	1st Aid	7:30A
	Watchmen	
	Playback Op.	

	Transportation		
	Car		1 Honeywagon
	Car		
	Car	AS PER TRANS	
1	Car (Co-ord)	↓	Picture Cars: AS PER TRANS
	Stretchout	↓	VIC'S ROLLS
1	Bus -Mini	↓	
	Bus	↓	
1	Camera-Sound	↓	
1	Prop- Trk.	↓	
1	Grip-Elec. Trk.	↓	
1	Generator	↓	
1	Utility Trk./Ward. Trlr	↓	
1	Set Dress. Trk.	↓	

No.	Meals	Ready
75	Lunch READY BY	1P
	Dinners	

Dept.	Special Notes
PROPS:	SCRIPTS, CAR PHONE, YELLOW PADS, SCHEDULE BOARD & EASEL, PLACARDS, VARIETY AD, COTTON CANDY MACHINE (MUST WORK), SKEEBALL, etc., MAILCART, INVITATION

UNIT PROD. MGR. E. WARD PHONE 475-9900 ASST. DIR. P. BERGQUIST/R. ABRAMITIS
ART DIR. MICHAEL CORENBLITH PHONE ______ SET DEC. K.C. FOX PHONE 559-0346
ISSUED BY OPERATIONS: DATE ______ TIME ______ APPROVED [signature]

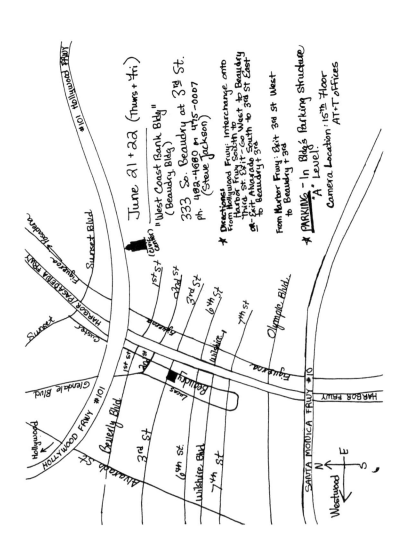

importance. Ideally, call times should cause an actor to arrive, prepare, and report to the set just as the shooting company reaches the work in which that actor is involved. It is impossibly difficult for any assistant director to estimate perfectly the work speed of the shooting company and to synchronize it exactly with the arrival of actors. Since it is preferable, except in rare instances, for the cast to be ready and waiting for the shooting company and not vice versa, the first assistant must allow enough or more than enough time in setting calls so that actors may complete makeup, wardrobe, and the like, without delaying the progress of shooting. Generally, the process of actor preparation may require from fifteen minutes to ninety minutes, but additional time must be allowed for any intricate or unusual makeup, wardrobe, or hairstyling. The abiding aim of the assistant directors is to have everything ready on time and all at the same time but never to have the shooting company waiting for the cast. In the sample the reader may note that actor #12 has an 11:30 A.M. call for a twelve noon report to camera. The call is later because the actor does not work until scene 51, the last work scheduled. All other actors are in the first scene, except #13. This actor could have been called later to work in the second scene scheduled. But as the first planned shots involved vehicles—which always increase the chances of malfunction —it was decided to have actor #13 ready early. In this way, if car problems did develop, the scene in which he was to work might be filmed first.

In detailing the atmosphere on the call sheet it is often necessary to specify the kind of persons (e.g., "women, 35–40" or "Asian youths") and whether they are required to bring a specific wardrobe or changes of clothing (e.g., "suit and tie" or "nurse's uniform"). The twelve EXT. ATMOS on the sample are pedestrians who will cross in the background of the modernistic mall and city streets. The "X" after the cast numbers designates that extras will work in those scenes.

The crew call is indicated at the top of the crew section; this is a general call time qualified by the parenthetical comment (unless noted below). All crew members must report at 6:30 A.M., unless a different time has been filled in next to that position. The assistant camera person, security guards, and driver coordinator all have special times and additional instructions. The camera assistant reports to the studio to load equipment onto the camera truck. Set dressers are often permitted their own call. This means they may determine what time to report for work based on their own estimate of the lead time needed to prepare the set before the shooting crew arrives. The *own call* may also be applied to drivers. In this instance, the second assistant has suggested a lead time of 5:15a for the driver coordinator but has left the other drivers at the coordinator's discretion (PER COORD), as long as they "leave studio 5:30a." Meal requests are also in the crew section and should include detail of how many meals, where served, and at what time.

The transportation and equipment section below explicitly details the items and times required. The special instructions are used in the sample to draw attention to the location map attached to the call sheet. The advance schedule is for the following day, Tuesday. It details the planned work and set descriptions. It is usually not necessary to list the characters, however, some production companies may prefer it. The bottom of the call sheet lists the production manager and assistant directors. It also has the initials of the production manager indicating approval.

Since everyone relies on the accuracy of the call sheet to prepare the day's work, double or even triple checking it may be essential. The originator's last step should be a thorough review of the scenes by rereading the script and verifying that all production elements are listed on the call sheet. Occasionally, the second assistant will discover something—a prop, a vehicle, a special item, or even an actor—that has inadvertently not been included in the shooting schedule.

RELEASING THE CALL

Once the call sheet has been completed and approved by both the first assistant director and the UPM, it may be copied for distribution. Once distributed, each crew member becomes responsible for meeting the call, i.e., being prepared to meet those demands which the planned work will make upon each department.

The UPM must insure that all supplementary crew members have been hired, that the set and facilities have been appropriately prepared, that all necessary equipment is arriving on schedule for shooting, and that any food, whether lunches, dinner, or merely coffee service, has been arranged for in accordance with the call. Not all crew members may be prepping or otherwise accessible to the production office to receive their calls for the first day. Ideally, the UPM will have instructed all crew at the time of hire to check with the production coordinator to receive these calls. Distribution of the first-day calls for the actors may be the responsibility of the casting department or the second assistant. In addition to call time it must be verified that the cast has any script revisions and correct directions to the studio or location. The casting department, when such exists, should provide the UPM and the assistant directors with a detailed cast list that includes addresses and telephone numbers for both the actors and their agents. Depending on the production it may also include the basic money deal for each cast member. As overtime and forced calls are affected by an actor's basic rate, such information is useful (particularly in episodic television) in guiding the assistant directors' production decisions when responding to scheduling problems. The casting department may also send day player contracts to the second assistant, who must then have them executed on the set. Run-of-the-picture cast have usually signed contracts before beginning work.

The second assistant may also work with a casting service regarding the atmosphere. Once the second assistant releases the call, including the details of type and wardrobe, to a service such as Central Casting, they may use their discretion in hiring individuals who fit the call. Even if the stand-ins or extras are being recalled from the set, the casting service should be informed so that they may print pay vouchers for all those hired. If no casting service is used (as was the case with *The Creature Wasn't Nice*), the production manager and producer will have to determine the method for hiring directly. For instance, a local drama school or club may be contacted and terms negotiated with the students. One of these persons may be engaged to coordinate the extras.

THE WORKING ROUTINE

Whether on a stage or distant or local location, the shooting progresses similarly, from first shot to last shot of the day as each scene or sequence is completed. The director, the first assistant, and the director of photography are the center of this routine. Following the planned schedule on the call sheet, the director informs the assistant director and cameraman of what and who are to be filmed and where the camera is to be placed for the shot. Once placement is decided, it is the job of the assistant directors and cinematographer to service the needs of the shot by supervising the cast and crew.

The crew's work concentrates on the changing positions of the camera whether it is moved a few feet or a few miles from the previous setup. The first shot of the day or on a new set is almost always the *master,* the angle that provides the widest view of the continuous action of the scene. The proper angle may be selected by bringing in the cast to block the action of the master (indicate positioning). The director, cinematographer, assistant director, and affected crew observe the blocking rehearsal. The director should be concerned with staging to establish the movements and actions of the cast. He or she may discuss performances, but in blocking the emphasis is on the technical operation of the shot. After blocking is completed, the actors may be dismissed from the set to complete their preparations. Once the director has blocked the action for the observers, he or she may also leave the set to discuss performance with the cast, review notes, or plan the next shot.

The first assistant director is now in charge of the set. The second team or stand-ins are summoned to walk through the scene for lighting and camera positioning. An assistant director should remain on the set during the entire shot preparation. Normally the first AD stays near the camera, but if he or she is called away to discuss the next shot or for any other reason, the second assistant may oversee the progress of the setup. The assistant director may some-times appear to be a spectator; but he or she should be watching and listening closely to insure that preparations are moving rapidly, safely, and accurately. Without the presence of the assistant directors to field questions and guide the work flow, the chances of inaccuracy and delay increase. In order to avert as well as solve problems, a calm vigilance of set operations is a prerequisite.

When the crew has completed its preparations, the cinematographer will signal the first assistant that the camera is ready. The second assistant is dispatched to inform the director and actors. Once the cast is assembled, there may be a final rehearsal of the shot during which the director may make adjustments. At the same time, the camera and lighting crew may ascertain that there are no technical problems with the setup. The first assistant supervises this fine-tuning and coordinates the movement towards the first take. The assistant directors may repeatedly call for quiet to put the set on standby. When both the camera operator and director have responded affirmatively to a final query of readiness, the first calls for a roll. After the sound mixer indicates speed and the camera operator engages the camera, a camera assistant slates the scene with clapperboard indicating scene number and take number.[25] The director may pause until all are settled. His spoken "action" indicates the actors' performances should begin. When the scene is completed or something goes wrong, the director cuts. Throughout, the first assistant stands by to repeat the cycle, call for technical adjustments, or instruct the company to move to the next setup.

Coverage shots most often follow the master. When time permits, the director, first assistant, and cameraman may discuss the coverage while the master is still being set up. Whether or not subsequent lighting changes and cast requirements have been anticipated, the first assistant must keep track of the shots, the cast on camera, and the progress of each setup. Resetting for coverage does not usually require extensive rehearsals. It may be sufficient for the second team to stand in while the crew makes slight alterations. If any of the cast wishes to leave the set, the first assistant should be aware of roughly how long it will be before a particular actor is needed again. Ideally, the coverage follows a logical pattern in which all the shots from one direction are taken before the camera and lights are repositioned in the opposite direction or reverse. However, the first assistant should be mindful of any operative restraints, such as the need to complete the coverage on certain actors first in order to avoid meal penalties or overtime or simply because the actor's status demands it.

DAY ONE—LOCATION WORK

The aim of the first assistant is always to accomplish the setup as quickly as possible. To this end, he must obtain the parameters of the setup from the director. Only with this information can the first assistant effectively oversee the preparations of cast and crew. The duties of the second assistant director key off those of the first. The second assistant must not only check that actors arrive on time and that they progress smoothly through the process of makeup, hairdress, and wardrobe, but also that the order of progression remains synchronized to the needs of the set. As in any procedure dependent on production decisions, priorities evolve from the demands of the work.

---

[25] Also indicated are the date and the director's and cinematographer's names. The closing of the clapper creates a synch-reference between the film and sound tape. By lining up the frame in which the clapperboard closes with the sharp sound on the track, the assistant editor will later be able to synch-up dailies.

In the specific instance of day one of *The Creature Wasn't Nice,* the first priority was to complete the makeup for character #8. Not only was he the principal actor working that day, but he also required special preparations. The second priority was the other cast involved in the first setup of the day: the hoods, characters #14 through #17. Since none of these men needed special attention, the assistant directors could decide the individual sequence in which they prepared arbitrarily. Within that sequence, wardrobe had priority over makeup. All the hoods would initially be photographed from a distance, as they rode inside a car. If the technical setup proceeded so rapidly that the camera should be ready before all four hoods were made up, it would still have been possible to interrupt the makeup process (since their facial features would be barely recognizable) and, as long as they were in the right wardrobe, make the first shot.

As might be imagined, the major threat to any first shot is an actor or key piece of equipment that does not arrive at the time called. When this occurs the second assistant must immediately inform the set via the first assistant. In the case of someone irreplaceable, such as a principal actor, no time is lost in telephone calls to the home, service, agent, or wherever there is a chance to verify that the actor is en route. If nothing materializes to reassure the assistant directors that the missing person will arrive momentarily, the day's planned work must be reexamined in search of some alternate scene to shoot in the interim. It is all too common, for the director, first assistant, and UPM to have to improvise a new schedule at a moment's notice.

When the important arrivals have been verified, the second assistant may check that the extra call has been met. The extras are under the direct supervision of the assistant directors throughout the day. While the second serves as liaison, the first assistant director generally stages the background action in the actual shots.[26] Once

---

[26] The casting service issues vouchers, a combination of contract and timecard, which the second assistant distributes on the set. Also sent to the set by the casting service are several copies of a list of the extras hired with detail about their report times and allowances (i.e., extra money paid for wardrobe, use of their cars). As the vouchers are handed out, the second assistant may inform the extras of the work for the day and where they should wait until needed for a shot. In certain instances, the extras may be required to change into wardrobe provided by the production company.

If any extras are late, the second assistant may check with the casting service or coordinator on their status. Upon being notified, the first assistant may ask that replacements be called in or that the number of extras who have reported will be sufficient for the needs of any shot.

the actors and extras are all checked in, the second may join the first assistant on the set to consult on what elements of the production need further supervision or on any changes in the planned work. On *The Creature Wasn't Nice*, it was discovered while setting up for scene 53 that the electric cart called for in the scene was not running. It was quickly decided to move on to scene 50. This was possible because all the cast needed for the morning's schedule, including #13, the punk, had been given first (i.e., earliest) call. Because the assistant directors were in constant contact with walkie-talkies, rapid communication and resolution of the electric cart breakdown was possible. It took only a few minutes for the second assistant to learn of the malfunctioning cart in the staging area, to radio the first who consulted with the director, and to receive a message back that scene 50 with actor #13 would be shot first instead.[27]

This change had to be passed on quickly to cast and crew. It is usually not enough that assistant directors transmit and receive instructions clearly; they must also confirm that the instructions have been carried out. As numerous preparations may be occurring simultaneously, it is essential that confirmation of critical details be part of the communication process between the assistant directors. If the production manager is present on the set, he or she may assume an active role. In this instance, in order for the assistant directors to turn their full attention to setting up for scene 50, the production manager took on the problems of the malfunctioning electric cart. After consulting with the drivers and deciding that the cart could not be repaired, the production manager secured a replacement which arrived within the hour. As a result, lost time was minimized.

As the day begins, all efforts are understandably focused on the first shot. It has significance beyond later setups, because the accomplishment of the first shot means that actors, crew, and equipment have reached a state of readiness which should in large part carry over to succeeding shots. If there are no pressing problems the second assistant may take advantage of whatever lulls occur after the first shot to begin the production paperwork. There are two priority items:

---

[27] Walkie-talkies have a particular value on a location, but they may also be part of the assistant director's equipment on a stage day. On a large soundstage, when the first assistant prefers to remain near the director and the camera throughout the workday, the second assistant may often remain on the perimeter of the stage to help keep the set quiet. In a sense, the second is the first assistant's courier, and that task may often be accomplished with greater efficiency if the courier is radio-dispatched.

the call sheet for the next day's work and the production report for the current day's work. As previously discussed, the call sheet must be submitted for approval as early as possible. The production report cannot be finished until the day recorded has ended. It is advisable to work on the report as the work progresses, since it may be difficult to recall all pertinent details at the end of the day.

THE PRODUCTION REPORT

As the reader may note, the two blank production reports which are reproduced here are fairly equivalent in their respective detail to the two earlier call sheet samples. Both formats include:

1. *Basic heading information*—Day and date; production number and picture (or episode) title; director and producer; date production began and date of scheduled completion.
2. *Schedule and status information*—Charts running totals of kinds of days, scheduled and actual.
3. *Set and location information*—Location(s) which the company worked; sets which were filmed.
4. *Time information*—Crew report, shooting call, actual first shot; lunch and/or dinner periods; first shot after lunch and/or dinner; time finished.
5. *Script information*—Taken from the script supervisor's report: pages filmed, minutes, scenes, and setups; totals of each to date; amounts remaining to be done; also scenes numbers, including retakes and added scenes.
6. *Film stock information*—Taken from the camera reports, compiled by the camera assistant: gross amount of film shot; amount printed; amount not printed ("no good"); and waste (film lost in loading and unloading the magazines).
7. *Film inventory information*—From the camera assistant's updated inventory, the amount of film on hand. A report on the ¼-inch tape used may be provided by the sound mixer.
8. *Cast information*—Names of actors and characters portrayed; work periods and meal periods. Blank columns may be used to note meal penalties, stunt, adjustments, etc.
9. *Sign-out information*—Space for the actors to sign in verification

CREATURE FEATURES

DAILY PRODUCTION REPORT

		1st Unit	2nd Unit	Rsn.	Test	Travel	Holidays	Change-Over	Retakes & Add. Scns.	Total	SCHEDULE	
(2)	No. Days Scheduled										AHEAD	
	No. Days Actual										BEHIND	

Title_____ Prod. #_____ Date_____
Producer___(1)_____ Director_____
Date Started_____ Scheduled Finish Date_____ Est. Finish Date_____

Sets ___(3)_____
_____ Location_____

Crew Call___(4)_____ Shooting Call_____ First Shot_____ Lunch_____ Till_____
1st Shot after Lunch_____ Dinner_____ Till_____ Last Shot_____
Company Dismissed: At Studio_____ On Location_____ At Headquarters_____

(5) SCRIPT SCENES AND PAGES			MINUTES		SET-UPS		ADDED SCENES		RETAKES		
	SCENES	PAGES							PAGES	SCENES	
			Prev.		Prev.		Prev.		Prev.		
Script			Today		Today		Today		Today		
Taken Prev.			Total		Total		Total		Total		
Taken Today			Scene No. (5)								
Total to Date			Added Scenes								
To be Taken			Retakes				Sound Tracks				

FILM USE (6)	GROSS	PRINT	NO GOOD	WASTE	1/4" ROLLS	(7) FILM INVENTORY		
Prev.						Starting Inventory		
Today						Additional Received		
To Date						Total		

CAST — WEEKLY AND DAY PLAYERS Worked—W Rehearsal—R Finished—F Started—S Hold—H Test—T Travel—TR			W H S F R T	Makeup Wdb.	WORK TIME		MEALS				SIGNATURE
(8) CAST		CHARACTER	TR		Report on Set	Dismiss on Set	Out	In			(9)

COMMENTS — DELAYS (EXPLANATION) — CAST, STAFF, AND CREW ABSENCE

(10)
_____
_____
_____
_____
_____
_____
_____
_____
_____
_____
_____

Assistant Director_Patrick Regan/Elizabeth Ward_ Production Manager_Alain Silver_

PICTURE THE CREATURE WASN'T NICE   NO. 002X   DATE

	NO.	ITEM			NO.	ITEM			NO.	ITEM	
			(11)	SOUND	1	MIXER		TRANSPORTATION	1	DRIVER CAPTAIN	
						RECORDER				DRIVERS	
PROD.	1	2ND ASST. DIRECTORS			1	MIKE BOOM MAN				CAMERA/INSERT CAR	
	1	SCRIPT SUPERVISOR			1	CABLE MAN				CAMERA TRUCK	
	1	DIALOGUE DIRECTOR								PICTURE CARS	
						PLAYBACK OPERATOR					
	2	Production Assts.				PLAYBACK MACHINE				MISC. CARS	
CAMERA	1	DIRECTOR OF PHOTOGRAPHY			1	PROPERTY MASTER					
	1	CAMERA OPERATOR		PROPERTY	1	ASST. PROPERTY MASTER			1	STANDBY CARS /Van	
	1	1ST ASSISTANT CAMERAMAN									
	1	2ND ASSISTANT CAMERAMAN			1	SET DECORATOR					
		EXTRA OPERATOR			1	LEADMAN				STATION WAGON	
		EXTRA ASSISTANTS			1	SWING GANG					
										STRETCHOUT	
		CAMERAS:			1	MAKEUP ARTIST					
										BUSSES	
				MAKEUP	1	HAIR STYLIST					
	1	STILLMAN								GOOSE WITH SOUND	
	1	ART DIRECTOR				BODY MAKEUP WOMAN				SOUND TRUCK	
		CONST COORDINATOR								ELECTRICAL TRUCK	
	1	KEY GRIP				COSTUMER (MEN)			1	PROP TRUCK(5-Ton)	
	1	2ND CO. GRIP		COSTUME						GRIP TRUCK	
	1	DOLLY GRIP								HORSE/WAGON TRUCK	
		EXTRA GRIPS			1	COSTUMER (WOMEN)					
		CRAB DOLLY								WATER TRUCK	
		CRANE				MUSIC REPRESENTATIVE				HONEY WAGON	
		HYSTER FOR HIGH SHOT				SIDELINE MUSICIANS					
OPERATIONS	1	CRAFT SERVICE MAN		MUSIC		SINGERS			6	DRESSING ROOM TRAILER	
		GREENSMAN				PROCESS PROJECTIONIST					
				PROCESS		PROCESS GRIPS					
		PAINTER				PROCESS EQUIPMENT					
	1	SPECIAL EFFECTS								RAMROD	
						STUDIO POLICE				HORSE TRAINER	
						WHISTLEMAN				ANIMAL HANDLER	
		PORTABLE DRESSING RMS.				MOTORCYCLE POLICE				WRANGLERS	
				POLICE/FIRE/MED.		FIRE WARDEN				WAGONS	
						FIREMAN				COACHES	
		SCHOOL ROOMS				FLAGMAN				HORSES	
						WATCHMAN				CATTLE	
ELECTRICAL	1	GAFFER				FIRST AID				OTHER ANIMALS	
	1	BEST BOY									
		GENERATOR OPERATOR									
	3	LAMP OPERATORS				BREAKFASTS		EXTRA TALENT	4	Stand-ins	
						BOX LUNCHES					
						HOT LUNCHES					
		GENERATOR		MEALS		DINNERS				(12)	
		WIND MACHINE				Coffee @					
	1	40 Man (Laird Stand-by)									

PRODUCTION REPORT ILLUSTRATION #2

DAILY PRODUCTION REPORT

NO. DAYS ESTIMATED (2)	NO. OF DAYS ON EPISODE INCLUDING TODAY						WEATHER
	TRAVEL	HOLIDAYS	IDLE	REHEARSALS	WORK	TOTAL	CLEAR _____ CLOUDY or FOG _____ RAIN _____

SERIES: (1) _____ PROD. NO. _____ TITLE: _____ DATE: _____

DIRECTOR _____ (1) _____ DATE STARTED _____ ESTIMATED FINISH DATE _____ STATUS: _____
CREW { CALL / LEAVING (4) _____ SHOOTING CALL _____ FIRST SHOT: ___ AM _____ PM _____
LUNCH FROM _____ TILL _____ DINNER FROM _____ TILL _____ TIME FINISHED: _____

SET: (3) _____ LOCATION: _____ | SPECIAL NOTES: _____
SET: _____ LOCATION: _____
SET: _____ LOCATION: _____
SET: _____ LOCATION: _____
SET: _____ LOCATION: _____

	SCENES	PAGES	MINUTES	SETUPS	(6)	PICTURE NEGATIVE			
							GOOD	NO GOOD	WASTE	COLOR PRINT
TODAY (5)									
PREVIOUS					USED TODAY				
TOTAL TO DATE					USED PREV.				
TOTAL IN SCRIPT					USED TO DATE				
TO BE TAKEN					TOTAL NEGATIVE USED TO DATE: (7)				

SCENE NUMBERS: (5)

CAST — Contract and Day Players						WORK TIME		MEALS		TRAVEL TIME				(9) ACTOR ACTRESS SIGNATURE
Worked - W Rehearsal - R Finished - F		W H S F R T TR	Makeup Wdbe.			Report on Set	Dismiss on Set	Out	In	Leave for Location	Arrive on Location	Leave Location	Arrive at Studio	
Started - S Hold - H Test - T														
Travel - TR.														
No.	CAST	CHARACTER												
(8)														

EXTRA TALENT — MUSICIANS, ETC.

No.	Rate	Adj. To	O.T.	T.T.	Ward.	MPV	No.	Rate	Adj. To	O.T.	T.T.	Ward.	MPV
(12)													

ASSISTANT DIR. _____ UNIT MGR. _____

SERIES:_____ PROD. NO._____ TITLE:_____ DATE:_____

Report ABSENCES on Account of Illness of Any Member of the Cast or Staff

(10) NAMES	REMARKS

(11) STAFF AND CREW	EXTRA PERSONNEL
___ Director	___ Electricians
___ Asst. Directors	___ Grips
___ Script Supvr.	___ Laborers
___ Dialogue Director	___ Mech. Effects Men
___ Technical Advisor	___ Prop Makers
___ Cameraman	___
___ Operator	___
___ Assistants	___
___ Camera Technician	
___ Constr. Coordinator	
___ Key Grip	
___ Grips	
___ Craft Service Men	
___ Landscape Men	EQUIPMENT
___ Painters	___ Cameras and Types
___ Prop Makers	___ Grip Truck
___ Mech. Effects Men	___ Prop. Truck
___ Gaffer	___ Camera Truck
___ Best Boy	___ Generator Truck
___ Electricians	___ Electric Truck
___ Mixer	___ Sound Recorder
___ Recorder	___ Passenger Cars
___ Boom Man	___ Stretchout
___ Cable Man	___ Station Wagon
___ Makeup Men	___ Station Wagon
___ Body Makeup Women	___ Bus
___ Hairdressers	___ Bus
___ Men's Costumer	___ P. A. System
___ Women's Costumer	___ Large Crane
___ 1st Property Master	___ Small Crane
___ Asst. Property Men	___ Crab Dolly
___ Set Dresser	___ Wagons/Stagecoaches/Et
___ Fixture Men	___ Horses
___ Wranglers	___ Cattle
___ 1st Aid/Nurse	___ Small Animals
___ Studio Police	___ Picture Cars
___ City Police/Firemen	___ Port. Dr. Rms.
___ Still Men	___ Dr. Rm. Trailers
___ Photo. Effects Men	___ Breakfasts
___ Lead Man	___ Lunches
___ Swing Gang Man	___ Dinners

SCRIPT REPORT FOR ADDITIONAL EPISODES

Series_____ Prod. No. _____

Title:_____

	Scenes	Pages	Minutes	Setups
Today:	___	___	___	___
Previous:	___	___	___	___
Total to Date:	___	___	___	___
Total in Script:	___	___		
To be taken:	___	___		

Sc. Numbers_____

SCRIPT REPORT FOR ADDITIONAL EPISODES

Series_____ Prod. No. _____

Title:_____

	Scenes	Pages	Minutes	Setups
Today:	___	___	___	___
Previous:	___	___	___	___
Total to Date:	___	___	___	___
Total in Script:	___	___		
To be taken:	___	___		

Sc. Numbers_____

SCRIPT REPORT FOR ADDITIONAL EPISODES

Series_____ Prod. No. _____

Title:_____

	Scenes	Pages	Minutes	Setups
Today:	___	___	___	___
Previous:	___	___	___	___
Total to Date:	___	___	___	___
Total in Script:	___	___		
To be taken:	___	___		

Sc. Numbers_____

DAILY PRODUCTION REPORT

No. of Days on Picture Including Today

	REH	TRAVEL	HOLI-DAYS	IDLE	RETAKES & ADD.SCNS.	WORK	TOTAL	AHEAD
								BEHIND

Director _____

Working Title _____

Picture No. _____

Set _____

Set No. _____ Location _____

Call _____ Leave _____ Arrive Location _____ 1st Shot: AM _____ PM _____ Wrap _____ Arrive Studio/Hotels _____

Crew Lunch _____ To _____ Crew Supper _____ To _____ 1st Shot _____

Camera Call _____ Camera Wrap _____ Sound Call _____ Sound Wrap _____

Date _____

Date Started _____

Estimated Finish Date _____

SCRIPT	SCENES	PAGES	MINUTES	SETUPS	ADDED SCENES	RETAKES	Scenes completed today:
Scenes In Script							
Taken Prev.							
Taken Today							
To be Taken							

FILM USE	GOOD	WASTE	N.G.	TOTAL	SOUND	ROLLS
Prev.					Prev.	
Today					Today	
To Date					To Date	
2nd Unit To Date					2nd Unit To Date	

CAST	W H S F R TR	MAKEUP WDBE.	WORK TIME — ON SET	WORK TIME — DIS. STUDIO	MEALS — 1ST MEAL IN	MEALS — 1ST MEAL OUT	TRAVEL TIME — LEAVE FOR LOCATION	TRAVEL TIME — ARRIVE LOCATION	TRAVEL TIME — DIS. LOC.	TRAVEL TIME — ARRIVE STUDIO

EXTRA TALENT — MUSICIANS, ETC.

NO.	RATE	ADJ. TO	O.T.	T.T.	WARD.	MPV	NO.	RATE	ADJ. TO	O.T.	T.T.	WARD.	MPV

Assistant Dir. _____ Unit Mgr. _____

ALTERNATE REPORT FRONT PAGE

DAILY PRODUCTION REPORT

	No. of Days on Picture Including Today							
	RCH	TRAVEL	HOLD DAYS	IDLE	RETAKES & ADD.SCHS.	WORK	TOTAL	AHEAD ⊖
	—	—	—	—	—	16	16	
								BEHIND 1

Director __DANNY DEVITO__ Date __JUNE 22, 1984 FRIDAY__
Working Title __THE RATINGS GAME__ Date Started __JUNE 1, 1984__
Picture No. __PP 101__ Estimated Finish Date __JUNE 29, 1984__
Set __INT. PARKER'S OFFICE, INT/EXT MBC, INT/EXT. ROLLS, INT VIC'S OFFICE, INT. PAISAN PROD.__ see ★★
Set No. __—__ Location __WEST COAST BANK (BEAUDRY BLDG) 333 S. BEAUDRY, L.A.__
Call __7:52 A__ Leave __—__ Arrive Location __—__ 1st Shot: AM __8:45 A__ PM __2:55 P__ Wrap __2:15 A__ Arrive Studio/Hotels __—__
Crew Lunch __1:50P__ To __2:20P__ Crew Supper __8:20 P__ To __8:50__ 1st Shot __—__
Camera Call __—__ Camera Wrap __—__ Sound Call __—__ Sound Wrap __—__

SCRIPT	SCENES	PAGES	MINUTES	SETUPS	ADDED SCENES	RETAKES	Scenes completed today:
Scenes in Script	306	113 3/8	—	—			194, 92, 193, 43,
Taken Prev.	139	71 5/8	86:42	453	/	/	44, 214, 215,
Taken Today	13	10 1/8	10:22	48			230, 879
To be Taken	154	31 5/8	tot: 97:04	Total: 501			68, 69, 70, 71

FILM USE	GOOD	WASTE	N.G.	TOTAL	SOUND	ROLLS	
Prev.	55,735'	4,485'	23,075'	83,295'	Prev.		
Today	6,150'	570'	2,480'	9,200'	Today	/	
To Date	61,885'	5,055'	25,555'	92,495'	To Date		
2nd Unit To Date					2nd Unit To Date		

CAST		W H S F R TR	MAKEUP WDRE.	WORK TIME			MEALS		TRAVEL TIME			
				ON SET	DIS. STUDIO	1ST MEAL IN	1ST MEAL OUT	2ND MEAL	ARRIVE LOCATION	DIS. LOC.	MILES
DANNY DEVITO	VIC	W	11:00A	11:00A	5:45P	1:50P	2:20P	—	—	—	12
RHEA PERLMAN	FRANCINE	W	11:00A	11:00A	5:45P	1:50P	2:20P	—	—	—	12
VINCENT SCHIAVELLI	SKIP	H	—	—	—	—	—	—	—	—	—
LOUIS GIAMBALVO	GOODY	W	11:00A	11:00A	2:10A*	1:50P	2:20P	8:20P	9:20P	—	12
FRED SCIALLA	RICHIE	W	11:00A	11:00A	2:15A*	1:50P	1:20P	8:20P	9:20P	—	12
FRANK SIVERO	BRUNO	W	10:30A	10:30A	6:00P	1:50P	2:20P	—	—	—	12
RONNY GRAHAM	CAP'N ANDY	H	—	—	—	—	—	—	—	—	—
MARK L. TAYLOR	KEN	W	8:00A	8:00A	11:05P	1:50P	2:20P	8:20P	9:20P	—	12
JEFFRY LAMPERT	GUARD	SWF	10:00A	10:00A	5:45P	1:50P	2:20P				
RANDI BROUGH	STACY	H	—	—	—	—	—	—	—	—	—
CANDI BROUGH	TANYA	H	—	—	—	—	—	—	—	—	—
PETER BROCCO	TAILOR	SWF	11:00A	11:00A	10:20P	1:30P	2:20P	8:20P	9:20P	—	12
ALICE BEASLEY	RECEPTIONIST	SWF	9:30A	9:30A	7:25P	1:50P	2:20P	—	—	—	12
GERRIT GRAHAM	PARKER	WF	7:45A	7:45A	11:10P	1:50P	2:20P	8:20	9:20	—	12
JACQUELINE CASSEL	TRISH	WF	8:30A	8:30A	4:15P	1:50P	2:20P	—	—	—	12

★ ADD 15 MINUTES FOR MAKEUP + WARDROBE REMOVAL.

EXTRA TALENT — MUSICIANS, ETC.

NO.	RATE	ADJ. TO	O.T.	T.T.	WARD.	MPV	NO.	RATE	ADJ. TO	O.T.	T.T.	WARD.	MPV
4	$30-	—	—	—	—	—							
11	$30-	—	$12-	—	—	—							
1	$30-	—	$36	—	—	—							
1	$50	—	$75	(set coord)	—								

Assistant Dir. __P. BERGQUIST / R. ABRAMITIS__ Unit Mgr. __E. WARD__

ENTERPRISE PRINTERS Telephone: 876-3530 57

★ INT. RECEPTION/PAISAN PRODUCTIONS, INT CORRIDOR.

PRODUCTION REQUIREMENTS

PICTURE *THE RATINGS GAME* NO. *PP 101* *FRIDAY* DATE *JUNE 22, 1984*

	NO.	ITEM	TIME		NO.	ITEM	TIME		NO.	ITEM	
PROD.	1	DIRECTOR	O/C	**SOUND**	1	MIXER	7:52A		1	DRIVER CAPTAIN	O/
	1	UNIT MANAGER	7:52A			RECORDER				DRIVERS	C
	2	ASSISTANT DIRECTORS	7:45A		1	MIKE BOOM MAN	7:52A				
	1	SCRIPT SUPERVISOR	7:52A			CABLE MAN				CAMERA/INSERT CAR	
		DIALOGUE DIRECTOR								CAMERA TRUCK	
	1	PGA Trainee	7:30A							PICTURE CARS	
						PLAYBACK OPERATOR			1	MINI BUS	✓
	2	Stand-ins	7:52A			PLAYBACK MACHINE					
CAMERA	1	DIRECTOR OF PHOTOGRAPHY	7:52A							MISC. CARS	
	1	CAMERA OPERATOR		**PROPERTY**	1	PROPERTY MASTER	7:52A				
	1	1ST ASSISTANT CAMERAMAN			2	ASST. PROPERTY MASTER	7:52A				
	1	2ND ASSISTANT CAMERAMAN								STANDBY CARS	
		EXTRA OPERATOR			1	SET DECORATOR	O/C				
		EXTRA ASSISTANTS			1	LEADMAN				STATION WAGON	
					2	SWING GANG	✓				
	2	CAMERAS: ULTRAVISION	7:52A							STRETCHOUT	
				MAKEUP	2	MAKEUP ARTIST	7:30A				
									X	BUSSES (PER CAPT)	O/C
					1	HAIR STYLIST	7:30A				
	1	STILLMAN	7:52A							GOOSE WITH SOUND	
OPERATIONS	1	ART DIRECTOR	O/C			BODY MAKEUP WOMAN				SOUND TRUCK	
	1	CONST COORDINATOR	O/C							ELECTRICAL TRUCK	
	1	KEY GRIP	7:52A			COSTUMER (MEN)					
		2ND CO. GRIP		**COSTUME**	1	WARDROBE	7:30A	**TRANSPORTATION**	1	PROP TRUCK	
		DOLLY GRIP			1	WARD. ASST	7:30A		1	GRIP TRUCK	
	2	EXTRA GRIPS			2	" "	O/C			HORSE 'WAGON TRUCK	
		CRAB DOLLY				COSTUMER (WOMEN)			1	CAMERA TRUCK	
		CRANE							1	MU/WARDROBE	
		HYSTER FOR HIGH SHOT				MUSIC REPRESENTATIVE				WATER TRUCK	
				MUSIC		SIDELINE MUSICIANS				HONEY WAGON	
	2	CRAFT SERVICE MAN	7:30A			SINGERS					
										DRESSING ROOM TRAILER	
		GREENSMAN		**PROCESS**		PROCESS PROJECTIONIST					
						PROCESS GRIPS					
		PAINTER				PROCESS EQUIPMENT					
		SPECIAL EFFECTS								RAMROD	
				POLICE/FIRE/MED.	1	STUDIO POLICE (LAPD)	8:00A			HORSE TRAINER	
						WHISTLEMAN				ANIMAL HANDLER	
		PORTABLE DRESSING RMS.				MOTORCYCLE POLICE				WRANGLERS	
					1	FIRE WARDEN	7:30A			WAGONS	
						FIREMAN				COACHES	
		SCHOOL ROOMS				FLAGMAN				HORSES	
						WATCHMAN				CATTLE	
ELECTRICAL	1	GAFFER	7:52A		1	FIRST AID	7:45A			OTHER ANIMALS	
		BEST BOY									
		GENERATOR OPERATOR									
	3	LAMP OPERATORS	7:52A			BREAKFASTS					
				MEALS		BOX LUNCHES					
					75	HOT LUNCHES READY @	1:00P				
	1	GENERATOR	O/C		60	DINNERS READY @	7:30P				
		WIND MACHINE									

DEPARTMENT	SPECIAL INSTRUCTIONS
	FIRST ASST. CAMERA TO OPERATOR RATE.

ASST. DIR. *P. BERGQUIST / R. ABROMITIS*   UNIT PROD. MGR. *E. WARD* of their work time. Some companies prefer to use a time sheet provided by the Screen Actor's Guild.[28] (*See* Appendix III.)

10. *Comments*—For notes on delays, absences, injuries, or any special problems.

11. *Crew/equipment/facilities information*—Personnel and equipment which worked. Late arrivals and/or early dismissals (i.e., times which vary from the general report and wrap noted in item 4) are logged by the appropriate person or item.

12. *Atmosphere information*—The numbers of extras used and their overtime and/or rate adjustments if any.

The report on production which the above information constitutes is the official record of each day's work. The data which the production report contains is used to verify employment and salaries, check on equipment rentals, account for production costs, and chart both the progress and difficulties of the filming. It is also proof for insurance claims based on cast or crew injuries or equipment malfunctions.

The report is completed by the second assistant and subject to amendment and approval by the production manager, who is then responsible for copying and distributing it. It is not a document that is normally copied for dissemination to cast or crew, although it is available for any that may wish to examine it. Usually only the producers, and studio operations, payroll, and legal departments receive file copies in addition to the production manager and assistant directors.

The production report for the first day of shooting of *The Creature Wasn't Nice* typically reflects that production's progress and problems. Most of it is simply a routine log of in-and-out times and totals. The reader may note the variety and succinctness of entries in the comments section:

1. "45 minutes lost due to electric cart malfunction. Repair attempted. Cart replaced." This summarizes in a few words the problem discussed earlier.

2. "40 minutes lost due to sun's glare . . ." This brings total time lost

---

[28] It is because SAG requires a copy of the work times and actors' signatures that many production companies use a separate sheet which lists only the cast times. Otherwise, it would be necessary to submit a copy of the entire production report to SAG, and most producers prefer to keep the contents of production reports confidential.

PRODUCTION REPORT ILLUSTRATION #1

CREATURE FEATURES
DAILY PRODUCTION REPORT

1st Day
Fair

	1st Unit	2nd Unit	Ren.	Test	Travel	Holidays	Change-Over	Retakes & Add. Sens.	Total	SCHEDULE
No. Days Scheduled	24	—	—	—	—	1			25	ON Sched
No. Days Actual	24	—	—	—	—	1			25	AHEAD / BEHIND

Title THE CREATURE WASN'T NICE   Prod. # 002X   Date Monday, 5/4/81
Producer Mark Haggard   Director Bruce Kimmel
Date Started May 4, 1981   Scheduled Finish Date June 5, 1981   Est. Finish Date June 5, 1981

Sets Ext. Streets #1,2,3, Ext. City Malls #1,2, Int. Board Rm
COMPANY REPORT TO LOCATION   Location Cypress College, 9200 Valley View, Cypress, CA.
Crew Call 6:30A   Shooting Call 7:00A   First Shot 8:27A   Lunch 12:30p Till 1:15p
Dinner Till — Last Shot 6:17p
Company Dismissed: At Studio —   On Location 6:30p   At Headquarters

SCRIPT SCENES AND PAGES			MINUTES		SET-UPS		ADDED SCENES		RETAKES	
	SCENES	PAGES							PAGES	SCENES
			Prev. 0		Prev. 0		Prev. 0		Prev. 0	Prev. 0
			Today 3:06		Today 28		Today 0		Today 0	Today 0
Script	127	97 3/8	Total 3:06		Total 28		Total 0		Total 0	0
Taken Prev.	0	0	Scene No. 50,51,52,53,50A							
Taken Today	5	2 6/8								
Total to Date	5	2 6/8	Added Scenes Need insert electric cart wheels for Sc. 53							
To be Taken	122	94 9/8	Retakes				Sound Tracks			

FILM USE	GROSS	PRINT	NO GOOD	WASTE	1/4" ROLLS	FILM INVENTORY	
Prev.	0	0	0	0		Starting Inventory	96,000
Today	3200	1710	860	630		Additional Received	
To Date	3200	1710	860	630		Total	96,000

CAST — WEEKLY AND DAY PLAYERS		W H S F R T	WORK TIME			MEALS				
Worked—W Rehearsal—R Finished—F Started—S Hold—H Test—T Travel—TR		Makeup Wdbe.	Report on Set	Dismiss on Set	Out	In				
CAST	CHARACTER	TR								
8 P. Brinegar	Old Man	SWF	6:30A	7:00A	4:30P	12:30P	1:15P			
12 K. Tobey	Board Member	SWF	12 Noon	12:30P	6:30P					
13 A. Abelew	Punk	SWF	6:30A	7:30A	4:30P					
14 B. Carpenter	Hood #1	SWF								
15 J. Mills	Hood #2	SWF								
16 P. DuPre	Hood #3	SWF								
17 R. Burke	Hood #4	SWF	✓	✓	✓	✓	✓			

COMMENTS — DELAYS (EXPLANATION) — CAST, STAFF, AND CREW ABSENCE

45 min lost due to Electric Cart malfunction. Repair attempted; cart replaced
40 min lost due to camera set up in sun's glare — waiting for change then moved set-up
Best boy electric ill; replaced by P. Trussell

Company Reported to Location unless otherwise noted

5/5/81 — NOTIFIED BY MGM LABS THAT INTERIOR SEQUENCES WERE UNUSABLE DUE TO HMI LIGHT FLICKER THROUGHOUT.

Assistant Director Patrick Regan/Elizabeth Ward   Production Manager Alain Silver

PICTURE THE CREATURE WASN'T NICE *Report to Location* NO. 002X   DATE *Monday 5/4/81*

	NO.	ITEM		NO.	ITEM		NO.	ITEM *Leave Studio 5:15*
		Report to Location @ 6:30A	SOUND	1	MIXER		1	DRIVER CAPTAIN */Craftservice*
		Unless otherwise noted			RECORDER		3	DRIVERS
PROD.	1	2ND ASST. DIRECTORS		1	MIKE BOOM MAN			
	1	SCRIPT SUPERVISOR		1	CABLE MAN		1	CAMERA/INSERT CAR *WJA*
	1	DIALOGUE DIRECTOR					1	CAMERA TRUCK
								PICTURE CARS *Lotus*
					PLAYBACK OPERATOR		1	*Pix Car- Electric Cart*
	2	Production Assts.			PLAYBACK MACHINE		1	*Cool Mobile*
	1	DIRECTOR OF PHOTOGRAPHY						MISC. CARS
	1	CAMERA OPERATOR	PROPERTY	1	PROPERTY MASTER			
	1	1ST ASSISTANT CAMERAMAN		1	ASST. PROPERTY MASTER			
	1	2ND ASSISTANT CAMERAMAN					1	STANDBY CARS */Van*
		EXTRA OPERATOR						
				1	SET DECORATOR			STATION WAGON
CAMERA		EXTRA ASSISTANTS		1	LEADMAN			
				1	SWING GANG			
								STRETCHOUT
		CAMERAS:	MAKEUP	1	MAKEUP ARTIST			
1		*Ultracam*						
1		*Arri 2 C*						BUSSES
				1	HAIR STYLIST			
	1	STILLMAN						GOOSE WITH SOUND
	1	ART DIRECTOR			BODY MAKEUP WOMAN			SOUND TRUCK
		CONST COORDINATOR						ELECTRICAL TRUCK
	1	KEY GRIP						
	1	2ND CO. GRIP	COSTUME		COSTUMER (MEN)		1	PROP TRUCK (5-Ton)
	1	DOLLY GRIP						GRIP TRUCK
		EXTRA GRIPS						HORSE/WAGON TRUCK
1		*Hustler Dolly*		1	COSTUMER (WOMEN)			
		CRAB DOLLY						WATER TRUCK
		CRANE						HONEY WAGON
		HYSTER FOR HIGH SHOT	MUSIC		MUSIC REPRESENTATIVE		1	*Motor Home*
OPERATIONS					SIDELINE MUSICIANS			DRESSING ROOM TRAILER
1		CRAFT SERVICE MAN			SINGERS			
		GREENSMAN	PROCESS		PROCESS PROJECTIONIST			
					PROCESS GRIPS			
					PROCESS EQUIPMENT			
	1	PAINTER						RAMROD
	1	SPECIAL EFFECTS *at studio*			STUDIO POLICE			HORSE TRAINER
			POLICE/FIRE/MED.		WHISTLEMAN			ANIMAL HANDLER
		PORTABLE DRESSING RMS.			MOTORCYCLE POLICE			WRANGLERS
					FIRE WARDEN			WAGONS
					FIREMAN			COACHES
		SCHOOL ROOMS			FLAGMAN			HORSES
					WATCHMAN			CATTLE
	1	GAFFER			FIRST AID			OTHER ANIMALS
	1	BEST BOY		4	*College Security*			
		GENERATOR OPERATOR */Grip truck Driver*	MEALS	ND	BREAKFASTS	EXTRA TALENT	2	*Stand-ins w/Adj $25.—*
ELECTRICAL	3	LAMP OPERATORS			BOX LUNCHES		9	*Atmos Punks @ $25.00*
				70	HOT LUNCHES *College Cafeteria*		2	*Silent Bits @ $100*
		GENERATOR			DINNERS		4	*Atmos Board @ $35*
		WIND MACHINE		60	*Coffee @ 6:15A*			
	1	*40 Man (Laird Stand-by)*						

to 85 minutes and partially accounts for the discrepancy between the 7:00 A.M. shooting call and the actual first shot at 8:27 A.M.

3. A crew member was replaced because of illness. This note is significant mainly to a payroll department or auditor.

4. "Company reported to location." This indicates also to a payroll department or auditor the work conditions, i.e., no travel time but a payment of mileage money.

5. The most portentous note is in another hand, "5/5/81: Notified by MGM labs that interior sequences were unusable due to HMI light flicker throughout." This note was added by the production manager on the following day, when, as mentioned earlier, it was discovered that the Board Room scenes had been ruined by a generator malfunction. The UPM made this note not merely as a record of the problem but also in anticipation of an insurance claim.[29]

THE LOCATION WRAP

The first assistant director calls the *wrap* after the last shot of the day has been completed. The director and first assistant may leave immediately (as their set work has also been completed) to attend dailies of the previous day's work and/or to discuss the work and plan for the next day. It is the function of the second assistant director to supervise the wrap. On a location set, each department must remove its equipment and load it for transportation to the following day's shooting site or for return to the rental outlet. Depending on the technical complexity of the last setup, this procedure may take from as few as fifteen minutes to as long as several hours. The second assistant may also be required to call in and notify the production office and/or studio operations that the picture has wrapped for the

---

[29] The claim was made against a policy covering faulty stock and equipment and *not* against the company who provided the lights and defective generator, although that company did agree to void all their rental charges to help offset the deductible amount not recoverable from the insurance carrier. As discussed earlier, the production manager was informed of the problem by the film lab early enough to arrange for retakes on Day Two. The insurance claim was based not just on the cost of wasted raw-stock and processing but also on the cost of recalling day players and the extra crew hours worked on Day Two.

day. The production office may request details of the day's work and wrap time preliminary to receipt of the full production report. While supervising the wrap, the second AD may collect crew timecards and extra vouchers. This is also an opportunity to finish the production report. When wrap is completed, the second assistant may package the production report, script supervisor's notes, camera reports, actors' contracts, SAG sheet, extra vouchers, timecards, and any other paperwork together and consign them to a driver who is returning to the studio.[30] The UPM usually requires the production paperwork to be on his or her desk the first thing the following morning for review and approvals. Finally, the second assistant should go over the call sheet for the next shooting day and check that actors, extras, crew, equipment rentals, and the like have been properly indicated and were not altered by the conditions at wrap.

DAY TWO—STUDIO WORK

The call sheet for the second day of *The Creature Wasn't Nice* was distributed at the end of the location day. As illustrated, it conforms to the production board and shooting schedule.[31] (See Production Board #3.) Shooting in the studio does not alter basic set operations. The work still proceeds from setup to setup. The interaction between director, first assistant, cast, and crew is also the same. A number of technical procedures do vary. Studio facilities must be notified to supply power to the stage[32] and heat or air conditioning if needed and to unlock the stage and makeup rooms on time. Dressing room trailers had been installed outside the stage on the previous day; the second assistant assigned these in the morning to various cast members.

The first actors to report were the three newspersons (#9, #10,

---

[30] Obviously, when the second assistant has been transported to the location the package may be returned personally to the studio. Typically, the envelope is dropped off at the production office or is left at the main studio gate.

[31] The reader may notice that scene 110 is not listed. It was determined by the director to be identical to scene 101 and was deleted at the director's request from the shooting schedule.

[32] The crew section lists a "40 Man" to be provided by Laird Studios. This refers to the electrician in the power house who is normally a member of Local #40 of the International Brotherhood of Electrical Workers.

CREATURE FEATURES
CALL SHEET

Tuesday

DATE __May 5th, 1981__

SHOOTING CALL __7:30A__   __2nd__ DAY OF SHOOTING

PICT. "THE CREATURE WASN'T NICE"

LOC. __Laird Studios, Stage 11__ PHONE 559-0346

9336 Washington Blvd. Culver City

BRUCE KIMMEL

PRODUCER __MARK HAGGARD__

ASSOC PROD __ALAIN SILVER/PATRICK REGAN__

ART DIRECTOR __LEE COLE__

SET #	SET	SCENES	CAST #	PAGES
	Int Talk Show	45pt, 73Bpt, 73C	9, 10, 11	2 3/8
	Int Corridors 12, 9	7Apt, 98pt, 101, 2, 70, 6	6	4/8
	Int Corridors 12, 9, Pit stop	98 comp 73D	3, 6	3/8
	Int Cockpit	5, 19, 43, 62, 96	3, 4	2 2/8
	Int Corridor (s)	23A, 10	2	6/8
			Total Pgs	6 0/8

CAST #	ACTOR	CHARACTER	MAKE UP	Report	SET	REMARKS
2	Bruce Kimmel (NEW)	John	—	to	1:00P	
3	Leslie Nielsen	Jameson	10:00A	Laird	10:30A	
4	Gerrit Graham	Rodzinski	10:30A	Studios	11:00A	
6	Ron Kurowski	Creature	10:00	Stage	10:30A	
9	Margaret Willock (F)	Linda	6:30A	11	7:30A	
10	Sheri Eichen	Grace	↓	↓	↓	
11	Carol Ann Williams	Mary	↓	↓	↓	

ATMOSPHERE & STANDINS: REPORT TO: Laird Studios, Stage 11

4	Stand-ins	7:00A		

CREW CALL: __7:00A__   (UNLESS NOTED BELOW)   REPORT TO: Laird Studios, Stage 11

1	SCRIPT SUP.		1	PROPMASTER		1	GAFFER
2	ASST. DIR.		1	ASST. PROPMAN		1	BEST BOY
1	CAMERAMAN		3	SET DRESSERS		3	LAMP OPER.
1	OPERATOR						GEN. OPER.
1	1ST ASST.			WRANGLERS		1	40 Man (Laird Stand-by
1	2ND ASST.			LIVESTOCK/WAGONS		1	KEY GRIP STG POWER BY 7AM
	EXTRA OPERATOR					1	2ND GRIP
	EXTRA ASSISTANT			FIRE WARDEN			GRIPS
1	STILLMAN			MOTORCYCLE POLICE		1	DOLLY GRIP
1	DIALOGUE COACH			POLICE			CRANE & CREW
1	MIXER		1	MAKE UP MEN	6:30A	1	CRAFTSERVICE/Trans. 6:30A
1	BOOMAN		1	HAIRDRESSER			GREENSMAN
	RECORDER		X	MAGIC LANTERN	10:00A		PAINTER
1	CABLEMAN			WARDROBE MEN		1	MAKEUP Taxes Room 6:30A
	P.B. & OPER.		1	WARDROBE WOMEN		/	CREATURE ROOM
	PHOTO FXS.		2	Prod. Asst.		X	GAL. COFFEE/DZ. DONUTS
1	EFFECTS MEN						LUNCHES
				1ST AID			DINNERS

SPECIAL INST. - EQUIPT. - REMARKS:

PROPS— PONG GAME, PORN MAGS FOR RODZINSKI
SET— WALL MAP, CORRIDOR SIGNS
FX— MOP BALLET

TRANSPORTATION:

1 Stand-by Van (IN REPAIR)

1 Set Dressing Truck (5-Ton)

6 Dressing Room Trailers

ADVANCE SCHEDULE: Wednesday 5/6/81 @ Stg. 11
Int. Cockpit   Sc. 12
Int. McHugh's Office   Scs. 8, 20, 57, 99
Thur + Fri, 5/7 + 8/81; Int. Corrs, Scs. 77, 82,
Int. Observ. Lab   Scs 79, 80, 83

Production Manager __Alain Silver__   Asst. Dir. __Patrick Regan/Elizabeth Ward__

#11) for the INT. TALK SHOW. As the cast call is 6:30 A.M., the makeup artist and hairstylist are given eighteen minutes to set up. This is .3 hour and reflects the preference of both studio operations and independent accountants for fractions of work hours to be indicated in tenths. The second assistant arrives with the first crew to make sure that stage and rooms have been opened and power turned on. The wardrobe person and craftservice also had early calls on the second day. This provided ample time for the wardrobe to be placed in the dressing rooms and for craftservice to prepare the stage for the general crew call. (This usually includes making coffee and setting out other food and beverage items.)

In the first scene of the day, the director changed his mind about a scripted character, Harvey Furman. The script called for a silent bit, but the director decided that the scene needed this character to speak lines of dialogue. This meant that an extra was converted to an actor under the terms of the SAG agreement and had to be given a contract to reflect this.[33]

Early in the morning the production manager notified the director and assistants that a retake of scene 51 would be necessary. While the first assistant announced that development to the crew, the second telephoned the actors involved. The production manager coordinated with the art director and set decorator in locating materials with which to construct a Board Room set on stage.

When working in the studio, it is normal to give the company an hour lunch period but not to provide meals. At most major studios,

---

[33] Because this production was a signatory to the SAG Basic Agreement, it had effectively agreed to hire only SAG members to work as actors. However, SAG is an open guild under the Taft-Hartley labor law, which permits anyone to accept work covered by collective bargaining and to continue working for thirty days before being required to join a union. SAG normally requires a producer letter detailing the reasons for employing nonmembers under Taft-Hartley. In this case, because an extra was converted in the course of lines being improvised on the set, SAG commonly makes allowances and requires no formal request if the proper notations are made on the contracts and production reports. The assistant directors are responsible for checking the status of extras who may be converted with the SAG "Station Twelve." Station Twelve is a computer index which reports, based on social security numbers, whether a person is a paid-up, dues-delinquent, or former SAG member; has no record, i.e., has never worked for a signatory company; or is a *must join*, i.e., has worked before under Taft-Hartley for more than thirty days. In the case of dues-delinquent or must join persons, the production company may ultimately be liable for payment of back dues or initiation fees if the person employed refuses to pay them.

the lunch report is called in by the second assistant detailing the first shot and the morning's work to the production office. Such reports are often made spontaneously whether working on stage or on location, as part of the second assistant director's ongoing liaison activity between the set and the production manager and/or production office.

THE PRODUCTION REPORT—DAY TWO

The second day's production report for *The Creature Wasn't Nice* lists all the work completed but makes particular note of the elements involved in the retake of scene 51. The reader may notice in the graph at the top of the report that ¼ day is listed in the box for "retakes and added scenes" and that this accounts for the "¼ day behind" noted in the schedule box. In the "retakes" section in the right center, scene R51, meaning retake of 51, is detailed. Below that, a scene 500 has been added. This number was assigned to a new, nonscript scene which was improvised on the set. An asterisk draws attention to the fact that the total page-count for the script as a whole has been revised.

In the cast section, character #21 has been added and marked with a "+" to indicate further explanation in the comments section below. This is the extra that was upgraded and made an actor: "Taft-Hartley for nonscript lines added by director on the set." Characters #8 and #12 are starred because they were called back only to perform in the retake of scene 51.[34] The asterisks after characters #9, #10, and #11 merely indicate that an "N.D. breakfast" was offered to offset any meal penalties. In the studio, SAG members must be broken for a meal within 5½ hours of their report time; on location, six hours are allowed. Without an "N.D. breakfast," the cast reporting at 6:30 A.M. would have been liable to incur meal penalties an hour before the crew. To synchronize cast and crew working times, SAG allows for nondeductible meals to be provided; nondeductible simply means that the time spent eating the breakfast may not be deducted from work time.

The final note—"30 minutes were lost due to several bulb blow

---

[34] This note would have greater significance if the retakes had been done on the following day. Two actors would then have been "SWF" on Day One and Day Three in apparent violation of SAG rules which would require Day Two to be paid as a hold day. However, SAG permits finished actors to be recalled for retakes or added scenes without payment of intervening days; but this must be noted on the SAG sheet or production report.

CREATURE FEATURES
DAILY PRODUCTION REPORT

2nd day

	1st Unit	2nd Unit	Reh.	Test	Travel	Holidays	Change-Over	Retakes & Add. Scns.	Total	SCHEDULE	
No. Days Scheduled	24	–	–	–		1	–		25	AHEAD	
No. Days SHOT	2	–	–	–	–	–	–	¼ day	2	BEHIND	¼ DAY

Title **THE CREATURE WASN'T NICE**   Prod. # **002X**   Date **May 5th, 1981**
Producer **Mark Haggard**   Director **Bruce Kimmel**
Date Started **May 4, 1981**   Scheduled Finish Date **June 5, 1981**   Est. Finish Date **June 5, 1981**

Sets **Int. Liv. Rm. Set; Int. Corridors, Int. Cockpit; Int. Board Rm**
Location **Laird Studios, Stage 11**

Crew Call **7:00A**   Shooting Call **7:30A**   First Shot **9:08ρ**   Lunch **1:00ρ**   Till **2:00ρ**
1st Shot after lunch **2:30ρ** Dinner _____ Till _____ Last Shot _____
Company Dismissed: At Studio _____ On Location _____ At Headquarters **7:27ρ**

SCRIPT SCENES AND PAGES			MINUTES		SET-UPS		ADDED SCENES		RETAKES	
	SCENES	PAGES							PAGES	SCENES
			Prev. 3:06	Prev. 28	Prev. 0	Prev. 0			R51
			Today 7:17	Today 29	Today 1	Today 1			
Script	126	98 3/8	Total 10:23	Total 57	Total	Total		
Taken Prev.	4	2 5/	Scene No. 45(pt), 73C, 73A(pt), 2, 101, 98(pt),					
Taken Today	7	6	23A, 10, 76 (pt) 5 (pt)					
Total to Date	11	8 5/	Added Scenes 500 *Revised Page Count					
To be Taken	115	89 9/	Retakes R51			Sound Tracks		

FILM USE	GROSS	PRINT	NO GOOD	WASTE	¼" ROLLS	FILM INVENTORY	
Prev.	3200	1710	860	630		Starting Inventory	
Today	4610	3170	1060	380		Additional Received	
To Date	7810	4880	1920	1010		Total	

CAST — WEEKLY AND DAY PLAYERS		W H S F R T	WORK TIME			MEALS			
Worked–W Started–S Travel–TR	Rehearsal–R Hold–H		Makeup Wdbe.	Report on Set	Dismiss on Set	Out	In		
CAST	CHARACTER	TR							
2. B. Kimmel	John	SW	12:00P	12:30p	3:30p	11:00p	2:00p		
3. L. Nielsen	Jameson	SW	10:00A	10:30A	6:30p	✓	✓		
4. G. Graham	Rodzinski	SW	10:30A	11:00A	6:30p	✓	✓		
+21. D. White	"Mr. Furman"	SWF	7:00A	7:30A	10:30A	–	–		
6. R. Kurowski	Creature	SW	10:00A	10:31A	4:21P	11:00p	2:00p		
*8. P. Brinegar	Old Man	SWF	4:00P	5:00P	7:30P	✓	✓		
*12. K. Tobey	Board Member	SWF	4:00P	4:30P	7:30P	✓	✓		
9. M. Wilock*	Linda	SWF	6:30A	7:30A	10:30A	–	–	* N.D. Brkfst
10. S. Eichen*	Grace	SWF				–	–		
11. C. William*	Marjorie	SWF	✓	✓	✓	–	–		

COMMENTS — DELAYS (EXPLANATION) — CAST, STAFF, AND CREW ABSENCE

★ Retakes due to H.M.I. Flicker @ Cypress Location, 5/5/81

+ Taft-Hartley for non-script lines added by director on set

30 min. Lost due to several bulb blow-outs

Assistant Director **Patrick Regan/Elizabeth Ward**   Production Manager **Alain Silver**

PICTURE THE CREATURE WASN'T NICE 2nd Day NO. 002X   DATE Tuesday May 5th, 1981

NO.	ITEM		NO.	ITEM		NO.	ITEM	
			1	MIXER		1	DRIVER CAPTAIN / Craftservice	
				RECORDER			DRIVERS	
1	2ND ASST. DIRECTORS		1	MIKE BOOM MAN				
1	SCRIPT SUPERVISOR		1	CABLE MAN			CAMERA/INSERT CAR	
1	DIALOGUE DIRECTOR						CAMERA TRUCK	
							PICTURE CARS	
2	Production Assts.			PLAYBACK OPERATOR				
1	DIRECTOR OF PHOTOGRAPHY			PLAYBACK MACHINE				
1	CAMERA OPERATOR		1	FISHER BOOM			MISC. CARS	
1	1ST ASSISTANT CAMERAMAN		1	PROPERTY MASTER				
1	2ND ASSISTANT CAMERAMAN		1	ASST. PROPERTY MASTER				
	EXTRA OPERATOR					1	STANDBY CARS / Van	
							(DISABLED)	
	EXTRA ASSISTANTS		1	SET DECORATOR				
			1	LEADMAN		1	STATION WAGON	
			2	SWING GANG				
	CAMERAS:						STRETCHOUT	
2	Ultra Cam		1	MAKEUP ARTIST				
							BUSSES	
			1	HAIR STYLIST				
1	STILLMAN						GOOSE WITH SOUND	
1	ART DIRECTOR			BODY MAKEUP WOMAN			SOUND TRUCK	
	CONST COORDINATOR						ELECTRICAL TRUCK	
1	KEY GRIP							
1	2ND CO. GRIP			COSTUMER (MEN)				
1	DOLLY GRIP					1	PROP TRUCK(5-Ton)	
	EXTRA GRIPS						GRIP TRUCK	
1	Hustler Dolly						HORSE/WAGON TRUCK	
	CRAB DOLLY		1	COSTUMER (WOMEN)				
	CRANE							
	HYSTER FOR HIGH SHOT						WATER TRUCK	
				MUSIC REPRESENTATIVE			HONEY WAGON	
				SIDELINE MUSICIANS				
				SINGERS		6	DRESSING ROOM TRAILER	
	GREENSMAN			PROCESS PROJECTIONIST				
				PROCESS GRIPS				
				PROCESS EQUIPMENT				
	PAINTER							
1	SPECIAL EFFECTS						RAMROD	
X	Magic Lantern			STUDIO POLICE			HORSE TRAINER	
				WHISTLEMAN			ANIMAL HANDLER	
	PORTABLE DRESSING RMS.			MOTORCYCLE POLICE			WRANGLERS	
				FIRE WARDEN			WAGONS	
				FIREMAN			COACHES	
	SCHOOL ROOMS			FLAGMAN			HORSES	
				WATCHMAN			CATTLE	
1	GAFFER			FIRST AID			OTHER ANIMALS	
1	BEST BOY							
	GENERATOR OPERATOR							
3	LAMP OPERATORS			BREAKFASTS		4	Stand-ins	
				BOX LUNCHES		4	Atmos Board	
				HOT LUNCHES			Members @ 35	
	GENERATOR			DINNERS				
	WIND MACHINE		6	Coffee @ 6:15A gals				
1	40 Man (Laird Stand-by)							

Side labels (left to right): PROD. | CAMERA | OPERATIONS | ELECTRICAL || SOUND | PROPERTY | MAKEUP | COSTUME | MUSIC | PROCESS | POLICE/FIRE/MED. | MEALS || TRANSPORTATION | EXTRA TALENT outs"—was made at the direction of the production manager. The lost time due to faulty bulbs continued on subsequent days and was later the basis for negotiating a rental discount from the company supplying the electrical equipment.

THE STAGE WRAP

At the close of the studio workday, the second assistant is responsible for alerting the production office that the set has wrapped; it may also be necessary to notify the operations desk or powerhouse to shut off the generators and to alert studio security that the company has finished work and the stage may be locked. The second assistant supervises the stage wrap just as on location, although the process is normally much less time-consuming. Except for timecards, the same package of production paperwork is prepared and delivered directly by the second assistant to the appropriate office(s). At the major studios, the crew will punch their own timecards on a stage day. Again the second assistant reviews the next day's calls and confirms that everyone concerned has received the proper information.

The overviews and the specific examples of the work of the production manager and assistant directors offered in this section are just that—overviews and examples. Even being present on a set and watching a shooting company at work will not reveal all the intricacies of crew function, scheduling concepts, contract administration, or the myriad other details with which production managers and assistant directors must deal. Many assistant directors claim that a day in which they made no mistakes was a day in which they did not push to do the best possible job. Mistakes, misstatements, miscalculations are part of any job and those under consideration here are certainly no exception. Perhaps it is the medium in which they work that can make a production manager's errors seem so costly or an assistant director's miscue appear so melodramatically wrong. As has been observed numerous times previously and will be observed again by others in the final portion of this book, in being part of the director's team, in assisting the director, the UPM and the AD must be more than just initials at the bottom of a call sheet or on a talent voucher. They share in many aspects of the number one job; in the glamour, in the stress, in the frustration, and, occasionally at least, in the satisfaction.

IV

The Working Professional: A Panel Discussion

What follows is an informal panel discussion among nine AD/UPM members of the Directors Guild of America. It was recorded on February 13, 1982, at the DGA Hollywood headquarters. Present in addition to the authors were unit production managers Carol Himes and Don Zepfel and assistant directors Harriette Ames-Regan, Stewart Lyons, Patrick Regan, Xavier Reyes, and Judith Vogelsang. These nine individuals are representative of the variety of background and experience of the DGA membership. Several of them have also worked as directors. Two are also members of the Writers Guild of America; one, of the Screen Actors Guild; and two, of the Producers Guild. Only three attended any film school; but five are graduates of the Assistant Directors Training Program. The others became assistant directors after work in commercials, regional television, documentaries, and in other capacities in the Hollywood film industry.

SILVER: What is an assistant director? It implies somebody that *assists* the director. But, as any assistant director will quickly tell you, you don't really spend most of your time assisting the director.

LYONS: The nomenclature has always bothered me too, ever since my first job. I've always thought "associate" director was more apropos because we associate with the director. But we really don't have the same direct levels of responsibility that the associate director in television videotape production has; they're really an assistant director in the sense that they line up the camera shot for the director moments before that director needs it in the video booth. The nomenclature is slightly misleading and more and more apparent as you're there at 5:30 in the morning for a start makeup call, which the director doesn't get involved in....

REYES: I think that depends a lot on the situation and certainly on the transition from trainee and 2nd assistant director to 1st AD. There's a big difference. When you're a 1st AD you are primarily an assistant director. I certainly see myself that way, and I experience my days that way. As a 2nd, you're hardly an assistant director.

LYONS: Absolutely granted. But I find that as a 1st I get into the assisting areas largely as a function of having discharged all of my actual responsibilities, in other words, all the management activities that I have on the set. You never really finish them at any given moment because you're going on to the next shot and the next set of problems, but it is the only time that I can move over and start looking more at what the director is doing and perhaps offering whatever I can offer in that particular area in terms of creativity.

REYES: But what you're talking about now is a protégé director. I'm talking literally about assisting the director to do his work.

LYONS: How do you see that?

REYES: By efficiently organizing the work to get the maximum amount of production value within a given day in a given budget to begin with, and then running the crew as efficiently as possible so that he gets the maximum of what he needs. Helping him dig up things that he thinks of at the last minute, or variations . . . to me, that's all *assisting* the director.

HIMES: Yes, I've always viewed it that way also.

LYONS: I do view my responsibilities that way too. But there is a nomenclature problem as well.

REYES: Also, just talking with the director, and finding out ahead of time what he really wants to do—how many shots he has, so you can calculate how quickly you can move the trucks to the next location—there's a lot of conversation that I would also call assisting the director. Sometimes you help him by making him lay out his shot. I've found occasions where it's my stimulation that makes him do it . . . otherwise, he'd sit back and wait till he had to decide and that would certainly be inefficient for me.

ZEPFEL: The question of allegiance, and who you really work for is one of the biggest problems in assistant directing. Are you working for the producer, the director, or the studio? There's often the sensation that you're torn between bringing it in for the price and trying to get the director's best picture. And I think it varies from case to case, in part, according to who hires you. In the last contract negotiations, it was made clear that the 1st AD should really be the choice of the director, and this was a landmark in changing his role. Aside from powerful directors who already had that choice of 1st AD because of their own stature, allowing the director to have the final say in his AD, does somewhat slant the loyalty of the 1st, leaning him a little more toward pleasing the director first, since that is where his next job may come from. Of course, he still must straddle the gap and satisfy the unit manager and the studio he's working for. But probably there's more of a sense now that the 1st AD is really out there to keep the director happy and will tend to lean a little more toward that side of the dichotomy.

LYONS: Isn't there a big chasm between television experience there and the feature experience, and even in TV, the TV series experience and the TV movies.

ZEPFEL: In series TV, a lot of the time the director is really a "guest star." They wheel in a new one each week and the crew kind of looks carefully at him. Some they like and some they don't.

HIMES: But that's when I think you really get into assisting directing because of the fact that you really know the show and you're really helping focus them on what they really need to do in a series. You're a member of the continuing process. You have a lot more to give and you have a lot more power too.

Also, from what I'm hearing from all of you, in talking about the director, it sounds like he's some sort of outside entity, who isn't paid by the same company. As though the AD team and the crew is paid by the producer but somehow the director is different from the continuation of it.

AMES-REGAN: The director gets away with murder. [*laughter*]

HIMES: They try many times. [*laughter*] Yeah, there are those that do that. But I've seen it more . . . maybe it's my own way of approaching it, . . . that we're all in it together and that we all function to make the best picture we possibly can in the amount of time and budget. Everyone is very aware of the budget . . . the director is just as aware of what his budget is and just where he is with it. I'm sure that on major features, they get a little bit more demanding and can go further beyond the budget. But in television it doesn't get that unreasonable.

LYONS: I think that assumption of good faith bears closer examination. Certainly, my experience is that there have been many examples where I felt that directors only gave lip service to the budget. They don't come in to honor the budget, they come in to make the best possible project for *them*, because it's going to have their name on it. And, if they happened to have agreed to twenty-five cars and they think they can get away with ordering fifty, they'll do it because it looks better. I have run into that on several movies-of-the-week which is unfortunate because that's really where questions of allegiance come in as an assistant director. I personally don't care whether they have fifty cars or a hundred. But, being charged with maintaining certain budget restrictions and communication with the production manager, it gets a little hairy in there.

ZEPFEL: Especially when the director sometimes makes promises that further on down the road things will be different. "Give me twenty-five today and we'll cut fifteen or twenty-five out of the big scene in two weeks!" And you say, "Well, o.k. . . . , but do you promise!" [*laughter*]

AMES-REGAN: In writing? [*laughter*]

REGAN: The real professional director, I've discovered, is the one who makes his deals at the production meeting. I'm talking about the episodic TV director now, who sees what he wants and sets it up: "Well, I could do that [scene] with a lot less, we'll just move that truck over to this [other scene]. I've got to have more extras here, in order to make the scene work." Those are the directors that everybody loves and hopefully they are working more than some of the other guys who we call 'screamers' because the screamers get through [with the show] and the screamers do work from year to year to year . . . there's something about them . . . somebody likes them. But basically we're dealing with two kinds of directors.

REYES: That's a good point . . . a lot depends on the director.

HIMES: Yes, but a lot depends on the producer. You've got the same combination going. Do they want to test each other constantly?

REYES: Yes, but I would basically disagree with your point. I don't often feel I'm on the same team [as the director]. I usually feel that I'm being pulled in two directions at the same time. On the one hand, I'm looking at my watch, wishing and hoping that the director is not going to do a lot of coverage, that he doesn't really need that shot . . . when I know that he really wants it, he really wants this and that. On the other hand, being somewhat of a protégé director myself, I want him to get as much as he can . . . I want the thing to be as good as it can be, so I feel myself torn throughout the whole day. Ideally, what you say is true [about everyone working together] but I don't experience it.

HIMES: Well, I've experienced an awful lot of what you're talking about. I used to experience a lot more of that. What's happening now is that I'm changing my places inside, too, about how I'm working with people. It may be that I'm coming to a finer place of balance within myself so I work differently now. Yes, I was always waiting for them to please get rid of that shot, so we could please get on and make the day.

REYES: So, how do you do it now?

HIMES: I'm not on the set, number one. [*laughter*] That changed some things. Number two, when you're the production manager you're the one making the deals about the entire production with the director in advance, not the assistant director, so much. The AD is usually caught in the middle of all that.

LYONS: I think there is also a perceptual thing here, too—you're looking at your watch [keeping track of the time throughout the day]. Basically, you present the unit production manager with what is happening at least two or three or sometimes four times a day, depending on what studio is involved, and by that time, as the assistant director, you may have worked out two dozen compromises. The net result is "Oh, we're going to get the day" [day's work]. Or, "We're about an hour behind," and that is what the unit manager hears. But they don't get into the actual [compromises]. I don't report "Oh, I talked him out of doing this and we moved it over here and we moved a backing and we didn't have to come all the way around and we saved ten minutes there." You don't mention all of those things, each one of which can be a struggle to accomplish.

HIMES: Then you're not having very clear communication with your unit manager at all.

LYONS: Oh, I would never bother. Why bother with the fact that you managed to cut fifteen shots to twelve shots?

AMES-REGAN: It makes you look good!, tell him! [*laughter*]

HIMES: Because it gives him a clear picture of what's happening with the day!

LYONS: Well, I think this is the same thing, even with perfect communication you don't summarize the day. You're answering their questions which are: Are things going smoothly? Are there any particular delays? Are you going to make it [the day's work]? That's the kind of information always asked for by the unit production manager, not a line-by-line reporting on my working relationship, no one is interested in that.

REYES: Are we still basically exploring the basic definition of the job?

HIMES: Everyone has their own viewpoint, as usual.

SILVER: But what we seem to have brought out is that there are occasions when we're going to swing one way or the other. There are screamers who don't elicit much sympathy from the production manager or the AD's on the set and who cause them problems which have to be resolved somehow. And then there are people who are respected directors, not only for the quality of their work but also for their efficiency, and then there's the difference between episodic TV and feature films. But, how do you make the decision of which way to go when you really are caught in the middle—when the production manager is telling you to pull the plug and the director is telling you, "I must finish this today, the actors aren't going to be able to give me this moment tomorrow, you can't pull the plug on me."

HIMES: I think you get a lot more of that in television and movies of the week that you get in major features, based on my experience in major features. Especially if you've got a hot director and big name people, they are given a free road. A lot of times you are told as an assistant director to forget everything you've ever learned, make sure they get what they need here. If they want seven hours to light [a shot] they get seven hours to light. That's really an attitude that comes down from the producers at that point.

ZEPFEL: I think it goes to show that each formulation of the directorial team is a different setup. For instance, one time you will have a producer who is a major factor and who is present, and is either in conflict with the director or who is backing him up against the studio. And the next time you'll have a nonexistent producer who is just the name—a part of the talent agency or part of the financing deal—who is off in Paris or somewhere while you're making the show. Each formulation is kind of like a roll of the dice, you get a different combination. And you have to go into it with your eyes open when you sign up and find out who really has the power, who really will fight for or against or with whom . . . is it a happy family of the studio, director, producer and the unit manager, are they all making the same picture? Or is the unit manager loyal to the studio but not to the producer . . . is the producer supporting the director but not the studio; the loyalties are really a mixed bag.

LYONS: I agree with Don, and there's another way of looking at this. There is a *core* that I feel, that I take to any particular job, whether it be feature, or episodic TV or special event TV like movies of the week . . . which is that there are certain *things* that I have loyalty to in terms of my profession and these do not change. By that I mean, I have to make the show efficient and efficiency means that I am going to be able to do the most with what I have been given by the unit manager, producer, and the studio. And the way to do that is to have as close communication with the director as possible to set things up. Now that is a loyalty to myself that I have got to have. And in order to do that job I have to do certain other things. Now, you get into special occasions where you're told by one power group to do something but the director wants you to do other things. I have certain loyalties there . . . I will not violate safety. And that has gotten to a big issue, I believe, in this town with people who do. I won't. And it's just a flat out thing—if I see a situation in terms of a stunt that is unsafe, I'll stop on my authority and let them fire me. But I think we've had too many situations where that has not occurred. So I won't risk any part of the safety aspect of the shoot. Now, if I'm told by a unit manager to "shut something down," in terms of you can only go to a certain time, I won't pull a surprise on the director, I'll say, "Look we have three more hours, or four more hours, let's sit and talk about what we can get within that time." If I make a judgment here that another 15 minutes or half an hour will enable us to get everything [in the day's work] then I'll go back and talk to the unit manager. If the UPM says no, then that is his or her responsibility and I am charged with carrying out those orders, but I won't make it a surprise to the director. What I'm talking about is a loyalty to the professionalism of the job—or assisting directing.

VOGELSANG: The interesting thing about communication with your unit manager if you're a 1st AD, if he or she comes to the set, the flood of remembrance comes over the UPM of what it feels like to be working there again. I find he often changes his mind and softens. [*laughter*] The UPM may even suggest a compromise and say: "Oh yeah, ok . . . one meal penalty . . ."—and everyone [on the set] feels better about things.

LYONS: It's a different psychology.

VOGELSANG: Yes, and often the more the unit manager stays away, the more difficult it is to communicate it to him or to communicate with him.

LYONS: If a director is saying, "Look, I need an extra hour," and the UPM is perhaps being caught in the middle [between the studio or the producers and the director], you can bring in other people. You can bring in the producer and let him know. However, you don't really want to tell the whole studio that you're doing that.

VOGELSANG: I was involved in a situation where we would often bring the producer down because the director was doing things that we knew were beyond our limits to approve.

ZEPFEL: And sometimes you can just tell the director, "Look, you'll have to go to the producer for additional clout to get what you want. This is where the production has drawn the line and if you want more bodies, or whatever, you'll have to appeal to the producer."

LYONS: Yeah, you don't want to be caught giving a flat out "no," because a lot of these people, once they're told "no," react by absolutely wanting to do what has been denied.

VOGELSANG: An aside to this, in regard to talking to the UPM on the phone is that another person is communicating with the UPM all the time: the *assistant* unit manager or the 2nd AD.

HIMES: Aha! A new title here! Assistant unit manager?

VOGELSANG: Yes, I think 2nd ADs often function as the assistant unit manager.

ZEPFEL: It's true that as a UPM you probably get ten calls a day from the 2nd AD for every one from the first AD. When you get one from the 1st AD, you know you're in trouble. When your first is on the phone, you know he's not on the set and he's got a big problem. Usually, the general flow of information is through the 2nd back to the office and into the set. Sometimes the trainee is delegated that responsibility.

VOGELSANG: Often there is another split in allegiance there. If you're supposed to be the 1st assistant's assistant, you're also describing the situation to the UPM or to the producer, or to whomever you're phoning and commenting on the relationship of the director and the 1st AD. This can get very important.

REGAN: In regard to safety, this is kind of a sideways reference to allegiance. Stewart was saying that he would shut anything down that wasn't safe. You can eliminate a lot of problems sometimes by reminding people that they are arguing about some contractual or money matter for which there's an industry-wide contract. I'm always amused about the arguing that can ensue over something that's really a contractual matter and that nobody can do anything about at that point.

REYES: Is it really possible to absorb useful concepts of how a production works by simply observing? I've been in the business a little over ten years and the changes that have occurred in that time are countless. I don't mean just a reordering within the Directors Guild, that's just one aspect. The whole structure is new. The crews are twenty years younger, the directors are often novices, the producers are writers more often than studio executives —the whole thing has changed. We've been talking as if this could be a very structured situation. But I've increasingly gotten the sense that there is no underlying structure, that the key to being an assistant director and dealing with whatever crops up is flexibility. You simply have to take a situation as it presents itself and make the best of it on a day-to-day basis. The director, the producer, the actors, the crew—they vary so much as to defy structuring.

AMES-REGAN: I work in a situation now where the director is also one of three producers, which works to the benefit of those of us in production. Not only because the director as producer has to have the budget in mind, and is constantly reminding himself that time is money, but also because when a decision about something has to be made [by a producer], I have him right there. There's no need to go to the phone; you just go to the director and get a yes or a no.

LYONS: I think Xavier has illustrated a point. Over the last ten years, the production process has demanded increasingly more of us as assistant directors because everybody else around us may have less production experience or knowledge. I'm not talking about the technicians. Cameramen and their crews are, by and large, wonderfully competent. They may be younger and there may be some prima donnas, but there were always some of them to contend with, someone who thought he was God's gift. But now we have producers emerging who know little about the production process, and directors who know as little or less. I've worked with two directors who *literally* did not know they were supposed to say, "Action."

AMES-REGAN: Or "Cut." Sometimes by the end of two shows they get that down. [*laughter*]

LYONS: Granted some of these novices have observed or sat in on production, but there's a limit to what can be absorbed that way. When you, as an assistant, are thrust into that situation of working with a totally inexperienced director, you do what you have to. You talk with the cameraman, on a three-camera show with the camera coordinator, and basically you all agree to carry these people. There's no way around it. Then after two or three episodes or, in the case of a movie of the week, after twelve days of shooting then they are really ready, they've completed their introductory course in directing. It takes 1st ADs a minimum of six years to get where we are, to say "Roll it" on a set; but in some minds a director can step in like that [*snaps fingers*]. There's just no way I can imagine a novice being asked to simply walk on and deal with one of the most complicated art forms ever created without having spent the days in apprenticeship.

REYES: When I first started, and saw things as people who might be reading this from another perspective, I think Stewart called it "from the bottom up" . . .

LYONS: Or "the outside in."

REYES: At that time and from that perspective, it seemed to me that I was overwhelmed by the monolithic aspects of filmmaking, the scope and organization and attitude of the "monster" that I was approaching. It took me a long time just to become reasonably comfortable in its company. What I find very interesting is that this monolithic creature is beginning to die off. I mean there are fewer and fewer places where you'll find the kind of structure and organization that I found when I first came into the business. For example, when I started, assistant directors did not sit [down]. Recently, I started work on a show where I had a chair.

REGAN: On my last job, the camera operator remarked to me that he had never seen an assistant director with a chair. I sat down and told him, "Well, now, that's a first for you, Jerry. And you've been around a long time."

REYES: Exactly what I mean. Lots of the crew remember when we as assistant directors were taught not to sit. To sit was a sin.

HIMES: Also a sin was not being the last one through the [food] line.

ZEPFEL: Not only are you the last, but you had to eat while standing.

REGAN: Or eat while phoning. [*laughter*]

HIMES: But you've also noticed that an awful lot of those guys are not around anymore because they did all that.

REYES: What do you mean?

ZEPFEL: The ulcers and varicose veins took them out.

HIMES: Right. The premature heart attacks and everything else.

REGAN: The other reason they're not around is because assistant directing ten years ago and before was a management training program that it isn't now. The studios then were run by former assistant directors and now they're run by agents and attorneys. There really is a qualitative difference now.

REYES: But aren't we talking essentially not only in terms of assistant directing but as an assistant director approaching the whole thing? The whole thing has changed for many of the same reasons. So what I'm trying to say is that when you come into this situation as an assistant director, you're not well-defined. It seems more complicated now. You can't just read the rules or talk to people and find out the right thing to do. There used to be a definite protocol and a method.

VOGELSANG: It's important to mention that a knowledgeable cameraman can be production's greatest ally. When the cameraman, AD and director all have the same goals for the day's work in mind, things run very smoothly. No one can save you more time than the cameraman. In any case, a good AD should be nearly as aware of the concerns of the picture as a whole as the director is. If a knowledgeable director trusts his AD, the director will talk a great deal to the assistant director.

ZEPFEL: If only as a sounding board. I find that often for the AD just to nod a lot is a valuable function. Because the director may just have to explain it to someone. Then he can say, "Ah. Now I can go talk to the actor."

HIMES: It gives him a chance to verbalize what he's been mulling over inside his head, and he finally comes out with it. And you haven't keeled over because it's so horrible.

LYONS: And you can play devil's advocate at that time, especially if you identify with that as part of your function. You can easily say, "Okay," and it's not that the idea is good or bad, but you can add, "What about this way, what about another way?"

REGAN: Enough said about directors, maybe we should move on to actors and discuss the trials and tribulations of getting them to come to the set.

SILVER: Certainly. Contractually, it's the second assistant's function to get actors. Practically, it often becomes the trainee's function. When the actor won't come to the set, the trainee gets the second, the second gets the first, who summons the production manager, so that he can get the producer. . . .

REGAN: And then the actor's attorney. [*laughter*]

LYONS: I think this is a situation that has gotten worse the last couple of years, at least in my experience.

ZEPFEL: There's a level of professionalism among actors that's changed. From a preponderance of old pros who had worked at it for years and years and understood the job, you now get a profusion of superstars who are made overnight.

LYONS: And they don't know the routine. I mean you can makeup "Frankenstein" in three hours, and I've had some actresses recently who take the same amount of time. You know, between the coffee and the cigarettes and the conversation, the time spent in makeup creeps up. Then that not only affects the start of the day's work, but also the turnaround situation regarding how late you can go before an actor is into overtime. Basically, the makeup on an average woman should not take more than an hour and a half, as long as people are doing it efficiently, just setting the hair, doing the makeup, and getting finished. Most contemporary makeup can be ready to shoot in about an hour, and that's allowing fifteen minutes of downtime for the bathroom.

REYES: That's generous.

ZEPFEL: Another factor is the "entourage effect." I've found that on shows where the actor or actress has their choice of makeup man and or hairdresser and or costumer, you tend to get the whole entourage system where the motorhome is crowded with camp followers, bowing and scraping and doing whatever to keep their job. And their job is just to please the star, with little sense of obligation to the production. You almost feel like you're intruding when, as an assistant director, you knock on the door and interrupt the breakfast chitchat. There's a lot of nonwork that goes on in there that can be very destructive to a show.

HIMES: Do you encounter this more often with someone that's a "real" actress or with someone that's a celebrity/personality turned actress?

LYONS: What's the difference? We've got to work with all of them.

ZEPFEL: I think you can expect the three-hour time to happen more often with the fading stars, concerned with maintaining the image.

REYES: The average actor or actress isn't paid to give a care about you or me. It's very rare they will do anything [consciously] to get us. They're primarily aware of themselves, and all the primping they do is for their own sense of security. They're not even aware sometimes when they cause a problem. You can say to them "You ruined me today." The reply is, "Oh, I did? I'm so sorry." Because they're not aware of you. You're like an ant.

ZEPFEL: They don't hear you when you knock on their door twelve times.

REYES: I think some actors are like the weather. [laughter] You try to propitiate the gods so it won't rain on you.

ZEPFEL: Sometimes, if you're lucky enough to be involved before they're cast and if the director isn't already committed, you might get an opportunity like I had once to try to veto an actor. I almost did and had I succeeded, it really would have helped. At least I got to warn the director. Going into a project, they are sometimes very unaware that this could be a factor. You can simply tell the directors that this actor has a reputation for being late or whatever, just make him aware of it, that it may cut into his time.

REYES: But in advance they consider it to be a very slight amount of time involved, and therefore not more than a potential nuisance which doesn't affect casting.

WARD: Just three minutes late for each scene affects a tight and heavy schedule very quickly. It can cost you dinner penalties every night.

ZEPFEL: But you have very little input in that area.

REYES: Almost none. The key is to learn how to deal with each particular character, because you can't do very much more than maybe throwing a barb in now and then.

VOGELSANG: I think that's a very good point. I think our main job in everything we do is dealing with people. It's managing the people and personalities around us so that all runs smoothly. You may not even know a particular rule and get by with that, but if you can't deal well with people, whether it's actors or the producer or the cameraman, you're going to have a problem.

REYES: I've even thought first assistant directors should have their own rooms, where they can go (leaving the set in charge of the 2nd) and meditate on the complexity of these problems.

REGAN: Are we going to talk about the "executive first," the guy who comes in each morning, lines up the first shot with the director and then disappears for a couple of hours. Because he exists. [*laughter*]

REYES: Seriously, though, we were talking about the unit manager being alone in the office and having a different perspective when coming down to the set. I think it's important for the first *and* even the second, although it's a very difficult thing to do, to try and get away from the set's immediate pressures at certain times, whether at the lunch period or whenever there's an opportunity. It's very important to try and remove yourself from that flow of information that's rushing by all the time. Otherwise, you get so caught up in it that you make stupid mistakes.

VOGELSANG: You need an overview.

REYES: Exactly.

ZEPFEL: But then again, I've found that, as a first, I was subject to that basic fear: one minute away from the set and that'll be when "it" happens.

REYES: But it won't.

ZEPFEL: Of course, it can run itself at times, but I still get that fear that if I leave, even for a few minutes, the whole show might fall apart.

WARD: We haven't talked about some of the roles which we women might have developed.

REYES: That's very interesting.

AMES-REGAN: It depends on with whom you're working. If your coworkers need a kind, loving mother and you don't mind being one, since you're getting paid to be there, you comply. If they need someone who's humorous or witty because they work better that way, then you try to give them that.

HIMES: I've found from my first days in the business that if I asked a crew member to do something rather than trying to order it done, that I got it done much faster and with more enthusiasm if they felt like they were contributing.

LYONS: Do you mean "ask" rather than "tell" them?

HIMES: You ask them to do something—to bring in the props, to take care of the wardrobe—you ask them for their assistance in this situation rather than just telling them you want something done.

WARD: You're being solicitous; I even solicit their opinion, like asking them if they don't think it's time to do a particular thing.

HIMES: And you're allowing them to be creative, to participate and assist in the entire process rather than presenting them with a simple task that you want done.

AMES-REGAN: I've gotten very good results by complimenting crew members for jobs well done and by discussing attitude or work problems quietly with individuals before the negative situation becomes apparent to the rest.

LYONS: The reason I asked you to clarify was that my experience has been that you shouldn't tell someone how to do something. You tell them what you would like to happen, but you don't tell them how to do it, because generally they'll know more about their job, and how to do it, than you. You hope that they will.

HIMES: Well, they better!

SILVER: But what happens when they don't?

HIMES: Well, to return to Elizabeth's question about how you deal with such things as a woman on the set, what role, what persona do you assume, I've found that asking for help got a lot more work accomplished than if I came in and stated what I wanted done. The major crew is predominantly male, possibly 80 or 90 percent male on some sets, so there are very few women. And many men do not like to take orders from women. They think of it as their mothers yelling at them again; and there are a lot of men who wonder about a woman's qualifications, so they test you. I've seen male assistant directors get tested also, but with a woman it's usually a test because they don't believe you really know all that you have to.

VOGELSANG: I'm not too comfortable with this idea of persona, of taking on some role.

HIMES: When Xavier was talking about role, I think he meant a method of working. I've never taken on a role in the sense of being other than who I am. What I did take on was an approach and an attitude.

REYES: I think there's always a relationship between a role and your real personality; you should be the same person on or off the set. I've found in my own experience, in starting to do this kind of work, that I was terrified. I suppose I still am terrified to some extent, but not as much as I first was. As an unconscious defense, I braced myself for work, and I had to get away from the set in order to relax, to be me. I've talked to a lot of assistants about this, and many of them really do play a certain part. They treat people on the job very differently from the way they treat their friends and their neighbors and their family.

VOGELSANG: I think that's right. And that's especially a problem with women. Many of them feel compelled to take on an extremely authoritative attitude.

AMES-REGAN: Many do, yes.

REYES: That's the most obvious.

VOGELSANG: I think a crew will do anything for you, once you get them on your good side. They will be asking you, "What can I do? Can I take this wall down? Can I prelight a set?"

HIMES: Or they'll come to you after they've figured out a solution to a possible upcoming problem that you haven't even considered. "We've got a great solution to this thing coming up."

VOGELSANG: And you say, "Oh, yeah, when are we doing that?"

HIMES: Or "Oh, wow, you guys are terrific."

REYES: It's ironic, but when I started I still thought film was an art form, and I was going to be doing something exciting and interesting.

VOGELSANG: It *is* an art form.

REYES: Well, that's not the way it struck me the first day on the set at Universal. That's not the way it struck me at all [*laughter*].

ZEPFEL: Are these the guys that build that cathedral? [*laughter*]

REYES: Or the pyramids. It was a shock. And I found that I really have to control my tongue so as not to be acerbic with people, because there were many "cathedral builders" whose actions seemed contemptible.

AMES-REGAN: Who seemed that way?

REYES: Everybody on the crew.

AMES-REGAN: But that may have been because you were insecure.

REYES: Certainly, that could be. But I think this is probably true of a lot of people who love film, who come into the business because they love film, and they may think that assistant directing is a step on the way to directing which, I think, a lot of us do. I do.

AMES-REGAN: So do I.

LYONS: But you're wrong. [*laughter*]

REYES: It's not that we're wrong in that assumption. It's just that you have to learn a lot in the process that you didn't expect to have to learn.

LYONS: To be an assistant director you must know a lot that you certainly don't have to know to be a director.

REYES: That's true. You may have thought you'd be learning things about aesthetics, about working with actors. Instead, you learn how to work within this big entity called the film company. Learning the reality of the situation and how to do your job as an assistant.

ZEPFEL: You basically have to submerge your ego. To have a first AD on the set, who has any ego problem or gets offended or anything of that sort, is disastrous. The first has to be a kind of superman who is able to sit up there and take the abuse or the snide remarks, whatever is necessary, and let it all roll off.

REYES: That's where the role comes in.

LYONS: Exactly, but there's too much of a pejorative attached to the word "role." I think "attitude" really sums it up. Are you going to take a humorous attitude, are you going to say, no matter what the problem is, "We're going to find a solution," or are you going to be a screamer? They're all extensions of personality. By knowing and being aware of your attitude or approach, if an actor or cameraman comes back at you, if the director blows up, you can step away from your persona. Let your persona get chewed out, while you avoid involvement in a contest of egos. After all, you are an assistant director; so in many instances, you're not a whole person. The cameraman is *the* cameraman, and the director is *the* director, they're not assistant anything, they have their "thing," we have our "thing," but it's not recognized as that.

REYES: We don't really have a skill, except . . .

LYONS: Except?

REYES: Manipulating other people. I didn't want to be an assistant director after the first day when I confronted the oppressive aspects of the job, and I tried to think of the shortest way out of it. But I'm still here after ten years, and I've learned to respect myself, to respect what I do, and to respect the people who work with me. I think people who read this book need to maintain some sense of the dignity and effectiveness and validity of the function. In the earliest traditions of the industry, it may not have been a job of much consequence; it was something to be done by second sons, people that couldn't make it as executives, and it was a poor relation's profession. And it's no longer that. It's emerged as something different.

ZEPFEL: Also, the whole industry is changing its structure. As the studio influence wanes and as producers change their roles, I think the assistant director and unit manager are expanding influences in a sense. You see a lot more UPM/Executive Producer or 1st AD/Associate Producer credits these days. I think all this is because a lot of the line producers or the people who get all of those other kinds of producer credits don't really know the job.

LYONS: There is a certain time factor that you have to put in to fully appreciate and *use* the "instrument" of the set adequately. Some people are not putting in that time. The real power rests with the people who are overseeing the development of the script. These are often people who may never have had the opportunity, time, or inclination to go out and actually watch what it takes to get "the German Army comes over the hill," which is a very easy sentence to write. This problem occurs often in police shows. The one-hour action-adventure episodic shows are, in my opinion, the hardest productions to do in this industry. On features you may get bigger scenes, but you'll have a whole day, or week, or month in which to do it. But in the one-hour police show, they just write in these chases with little idea of what it takes to shoot. They give these people titles like "vice president in charge of production," but they're really development people, basically, graduated script readers. They know how to make the deals and they know how to find the properties, which is extraordinarily important. But they don't know how to *make* the movie. And we're the ones it finally comes down to. In business school, they talk about the discrepancy between authority and responsibility. We have a tremendous amount of responsibility and the level of authority is not commensurate with that.

AMES-REGAN: I think you've got to assume you've *got* the authority. You've got to tell them you're in charge.

HIMES: Yes, just pick up and go with it.

LYONS: Assuming authority and *having* authority are different.

WARD: You're not making policy, you have to make sure that other people's policies are carried out.

AMES-REGAN: But if the policy is not correct, you've got to fix it.

HIMES: And, sometimes, a policy has not been dictated when it's badly needed . . . so many times you're inventing it as you go.

REYES: I've found often that there'll be a vacumn of authority, and I'll step in bearing only responsibility and get into a lot of deep trouble. Not because I didn't come up with a good way to handle the situation but because the people with authority resented the fact that I took charge, that I came up with a viable idea. They don't care how viable the idea is; we're dealing with exaggerated egos.

HIMES: I'm not denying that. I'm not saying the world isn't filled with a lot of land mines.

LYONS: And we're the ones who have to clean up the mess. And it's happening more and more. The turnover is so rapid in television. The people with experience leave for independent production deals. The inexperienced people who are left think they can make decisions the night before that can completely change the following day's shooting. You get no notice until the script pages arrive on the set and then you're stuck having to do these scenes without enough time to really prepare these changes. No wonder that episodic TV loses its good people. Once you can get away from that insanity, you *get* away from that insanity! It used to be when you were an AD ten years ago, and if you had done an episodic show for a couple of years, the last show of that season was "yours," you got to break in as a director. That's how guys like Bruce Bilson came up; I think we can name about a half dozen of now-successful directors who came up that way.

ZEPFEL: Yeah, stay with the show for a couple of years and you get your directing break . . .

LYONS: Now, they've got six producers, all of whom are going to get a shot before you.

ZEPFEL: And they [the network] only order six shows at a time anyway, so . . . [general laughter]

WARD: And the writing staff may have their chances first . . .

REYES: And the stars . . .

WARD: But is that the real ambition of an assistant director: to be a director? to be a producer? to be . . . what?

ZEPFEL: Is there a future in being a 1st AD?

REYES: How many of us here want to be directors?

AMES-REGAN: I'd like to. Some of the time. When I'm not producing. [*general laughter*]

REYES: We do learn a lot as assistant directors and unit managers. Eventually, that will show on the screen if we do direct. We do have something valuable that will eventually be acknowledged.

LYONS: But not necessarily within the confines of the job.

HIMES: Not for everyone . . .

LYONS: I believe it is the expectation of most of those AD trainees that they're not going to wind up as 1st ADs.

HIMES: How many people remain 2nd ADs? Men used to come into the guild and they would remain 2nd ADs for their career life. They would accept that as the position and the job and stay there, and not even think of moving to 1st AD.

ZEPFEL: Now when you see people who consider themselves professional 2nd's (they do still exist), there's a suspicion that they're limited. Why haven't they moved up? Is it because there's something wrong with them? Obviously, they have their reasons. Some of them are very good at their job and it's a shame that there isn't more of a stabilizing influence that's acceptable.

REYES: Is there anything wrong with assisting directing and unit managing as being a ladder toward something else?

AMES-REGAN: No, not if you do your job well in the meantime.

REGAN: Not if you do the job for a certain length of time to gain knowledge, experience, and maturity.

HIMES: Whatever you need to move up!

VOGELSANG: What time is it now? [*laughter*]

LYONS: You take a different attitude toward the job you're passing through than you would if it were your ultimate goal. I think that that is reflected in considering what people are willing to put up with in any job situation. We do a lot of things for promises, I believe. Especially in entertainment; you do things for the promise that you'll get to be the producer. As a trainee, when you're putting up with the really impossible working conditions, the way to get through it is to count the days; 400 days to go at the beginning, and then you'll have 200 days through and it's cognitive dissonance . . . you convince yourself that at the end of this rainbow is a pot of gold . . .

AMES-REGAN: You're paying your dues . . .

WARD: Everyone is telling you that constantly . . .

HIMES: Are we, as assistant directors and unit managers, a group of people that defer our possibilities?

LYONS: I think so, by and large, the people I know are willing to put up with a lot now because in five years they'll get what they want.

REYES: Do you think that it lowers or raises the quality of the workers?

LYONS: I'm not sure. But I do know that it changes what we're willing to put up with. If a situation is not very good, you take a different attitude if you're going to be stuck there for the rest of your life.

REYES: No, you don't. You very quickly develop a slave mentality and most of the career 2nd's were like pyramid builders.

LYONS: And they thought the Pharaoh knew what he was doing.

REYES: No they didn't.

LYONS: They never built one upside down! They all had the broad base on the ground. And we have all worked on productions that had the pyramid sitting on its tip. [*general laughter*]

REYES: I'm not so certain that you don't develop more of a tolerance and an indifference in a slave mentality when you're hopelessly confined but you know that you've got to keep getting work.

SILVER: But you don't know exactly where it's leading to; that's what we've all been hinting at. When you come into the industry as an electrician cable man, or camera assistant, there's always a job objective and role model right there within your department. You know that if you do your job for a certain number of years, 15 or 20 as specified in the union rules, you will become a director of photography [or head of your technical department]. Anywhere along the line you may stop; there is no stigma attached. If you want to stay a camera operator, or 1st camera assistant, fine. If you want to stay best-boy grip, fine. There are plenty of career people in those categories. But it is not clear what's next after unit production manager. Are you working toward production supervisor of a studio? Producer? Director? The training program is called the "Directors Guild of America Producers Training Program." What does that mean? "Well, it's the DGA training you to be a producer" is what they told me. Why is the Directors Guild training me to be a producer instead of a director? And why are they doing that by making me an assistant director? Why don't they train me by making me an assistant producer? There is a confusion of goals that is difficult to comprehend because you have to make deals that aren't in writing. You can't say to yourself, "Well, if I do this for twenty years I get to be a director." You can maybe do it for two months and get to be a director; or forty years and never make it.

APPENDIX 1

Three-Camera
Film Production

The three-camera film show may often be confused with similar programming that is produced on videotape; but it remains, from the point of view of both the reproductive process and staffing, a film medium. Since its popularization by Desilu for the production of *I Love Lucy*, three-camera methods have been used almost exclusively to film episodes of half-hour comedy series. The refinement of videotape processes and the success of such early tape sit-coms as *All in the Family* has long since removed the last vestiges of network resistance to the use of videotape for prime-time programs. As a result, only MTM Productions and Paramount have in recent years continued to employ the three-camera film format, as the majority of multi-camera, live-audience sit-coms have been recorded on videotape.

Multi-camera programs, whether filmed or taped, do share certain operating procedures, most notably the use of proscenium-style sets erected on soundstages in a manner that can be viewed by a live audience from raised bleachers.[1] Three-camera film shows employ personnel under the terms of the guild and union film agreements, but the management and set supervision of such productions, that is the work of the unit production manager and assistant directors, includes requirements quite distinct from those of the one-camera format.

Three-camera half-hour shows work on a five-day production schedule; one-camera half-hour episodes are typically budgeted to accommodate three or four shooting days. A three-camera show has only *one* shooting day, which follows three days of reading and

[1] In should be noted that some tape shows do not record before an audience but merely "block and shoot" using multiple cameras. This can also be done with three-film cameras, and the result bears a much closer resemblance to a one-camera operation, as the reader may note from the reproduction of a "block and shoot" call sheet.

W. A. 5736				Day FRIDAY, FEBRUARY 15, 1980	
Series ANGIE				5th Day out of 5 days	
Producer MILLER/MILKIS/BOYETT; THUNA/CAULEY/BANTA		**CALL SHEET**		CREW Call 10:30 A	
Director JOHN TRACY				CAST Call 11 A	
Title FRIENDS IN NEED		Prod. No. 60432-037		Location Stage 30 (x1930)	

SET # SET	SCENES	CAST	D/N	PAGES	LOCATION
	CLOSED SET - NO VISITORS				
	FINAL REHEARSAL			11A	Stage 30
	RUN THROUGH			2P	
	SHOOT SHOW #037			6:30P	

CAST & DAY PLAYERS	PART OF	MAKE-UP/LEAVE	SET CALL	REMARKS
DONNA PESCOW	ANGIE		11A	Report to Stg. 30
ROBERT HAYS	BRAD		11A	
DORIS ROBERTS	THERESA		11A	
SHARON SPELMAN	JOYCE		11A	
DEBRALEE SCOTT	MARIE		12N	
EMORY BASS	PHIPPS		11A	
SUSAN DUVALL	MARY G.		11A	
NANCY LANE	MARY K.		11A	
VALRI BROMFIELD	MARY M.		11A	
MICHAEL MCMANUS	DOUGIE		11:15A	
MARTIN FERRERO	FR. TORTELLI		11:15A	
*JASON SEMELENG	CHUCKIE		1:00P	
*TERRI WAGNER OTIS	DEBBIE		1:00P	
*MINORS				

ATMOSPHERE AND STANDINS			SPECIAL INSTRUCTIONS	
9	STAND-INS	@ 11A	Report to STAGE 30	
1	BEAUTICIAN	@ 12P		
3	BEAUTY SHOP PATRONS			
6	CHILDREN	@ 1P		
1	TEACHER	@ 1P		

ADVANCE SHOOTING NOTES

SHOOTING DATE	SET NO.	SET NAME	LOCATION	SCENE NO.
2/18/80 MONDAY		HOLIDAY - WASHINGTON'S BIRTHDAY		
2/19/80 TUESDAY		WRAP SHOW		

UNIT PROD. MGR. A. McCULLOUGH   PHONE 1066   ASST. DIR. A. SILVER/W. SHEAR PHONE 1930/2425
ART DIR. K. DAVIS   PHONE 2687   SET DEC. B. GIBESON   PHONE 2474
ISSUED BY OPERATIONS: DATE 2/13/80   TIME 8:00PM   APPROVED

© 1979 Paramount Pictures Corporation.

rehearsal and one day of camera blocking. With only one shooting day, there is no need for a formal breakdown of the script or to establish a production board or shooting schedule. The script itself is typed in a slightly different format (see illustrations); and it is not unusual for it to undergo three revisions in the course of four days. The final draft script is normally distributed at the beginning of the shooting or "show" day. The revisions, which may range from minor line changes to complete restructuring, are based on the rehearsals and run-throughs staged by the director and cast for the producers and writing staff. Typically, three-camera productions operate as follows:

DAY ONE—Director, cast, producers, writers, production manager, assistant directors, and department heads assemble in a conference room or rehearsal hall to "read" the script. After the reading, the cast is dismissed and a variant of the production meeting takes place in which the particular requirements of the episode are discussed. On some shows, the cast reassembles later on stage for an initial walk-through for the director on the actual sets. If the show's home stage is unavailable due to set construction, this activity may be temporarily relocated to a rehearsal hall or open stage.

DAY TWO—The Director of Photography and his lighting crew take an earlier call. Director and cast arrive mid-morning, go over script changes, and rehearse. In the late afternoon, the entire show is run through for the producers and writing staff.

DAY THREE—A revised final draft incorporating changes based on Day Two run-through is distributed. Between scene rehearsal, stand-ins work with the director of photography and crew. At day's end, Director and cast hold another run-through.

DAY FOUR—A shooting script with changes based on Day Three is delivered. "Camera blocking" is the first day of work for the camera crews (three operators and three camera assistants), camera coordinator, dolly grips, sound crew, makeup and hair, and extra lamp operators. After the cast runs each scene, the director uses the stand-ins to set camera positions and coordinate their movements within the scene. The camera coordinator notes and assigns numbers to all the positions, so that he may cue the camera operators and dolly grips over headsets. The dolly grips put color-coded marks on the stage floor. The camera assistants

---

DOING OUR THING

CAST

	A	B	C	D	E	G	
BERT CARSON	A	B	C	D	E	G	WALTER NEFF
DOUG PETERS	A	B	C	D		G	SCOTTY FERGUSON
ELEANOR "TEDDY" PETERS	A	B	C	D	E	G	MELANIE DANIELS
MOE DUSENBERG		B			E	G	GABRIELLE GIRARD
COOLIDGE HUNTER		B			E	G	JONATHAN SHIELDS
CONNIE BAKER			C			G	CARMEN STERNWOOD
FRANK BAKER			C			G	JEDEDIAH LELAND
VINNIE	A				E		NICK BIANCO
JUNKMAN	A			D			MARTIN ROME
CUSTOMER				D			NOAH CROSS
ELDRIDGE				D			JONATHAN HARKER

SETS:	PAGE:		
BARBER SHOP	(1)	(A)	INT. BARBER SHOP - DAY
HOTEL LOBBY	(12)	(B)	INT. HOTEL LOBBY - DAY
BAKERY	(18)	(c)	INT. BAKERY - DAY
	(24)	(D)	INT. BARBER SHOP - A WEEK LATER
	(37)	(E)	INT. HOTEL LOBBY - LATER
	(42)	(G)	TAG - INT. BARBER SHOP - EVENING

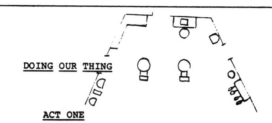

DOING OUR THING

ACT ONE

4 CUES: 2 on p 1   A
        1 on p. 5
        1 on p. 8

FADE IN:

INT. BERT'S BARBERSHOP - DAY

BERT'S IS AN OLD STYLE BARBERSHOP, WHICH STILL FEATURES RAZOR
STROPS AND A CASE FULL OF PERSONALIZED SHAVING MUGS ON THE
WALL. IT'S A DOUBLE STORE FRONT OVERLOOKING THE BOARDWALK
IN VENICE, CA. THE FOUR SWIVEL CHAIRS AND SHOESHINE STAND
ARE FLANKED BY THE FAMILIAR BROWN VINYL, SPRING-LEGGED
WAITING CHAIRS INTERSPERSED WITH STEEL TABLES STACKED WITH
BATTERED "ESQUIRES" AND "FIELD AND STREAMS." THE CALENDAR
ON THE WALL FEATURES A TANNED BLONDE IN A CATALINA SWIMSUIT
SIPPING A FROSTY ROOT BEER. THE MONTH IS: "JANUARY, 1965."   # 4

VINNIE VARELA SHUFFLES OUT FROM THE BACK ROOM. HE WEARS A
COAT OVER HIS WHITE SMOCK AND AN OLD FEDORA PERCHED ON HIS
BROW. VINNIE NOTICES THE CALENDAR, REFLECTS, THEN TEARS
OFF A SHEET TO ADVANCE IT TO FEBRUARY. THE OWNER, BERT ———— # 4
CARSON, ENTERS FROM THE BACK. BERT IS JUST SHY OF THIRTY
AND CLEAN SHAVEN. HE HANDS VINNIE A RUMPLED ENVELOPE.

                    BERT

        It's all there. Want to count it?   V Q B

                    VINNIE

        (ITALIAN ACCENT) Thirty two years I   V XR

        work for you and your father. (TO

        THE SKY) He asks if I want to count

                    (MORE)

2.
(A)

                    VINNIE (cont'd)

      my last pay envelope. (TO BERT)

      You're gosh-darned right I want to

      count it!

AS VINNIE COUNTS, BERT INDICATES THE SHORT HAIRS AROUND
HIS EARS. VINNIE GIVES HIM AN ANNOYED NOD. THEY CROSS TO
A CHAIR, AND BERT SITS DOWN TO RECEIVE A TRIM. VINNIE
TAKES A COMB AND SCISSORS FROM A GLASS DISPENSOR AND STARTS
TO CUT.

                    VINNIE

      Fourteen years I used these scissors.

                    BERT

      Okay. Take them with you.

                    VINNIE

      And this comb. . .

                    BERT

      It's yours. It's yours.

VINNIE ACTS HURT.

                    BERT

      I'm sorry, it had to come to this.

                    VINNIE

      (AS HE CUTS) Why be sorry? Nobody

      wants haircuts, you don't need an

      old man sitting around reading maga-

      zines. Besides, I'm gonna like it

      at Golden Acres.

                    BERT

      Really?

note focus changes and zooms; the camera operators do the same for pans and tilts. If at any point in the scene the actors shift too radically for the cameras to follow comfortably, there may be a "reset" in the blocking: the cast will pause in the action while cameras shift, then recommence overlapping their movements slightly. After each scene is blocked, it is run with the cast so that marks may be checked. At day's end, there is another run-through for producers and writers. On some shows, a detached or unusual scene may actually be filmed on blocking day.

DAY FIVE—"Show Day" requires additional crew: second camera assistant; extra costumers, makeup, and hair; standby first-aid person and fireman. Cast and crew report around midday in anticipation of an evening filming before an audience. A revised shooting script is delivered for review. There is a final rehearsal and final adjustments. The early audience is then admitted to view the formal run-through. Occasionally, "pick-ups" or entire scenes may be filmed at this time. Normally, this run-through is only for director, cast, and crew to adjust their timing based on audience response. There is a last conference with producers and writing staff for notes based on this audience response. After a dinner break, the show is filmed before a second audience. Ideally, each scene will be filmed only once. If there are problems, the director may re-do or "pick-up" portions of any scene. After the audience leaves, planned pick-ups of additional reaction shots or inserts and unplanned pick-ups due to technical problems will be shot. If needed, wild lines will be recorded.

On the surface, this operating procedure differs radically from the one-camera production format. However, the job functions of the production manager and the assistant directors, although clearly not encompassing most of the duties listed in the DGA Basic Agreement, do correspond to the thrust of their work in a one-camera situation. The production manager still supervises the show's budget and approves personnel and equipment requirements; the second assistant director still prepares call sheets and production reports and disseminates information to cast and crew. It is the first assistant director who, while still running the set for the director in the sense of calling for quiet and rolling camera, must assume the widest range of "new" duties in the three-camera format.

Although a production board or shooting schedule would be

superfluous, many of the myriad details which would have been annotated on a board or schedule carry over to the three-camera format and must be tracked by the first assistant. Whether the scenes are given number or letter designations, the first assistant must be aware of which actors are needed for them. Typically, the front page of each draft is marked as in the illustration to provide quick reference. Because the actors cannot be certain of hearing dialogue cues over audience reaction, all entrances are cued by lights connected to a central control in the hands of the first assistant, who must note where the director wishes the cue to be given. Hence, the numbers on the margins of the sample script page refer to the buttons on the cue light control box which must be depressed at that point. Typically, the first assistant will watch each rehearsal with considerable attention and may note only light cues but also the actors' crosses and exits in anticipation of blocking. The comparative samples from first and final drafts show the development of blocking of both actors and extras (for whose staging, the first assistant is responsible) in an opening scene.

During the first three days, as the episode progresses through rehearsals, run-throughs, and rewrites, the first assistant director must act as a liaison between director and cast on stage and the producers and writing staff in their offices. An additional line-of-communication is needed between the director, and the UPM and department heads concerning such things as personnel, set dressing, and like needs not contained in the script but developing out of the director's staging. On some shows, the first assistant will attend the major rewrite conference on the evening of Day Three to be kept up-to-the-minute on significant changes. As diverse as these duties are, the slower pace and shorter hours of the three rehearsal days should allow the first assistant ample time to keep track of the staging and respond to potential problems. The pressures of Blocking Day and Show Day are considerably greater.

During camera blocking, the camera coordinator is the only person who must make detailed notes throughout. The first assistant must nonetheless be aware of all resets and pick-ups and should add these notations to the script margin. Although the resets involve all the cameras, the planned pick-ups may involve just one or two and selected cast, which should also be noted. If possible, the first assistant may write the planned pick-ups on the light-plot prepared by the script supervisor (see the sample on pages 147–148). At day's end, the first assistant may participate in any consultation among director, cast, and

Appendix 1

147

LIGHT PLOT

PARAMOUNT TELEVISION   SERIES _ANGIE_   EPISODE _FRIENDS IN NEED_

PROD # _6032-037_   DIRECTOR _JOHN TRACY_   DATE FILMED _2/15/80_

Sc.	Set	Time	Pick-ups
A	BEAUTY SHOP	DAY	1) 3 CAM — "A" MARIE / "B" MARY M. / "B" 2 SHOT 2) 2 CAM — "A" MARY G. / "C" MARY K.
B	DAY CARE CENTER	DAY	1) 2 CAM — "A" MARY G. / "B" MARY K.
C	BENSON LIVING ROOM	NIGHT	1) 1 CAM — "A" BRAD IN KITCHEN
D	BENSON LIVING ROOM	DAY	1) 1 CAM — "A" JOYCE BY TABLE 2) 1 CAM — "C" MARY M.
E	DAY CARE CENTER	DAY	
G	BENSON LIVING ROOM	NIGHT	1) 2 CAM — "B" MARY G. / "C" MARY K.

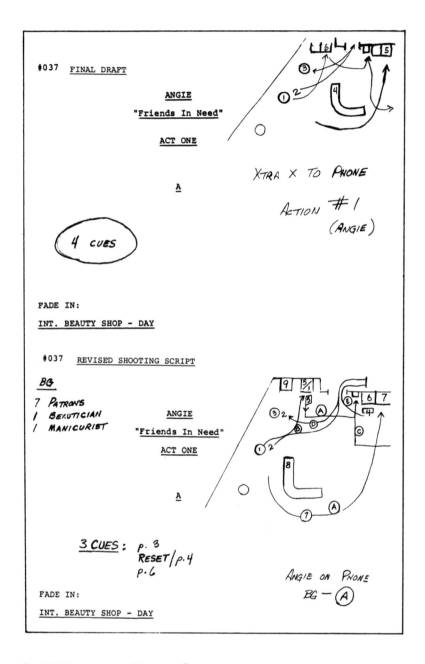

#037   FINAL DRAFT

ANGIE

"Friends In Need"

ACT ONE

A

4 CUES

XTRA X TO PHONE

ACTION #1
(ANGIE)

FADE IN:

INT. BEAUTY SHOP - DAY

#037   REVISED SHOOTING SCRIPT

BG

7 PATRONS
1 BEAUTICIAN
1 MANICURIST

ANGIE

"Friends In Need"

ACT ONE

A

3 CUES: p. 3
RESET/p.4
p. 6

ANGIE ON PHONE

BG — (A)

FADE IN:

INT. BEAUTY SHOP - DAY

producers about which, if any, of the pick-ups will be "hot," i.e., filmed before the audience.

The actual shooting of the episode is the culmination of four and one-half days of effort and, as might be expected, will make the heaviest demands on the first assistant director's organizational *and* improvisational abilities. The final rehearsal and afternoon run-through must proceed at the planned pace, or there will be meal penalties before the dinner break. Further, if the predinner notes are lengthy, the cast may be delayed in returning for wardrobe and makeup before shooting, a time that is fixed by the arrival of the audience. On returning to the stage after dinner, the first assistant may meet with the director, camera coordinator, and script supervisor for a final review of script annotations. After cast introductions, the first scene is shot. The first assistant follows the script not just to give cues but also as a back up to the director, script supervisor, and camera coordinator in checking for possible errors in line reading or camera moves. Ideally, after the cut, the director and first assistant will begin by consulting the A and C camera operators. These are the outside cameras which film the action in two-shots and singles. When they meet at B camera, the director will actively consult with the first assistant over the camera operators' reports of problems and whether unplanned pick-ups must be made. The camera coordinator and sound mixer are in a control booth, but they may communicate problems to the first over their headsets.

ANGIE Show #022
Production Time Breakdown for 10/2/79

Cast introductions	6:35 P	
First shot	6:45 P	(two pick-ups from B during show; script timing: 22:15)
Audience released	8:10 P	Approximate time for redress/ward change/retouch makeup/other changeovers: 65 *minutes*
10-minute camera break while audience exits.	8:10 to 8:20 P	
Wild line	8:15 P	
3 pick-ups in G	8:20 to 8:50 P	(No ward/makeup wait)
Ward change/makeup (Angie; Brad; Theresa)	8:50 to 9:05 P	
Redress extras	8:50 to 8:55 P	(10-minute ward/makeup wait)

2 retakes/3 pick-ups in D (1 redress)	9:05 to 9:55 P	
Wild track—casino	9:55 to 10:00 P	
2 pick-ups in A (Theresa off-camera in 1)	10:00 to 10:25 P	(No ward/makeup wait)
Retouch makeup (Angie)	10:25 to 10:35 P	(10-minute ward makeup wait)
1 retake/1 pick-up in E	10:35 to 10:55 P	
Wild line (Brad)	10:55 to 11:00 P	
1 retake/2 pick-ups in C	11:00 to 11:20 P	(10-minute ward/makeup wait)
Wild line (Angie)	11:20 to 11:24 P	
WRAP	11:24 P	(No ward/makeup wait) Approx. ward/makeup/ changeover time: 30 *minutes* Ward/makeup wait time only: Show—45 minutes Pick-ups—20 minutes

If unplanned pick-ups are not done "hot," the first assistant is responsible for remembering that they must be done later. In running the set, the first assistant is the one who informs the cast and crew to prepare for a pick-up or for the next scene. As the audience leaves after the show, the first and second assistants will confer over the order in which remaining pick-ups and wild lines should be obtained. Normally, pick-ups will be executed in the sequence which necessitates the minimum amount of set redressing and costume changes.

Realistically, it cannot be expected that a cast will remember perfectly lines which may have just been changed, or that camera crews will avoid any missteps in their technical ballet of people and equipment. Consequently, the three-camera format relies heavily on preparedness in-depth to avert catastrophe. From the standpoint of both director and his or her assistants, who never have the luxury of finishing tomorrow, the format makes unique demands on creative thinking and planning, all focused on those few hours of actual filming.

W. A. __2908__
Series __ANGIE__
Producer __MILLER/MILKIS/BOYETT; THUNA/CAULEY__
Director __DORIS ROBERTS__
Title __"ANGIE AND JOYCE GO TO JAIL"__

CALL SHEET

Prod. No. __60432-026__

Day __MONDAY, NOVEMBER 5, 1979__
__4TH__ Day out of __5__ days
Crew Call __7:30 A__ ~ 10 AM SHOOTING
Cast Call __9:00 A__
Location __STAGE 30 (x 1930)__

SET # SET	SCENES	CAST	D/N	PAGES	LOCATION
	CLOSED SET ~ NO VISITORS				
	BLOCK & SHOOT:				
INT DEPARTMENT STORE	A	1, 3, 13, 14, X	D	7⁶/₈	STG. 30
INT JAIL	B	1, 3, 9, 10, 11, 12	D	7³/₈	
" "	D	1, 3, 9, 10, 11, 12	N	2⁴/₈	
" "	E	1, 3, 9, 10, 11, 12	D	6 -	
" "	H	1, 2, 3, 9, 10, 11, 12	D	—	
IF TIME PERMITS					
INT LIVING ROOM	C	2, 4, 5	D	3⁴/₈	

CAST & DAY PLAYERS	PART OF	MAKE-UP	SET CALL	REMARKS
1. DONNA PESCOW	ANGIE	8:30 A	9A	
2. ROBERT HAYS	BRAD		W/N	
3. SHARON SPELMAN	JOYCE	8:30 A	9A	
4. DEBRALEE SCOTT	MARIE		W/N	
5. EMORY BASS	PHIPPS		W/N	
6. SUSAN DUVALL	MARY G.	~ HOLD ~		
7. NANCY LANE	MARY K.			
8. VALRI BROMFIELD	MARY M.			
9. JANE CONNELL	BELLA	9A	10:30 A	
10. PATTI COLOMBO	GINGER			
11. ANNIE McGREEVEY	BLUE			
12. ALEX HENTELOFF	GUARD	9:45 A		
13. JAMES MURTAUGH (F)	DETECTIVE	8:30 A	9A	
14. JOAN ELIZMAN (F)	SALESLADY			
15.	MESSENGER		W/N	

ATMOSPHERE AND STANDINS	SPECIAL INSTRUCTIONS
6 STAND-INS @ W/N	
X STORE PATRONS @ 9A	

ADVANCE SHOOTING NOTES

SHOOTING DATE	SET NO.	SET NAME	LOCATION	SCENE NO.
TUES, 11/6		BLOCK, SHOOT, FINISH SHOW #026	STG. 30	
WED, 11/7		READ & REHEARSE SHOW #027	T.B.A.	

UNIT PROD. MGR. __DON TORPIN__ PHONE __1570__ ASST. DIR. __Herbert AMES/Alan SILVER__ PHONE __1930__
ART DIR. __KEN DAVIS__ PHONE __2607__ SET DEC. __BRUCE GIBSON__ PHONE __2479__
ISSUED BY OPERATIONS: DATE __11/1/79__ TIME __8:35 AM__ APPROVED _____

APPENDIX 2

Qualification, Training and Internship

Under the terms of the Basic Agreement between the Alliance of Motion Picture and Television Producers (AMPTP), representing the major industry production companies, and the Directors Guild of America, there are four "qualification lists" which restrict who may be employed by the signatory companies as Unit Production Managers and Assistant Directors. These lists separately cover Commercial and Entertainment productions for areas designated as East and West Coast, but actually pertain only to Los Angeles and New York and only to the AD/UPM category because employers may hire anyone they deem qualified to direct a motion picture. Employers based in those areas or based elsewhere and working in those areas may only employ persons who are both members in good standing of the DGA and whose names appear on the appropriate qualification list. Persons not on the qualification list may work for signatory companies based outside the restricted areas or for Los Angeles or New York companies shooting outside the area in an "off-roster" category such as Additional 2nd Assistant Director. Days worked in this capacity count toward the requirements outlined below.

The key criterion for placement on the Entertainment lists, which govern employment in features and filmed television, remains 400 days (350 on the East Coast) of industry experience in the capacity for which a person seeks placement. For example, to be placed as a 2nd Assistant Director, a prospective listee must provide proof of 400 days of work as a 2nd Assistant Director (or 1st, UPM, Technical Coordinator, Director, or any combination). Such work may be for (1) non-DGA employers; (2) DGA employers outside the jurisdiction of qualification lists; or (3) as a DGA/AMPTP "Trainee" or as a DGA or non-DGA stage manager or associate director in videotape production. At least 75% of the days must be "shooting" days.

If all this seems complicated, doing the work is only the beginning of the process. In addition to check stubs and other production paperwork, applicants are expected to submit letters from the various employers confirming the work dates and duties performed for review by the Directors Guild of America Contract Administration (DGACA). The "Internship" program was suspended in 1984 and is unlikely to be revived. Most recently, a side letter to the Basic Agreement effectively precludes anyone not working in a DGA capacity for a signatory employer from counting such days towards qualification list placement. What this means is that Production Assistants, who despite prohibitions in the Basic Agreement may do some of the work of Assistant Directors on DGA shows, can no longer "use" those days to qualify.

For those who lack the connections or the determination to cut through the list system and its regulations, the surest and simplest alternative is the Assistant Directors Training Program. Since its inception in 1965, this program has provided the industry with a steady source of assistant directors. Both the East and West regions have training programs, although the number of persons working in the West, where most filmed television is based, is always higher. (In fact, the Eastern Training Program did not accept new applicants in 1991 due to lack of work.)

To make application to the West Coast program persons must be at least twenty-one years of age, U.S. citizens or resident aliens with work permits, and hold a minimum of an Associate degree (in any discipline) or have an "equivalent" amount (i.e., two years) of actual, paid work experience in the film industry. There were over fourteen hundred applicants to the 1992 West Coast program who qualified for the first stage of evaluation—a series of written tests. These are administered in Los Angeles and one other city (most recently Chicago). Those who qualified for testing completed and returned all supporting documents and the basic application by the deadlines indicated. Over the years, many have been denied the opportunity to even take the annual test simply because colleges or industry employers failed to send transcripts or letters in time.

The test is a battery of examinations similar to a basic aptitude test with both verbal and mathematical portions and sections on problem solving and spatial relations. On the East Coast, the top scorers on the test are invited to a personal interview. On the West Coast, approximately one hundred persons with the top test scores are invited to attend an assessment center, where they are presented with practical problems in group situations and observed by evaluators. Finally thirty to fifty persons from the group assessments are invited to individual interviews conducted by the Board of Trustees of the Training Program. Of these, eight to twenty persons are accepted as Trainees. Persons who fail to make the cut at any stage may reapply as many times as they wish.

Those accepted into the program are effectively working under probationary status and assigned to actual feature and television productions, where they are evaluated by the UPMs and ADs. The rate of pay is set by the Basic Agreement with increases every 100 days. The 1992 West Coast rates (effective July 1, 1992) start at $377 per week (which is $6.18 per hour with a minimum guarantee of fifty-four hours per five-day week) and increase every 100 days in 7.5% increments. After 400 days of work and concurrent attendance at a series of job-related seminars, graduates of the Training Program are automatically placed on the Los Angeles County entertainment qualification list as 2nd Assistant Directors. Those with sub-standard evaluations are counseled but the ultimate result can be trainees being dropped from the program, particularly in recent years.

The application period for the Assistant Directors Training Program normally begins September 1 for testing sometime in March. Readers may make inquiries and obtain applications by writing or telephoning the Assistant Directors Training Program.

APPENDIX 3

Paperwork

The authors cannot reproduce the entire budget from *The Creature Wasn't Nice* or budgets from any motion pictures or television productions on which they have worked, without detailing the individual salaries of cast and crew members and violating their confidentiality. Reproduced instead is a second draft budget for a project in development.

Also reproduced are variant formats of breakdown sheet and cost reports and samples of camera and script reports.

THE FUNCTIONS OF THE PAPERWORK TOOLS

While there is considerable overlap, even redundancy of information among the various forms and reports used in production, the reader should not assume that this is the result of poor logistical planning by scores of forms' originators. Each of the major tools are designed to work both individually, as complete units, and in a collective context with the other tools, as part of a system of cross-checking.

Most of the cast and crew will consult only specific forms during the course of production. The production manager and assistant directors will need to be familiar with all of them. The following chart graphically illustrates the use of the various items of paperwork at different phases in preproduction, production, and post-production.

FUNCTIONS OF PRODUCTION PAPERWORK

ITEM	ORIGINATOR	USED BY	Use During PRE-PRODUCTION	Use During PRODUCTION	Use During POST-PRODUCTION
SCREENPLAY	WRITER PRODUCER DIRECTOR	ENTIRE COMPANY	------- THIS	IS THE PRODUCTION	-------
BUDGET	UPM	PRODUCER & AFFECTS ENTIRE CO.	ALLOCATE COSTS	RELEASE EXPENDITURES	ACCOUNT FOR COSTS
BREAKDOWN PAGES	UPM or 1st A.D.	UPM & AD's	DETAIL & CATEGORIZE SCRIPT; TYPE SCHEDULE FROM IT	A CHECK THAT ALL ELEMENTS ARE PREPARED AND UTILIZED ACCORDING TO THE SCRIPT	OBSOLETE
PRODUCTION BOARD	UPM or 1st A.D.	UPM & AD's	VISUAL DISPLAY OF SCRIPT; FLEXIBLY ORGANIZES ALL SCRIPT ELEMENTS FOR BUDGETING & SCHEDULING	KEEPS TRACK OF WORK PROGRESS; FLEXIBILITY TO ADJUST TO PROBLEMS; DAILY CALL SHEET PREPARED FROM IT	OBSOLETE
SHOOTING SCHEDULE	UPM or 1st A.D.	ENTIRE COMPANY	ORGANIZES THE SCRIPT INTO DAYS OF WORK	CHECKLIST OF ELEMENTS TO BE PREPARED AND UTILIZED ACCORDING TO PLAN	OBSOLETE
DAY OUT OF DAYS	UPM or 1st A.D.	PRODUCER & CASTING	SCHEDULE ACTORS; PLAN COSTS; MAKE DEALS or ARRANGE CONTRACT TERMS	CHECK AGAINST SCHEDULE	OBSOLETE
ONE LINER SCHEDULE	UPM or 1st A.D.	OPTIONAL ENTIRE CO.	TYPED ESSENTIALS OF PRODUCTION BOARD	QUICK CHECK AGAINST SCHEDULE	OBSOLETE
DAILY CALL SHEET	2nd A.D.	ENTIRE COMPANY	· PREPARE WORK	THE PLANNED WORK; DERIVED FROM PROD'N BD. THE SHOOT SCHED. & DOUBLECHECKED w/SCRIPT	OBSOLETE

FUNCTIONS OF PRODUCTION PAPERWORK

Page 2

ITEM	ORIGINATOR	USED BY	Use During PRE-PRODUCTION	Use During PRODUCTION	Use During POST-PRODUCTION
DAILY PRODUCTION REPORT	2nd A.D.	PRODUCER PAYROLL & STAFF	-none-	DETAILS THE ACTUAL WORK CHARTS PROGRESS RECORDS PROBLEMS	PROVIDES OFFICIAL RECORD; PAYROLL VERIFICATION
SCRIPT SUPERVISOR'S FORMS	SCRIPT SUPERVISOR	2nd A.D. EDITOR ASSOC.PROD.	MAY PROVIDE TIMING OF SCRIPT AND PAGE AND SCENE COUNT	KEEPS LOG OF ALL SHOTS; KEEPS STATISTICS OF WORK	PROVIDES EDITOR w/LOG OF FOOTAGE; BACK-UP FOR PRO-DUCTION REPORT
COST REPORTS	UPM or PRODUCTION ESTIMATOR/ ACCOUNTANT	PRODUCER & AFFECTS ENTIRE COMPANY	-------------	-- KEEP APPRISED OF FINANCIAL SITUATION AS PRODUCTION PROGRESSES	

SAMPLES

Many of the breakdowns and budgets prepared in Hollywood are for motion picture and television projects that never get made. Producers making presentations to production companies or independent inventors often submit "packages." These may consist not merely of proposed scripts but also of one or more "attachments" and details on the proposed project. Typically the attachments come in the form of letters of intent from actors, directors, and other craftspeople who are committed to working on the production. The "details" vary, but a budget and occasionally a breakdown are high on the list of supporting documentation which producers use to convince companies or investors of the feasibility of their projects.

In turn, studios, distributors, private investors, even bond companies may commission budgets and/or breakdowns to independently verify whether the fiscal basis of a proposal is sound. Once the range of costs is established, the budget preparer may be asked to adjust the figures to a particular point in that range.

There are several general criteria to be considered in preparing budgets for presentation purposes. Of prime importance is the ratio of above- to below-the-line. Currently, the cost of films ranges from under $4 million at the low-budget end to over $12 million at the high end with medium occupying the considerable area between. Since higher budget pictures usually involve "star" salaries, the proportion of costs above and below also shifts from 40/60 at the low end to 60/40 at the high end. As budgets drop toward $2 million and below, the normally higher fees for the creative personnel above-the-line must bear the more drastic cuts because there are fixed costs below the line such as film stock, processing and the salaries of technician's which have accepted floors. In some low-budget situations, writers, producers, directors, and actors who have a vested interest in the success of a project and/or a proprietary interest therein may elect to defer all or part of their salaries. In extreme situations, all salaries may conceivably be deferred; but raw stock, equipment rental, permits, food, gasoline, and the like prevent the below-the-line from reaching zero. Since "presentation" budgets are, however, meant be to be demonstrations of feasibility, anticipating too many deferred salaries, cut-rate prices, or other "favors" undercuts the validity of the process. Conversely, above-the-line persons who allot themselves disproportionately large salaries on modestly budgeted projects may give the appearance of being more interested in guaranteed fees than getting the picture made, which, in turn, often discourages investors. Through all of this the equation of time and money to production value continues to hold true. Slashing schedules to reduce a projected negative cost is as unrealistic as hoping for gifts of raw stock or snack packs. Feature films can still be shot in ten days or less, but they very seldom are and rarely, if ever, when seven-figure budgets are involved.

As in all budgeting and scheduling, those attached to packages must remain balanced. The music account on a $4 million picture cannot be arbitrarily reduced to nothing in anticipation of a deal for a soundtrack album (as was the case in one of the budgets discussed below). Not only does this imbalance the budget, but, if funding is obtained based on this expectation, it creates the risk of a catastrophic overage.

The budgets and schedules examined below were produced for various purposes. The most recent were part of presentation packages and are reproduced as examples of low and high budgets, the former in its entirety as a guide to preparers. Such preparers are cautioned, however, that the requirements of the particular script are relatively more significant at the $1.2 million level. Many, but certainly not all, scripts may be realistically produced for such a total cost. The keys to making such a determination are multiform, but one is preeminent: cast. As the ratio of costs shifts heavily below the line, the actors' compensation, which is almost always the largest single account above or below, is the main impediment. Too many actors, even when paid scale under the Screen Actors Guild Low Budget Agreement, increase cost. This may tempt preparers to cut the days that actors are scheduled to work, which is a perilous strategy. For those who would cut the overall schedule, a similar peril exists with even a limited number of actors if many of them speak lines in numerous scenes and make seven-, six-, or even five-page shooting days unworkable. On average, nothing consumes contingencies faster than actors on overtime.

A final note: there are several commercially available but relatively costly computer programs designed to assist the preparer of breakdowns and budgets. Most also can produce a day-out-of-days, one-liner, or shooting schedule, and some can produce call sheets and productions reports. The breakdowns and two of the budgets in the illustrations that follow were done with a prefabricated program. Most of the budgets were produced with a spreadsheet program and templates based on the two basic forms described in the body of the book.

Budgets

SCHOOL DAZE

A template was used for the illustration from *School Daze*.

The budget submitted by Spike Lee to Island Pictures was for just under $4.5 million dollars on a 40-day shooting schedule. Concerned about several factors in the week before pre-production was set to begin in Atlanta, Island commissioned a new budget. Primarily because of concern over the length of the script and the scheduled days, and despite the fact that the two draft budgets were within a few thousand dollars, Island pulled out of the project. The following week, a revised budget for $4.6 million was requested by the production company and submitted by them to David Putnam at Columbia, who took over the project.

BUDGET TOPSHEET

TITLE: "SCHOOL DAZE"   IP 87-002

PICTURE NO.

ACCT.#	DESCRIPTION	PG.		TOTAL	TOTALS
1.00	Story/Screenplay	1		104,057.50	104,057.50
2.00	Producer/Staff	1		150,000.00	150,000.00
3.00	Director/Staff	1		109,000.00	109,000.00
4.00	Cast	2		644,798.06	644,798.06
5.00	Extras	3		71,650.50	71,650.50
6.00	Travel/Living	3		147,212.00	147,212.00
7.00	Fringe Benefits	3		98,208.82	98,208.82
	TOTAL ABOVE-THE-LINE				1,324,926.88
8.00	Production Staff	4		210,616.00	210,616.00
9.00	Production Operating Staff	5		411,109.60	411,109.60
10.00	Set Designing	8		111,090.00	111,090.00
11.00	Set Operations	9		303,275.00	303,275.00
12.00	Cutting/Film/Laboratory	11		368,010.20	368,010.20
13.00	Music	13		0.00	0.00
14.00	Sound	13		81,350.00	81,350.00
15.00	2nd Unit/Tests/Inserts	13		12,500.00	12,500.00
16.00	Transportation	14		134,874.00	134,874.00
17.00	Publicity	14		6,750.00	6,750.00
18.00	Location	15		322,292.00	322,292.00
19.00	Stage/Studio Operations	15		750.00	750.00
20.00	Insurance/Taxes/Licenses	16		132,969.15	132,969.15
21.00	General Overhead	16		75,000.00	75,000.00
22.00	Miscellaneous	16		2,500.00	2,500.00
	TOTAL BELOW-THE-LINE				2,173,085.95
	TOTAL DIRECT COSTS				3,498,012.83
	Contingency		10.0 %		349,801.28
	Completion Bond		6.0 %		209,880.77
	GRAND TOTAL				4,057,694.88

Prepared   January 15, 1987

From   128   Page Script Dated   Sept. 14, 1986

   40   40

     Day Shooting Schedule (Distant   Local Location/Studio   )

Director   Producer

Budget   Alain Silver

REVISED TOPSHEET

BUDGET TOPSHEET

"SCHOOL DAZE"

TITLE:_____PICTURE NO._____

ACCT.#	DESCRIPTION	PG.		TOTAL	TOTALS
1.00	Story/Screenplay	2		204,057.50	204,057.50
2.00	Producer/Staff	2		250,000.00	250,000.00
3.00	Director/Staff	2		109,000.00	109,000.00
4.00	Cast	3		644,798.06	644,798.06
5.00	Extras	4		71,650.50	71,650.50
6.00	Travel/Living	4		147,212.00	147,212.00
7.00	Fringe Benefits	4		98,208.82	98,208.82
	TOTAL ABOVE-THE-LINE				1,524,926.88
8.00	Production Staff	5		210,616.00	210,616.00
9.00	Production Operating Staff	6		411,109.60	411,109.60
10.00	Set Designing	9		111,090.00	111,090.00
11.00	Set Operations	10		303,275.00	303,275.00
12.00	Cutting/Film/Laboratory	12		368,010.20	368,010.20
13.00	Music	14		275,000.00	275,000.00
14.00	Sound	14		81,350.00	81,350.00
15.00	2nd Unit/Tests/Inserts	14		12,500.00	12,500.00
16.00	Transportation	15		134,874.00	134,874.00
17.00	Publicity	15		6,750.00	6,750.00
18.00	Location	16		322,292.00	322,292.00
19.00	Stage/Studio Operations	16		750.00	750.00
20.00	Insurance/Taxes/Licenses	17		146,969.15	146,969.15
21.00	General Overhead	17		130,000.00	130,000.00
22.00	Miscellaneous	17		2,500.00	2,500.00
	TOTAL BELOW-THE-LINE				2,517,085.95
	TOTAL DIRECT COSTS				4,042,012.83
	Contingency		10.0 %		404,000.00
	Completion		6.0 %		242,520.77
	GRAND TOTAL				4,688,533.60

Jan. 28, 1987
Date Prepared_____

From_____Page Script Dated_____
40   0   40
_____Day Schedule (Rehearse____Distant_____Local Loc._____ Studio_____)
        Spike Lee
Director_____Producer_____
        Alain Silver
Budget_____

Form SB001, Copyright (c) 1984, PENDRAGON FILM LTD.

HOMEFRONT and THE BIG EASY

Budgets were produced in the early stages of these Kings Road Productions as draft estimates and to furnish Universal, the distributor and guarantor of negative costs, with appropriate topsheet summaries of cost for *Homefront*, *The Big Easy*, and *Rent-a-Cop*. In instances such as these, topsheets as well as scripts are reviewed before projects in advanced stages of development are given a final go-ahead. Unlike the case of *School Daze*, the review process here was part of a package of several pictures. Since there was no underlying apprehension about the projects, the presumption was that the process was merely the final stage in obtaining formal approval, which was forthcoming. *Homefront* was prepared by amending an existing rough draft done with a budgeting program—an original topsheet with pencil notes is reproduced. At the production company's request, the first revised draft was then transferred from a long-form budget to a short-form and manipulated to reflect various union conditions. Topsheet from long and short form revisions are given as illustrations. [Note: the script of *The Big Easy* was, at the time this topsheet was prepared, called *Nothing But The Truth* and situated in Chicago rather than New Orleans.]

HOMEFRONT
Kings Road Productions

FRINGE
DIFFERENCES

ACCT	DESCRIPTION	Adj. Nos	BUDGETED	SPENT	BALANCE	
1100	STORY		0	0	0	
1200	WRITERS	383,100	345000	(WGA) 0	345000	20,000
1300	DIRECTION & SUPERVISN	133,265	145250	(DGA) 0	145250	8,834
1400	CAST	829,964	745496	(SAG) 0	745496	50,744
1500	TRAVEL & LIVING	132,295	132295	0	132295	
1600	PRODUCTION FEE		0	0	0	
1900	FRINGE BENEFITS ABTL		0	0	0	
	TOTAL ABOVE THE LINE		1368041	0	1368041	
2000	PRODUCTION STAFF		224098	0	224098	
2100	EXTRA TALENT		239876	(SEG) 0	239876	(1,342)
2200	ART		90600	0	90600	
2300	SET CONSTRUCTION		77500	0	77500	
2400	SET STRIKING		0	0	0	
2500	SET OPERATIONS		77600	0	77600	
2600	SPECIAL EFFECTS		45450	0	45450	
2700	SET DRESSING		188675	0	188675	
2800	PROPERTY		79625	0	79625	
2900	MEN'S WARDROBE		80500	0	80500	
3000	WOMEN'S WARDROBE		51600	0	51600	
3100	MAKEUP & HAIRDRESS.		52012	(IA) 0	52012	(5,277)
3200	LIGHTING		149000	0	149000	
3300	CAMERA		102655	(NABET) 0	102655	(585)
3400	PRODUCTION SOUND		52660	0	52660	
3500	TRANSPORTATION		244081	(TEAM) 0	244081	23,862
3600	LOCATION		456000	0	456000	
3700	PROD. FILM & LAB		126014	0	126014	
3800	STAGE FACILITIES		6000	0	6000	
3900	PROCESS-REAR PROJECTN		0	0	0	
4000	SECOND UNIT		12500	0	12500	
4100	TESTS		2500	0	2500	
4400	PROD.PERIOD FR.BEN.		0	0	0	
	TOTAL PRODUCTION		2438946	0	2438946	
4500	FILM EDITING		201575	0	201575	
4600	MUSIC		150000	0	150000	
4700	POST PROD. SOUND		96275	0	96275	
4800	POST.PROD.FILM/LAB		42960	0	42960	
4900	MAIN & END TITLES		20000	0	20000	
5900	POST.PROD.FRIN.BEN.		0	0	0	
	TOTAL POST PRODUCTION		510810	0	510810	
6500	PUBLICITY		15000	0	15000	
6700	INSURANCE		140000	0	140000	
6800	GENERAL EXPENSE		63000	0	63000	
6900	RETROACTIVE SALARY		0	0	0	
7400	OTHER FRINGE BENEF.		0	0	0	
7500	FEES & CHARGES		50000	0	50000	
7700	INTEREST & MISC		0	0	0	
8000	COMPLETION FEE		0	0	0	
9000	CONTINGENCY		0	0	0	
	TOTAL OTHER		268000	0	268000	

TOTAL BELOW THE LINE - - - - - - - -	3217756	
TOTAL TAXES AND FRINGE BENEFITS - - - -	334134	
SUB-TOTAL (budgeted + fringes) - - - -	4919933	
CONTINGENCY 0 %		0
COMPLETION BOND 0 %		0
TOTAL SPENT		0
COST TO COMPLETE		4919933
TOTAL		4919933

GOV'T FRINGES 133,137

TOTAL 229,373

PRODUCTION BUDGET

DATE: _____ July 7, 1985

TITLE: HOME FRONT _____ PICTURE NO. _____ 85002

DAYS
Travel: 2
Rehearse: 5
Distant: 43
Local Loc:
Stage:
TOTAL: 50
UPM: Patrick McCormick
1st AD:

Exec Producer:
Producer: Steve Friedman
Director: Terry Winsor
Start Date: Sept. 23, 1985
Finish Date: Nov. 4, 1985
Script Dated: May, 1985
Script Pages: 122
Exec V.P. Prod: John E. Quill

ACCT.#	DESCRIPTION	PG.		TOTAL	TOTALS
1100	Story, Rights, & Continuity	1		345,000.00	345,000.00
1200	Producers Unit	1		23,000.00	23,000.00
1300	Direction	1		122,250.00	122,250.00
1400	Cast	2		745,496.00	745,496.00
1500	Travel and Living	3		132,295.00	132,295.00
1600	Miscellaneous	3		0.00	0.00
1900	Fringe Benefits	3		52,146.00	52,146.00
	TOTAL ABOVE-THE-LINE				1,420,187.00
2000	Production Staff	4		304,098.00	304,098.00
2100	Extra Talent	5		279,876.00	279,876.00
2200	Art Direction	6		110,000.00	110,000.00
2300	Set Construction	6		99,500.00	99,500.00
2400	Set Striking	6		0.00	0.00
2500	Set Operations	7		107,600.00	107,600.00
2600	Special Effects	8		65,450.00	65,450.00
2700	Set Dressing	8		188,675.00	188,675.00
2800	Property	9		94,625.00	94,625.00
2900	Men's Wardrobe	9		91,500.00	91,500.00
3000	Women's Wardrobe	10		61,600.00	61,600.00
3100	Make-up/Hairdressing	10		78,012.00	78,012.00
3200	Electric/Lighting	11		164,000.00	164,000.00
3300	Camera Operations	12		207,655.00	207,655.00
3400	Production Sound	12		69,660.00	69,660.00
3500	Transportation	13		302,081.00	302,081.00
3600	Location	14		486,000.00	486,000.00
3700	Production Film and Lab	15		141,014.00	141,014.00
3800	Stage Facilities	15		35,000.00	35,000.00
3900	Process and Rear Projection	16		0.00	0.00
4000	2nd Unit/Miniatures/Effects	16		12,500.00	12,500.00
4100	Tests	16		2,500.00	2,500.00
4900	Fringe Benefits	16		241,968.00	241,968.00
	TOTAL PRODUCTION PERIOD				3,143,314.00

ACCT.#	DESCRIPTION	PG.		TOTAL	TOTALS
5000	Editorial	17		201,575.00	201,575.00
5100	Music	18		150,000.00	150,000.00
5200	Post-production Sound	18		116,275.00	116,275.00
5300	Post-production Film & Lab	19		42,960.00	42,960.00
5400	Main and End Titles	19		20,000.00	20,000.00
5900	Fringe Benefits	19		36,884.00	36,884.00
	TOTAL EDITING PERIOD				567,694.00
6500	Publicity	20		15,000.00	15,000.00
6700	Insurance	20		140,000.00	140,000.00
6800	General Overhead	21		63,000.00	63,000.00
6900	Fringe Benefits	21		3,146.00	3,146.00
7500	Fees/Charges/Miscellaneous	21		50,000.00	50,000.00
	TOTAL OTHER CHARGES				271,146.00
	ABOVE-THE-LINE				1,420,187.00
	BELOW-THE-LINE				3,982,154.00
	DIRECT COSTS				5,402,341.00
	CONTINGENCY				0.00
	OVERHEAD FEE				
	COMPLETION BOND				0.00
			TOTAL		5,402,341.00
	DEFERMENTS TOTAL	22			
			TOTAL NEGATIVE COSTS (Deferments Included)		5,402,341.00

PICTURE BUDGET DETAIL

TITLE: HOMEFRONT [NABET]   85002
                           PICTURE NO.

ACCT.#	DESCRIPTION	PAGE	TOTAL	TOTALS	TOTALS
1.00	Story/Screenplay	1	383,100.00		383,100.00
2.00	Producer/Staff	1	18,500.00		18,500.00
3.00	Director/Staff	1	114,764.80		114,764.80
4.00	Cast	2	829,963.93		829,963.93
5.00	Travel/Living	3	132,295.00		132,295.00
6.00	Fringe Benefits	3	52,146.31		52,146.31
	TOTAL ABOVE-THE-LINE				1,530,770.04
7.00	Production Staff	4A	304,630.74		304,630.74
8.00	Extras	4B	252,534.04		252,534.04
9.00	Production Operating Staff	5/6	639,390.62		639,390.62
10.00	Set Designing	7	169,958.17		169,958.17
11.00	Set Operations	8	444,775.00		444,775.00
12.00	Cutting/Film/Laboratory	9	429,495.69		429,495.69
13.00	Music	10	150,000.00		150,000.00
14.00	Sound	10	81,375.00		81,375.00
15.00	Transportation	10	325,434.49		325,434.49
16.00	Tests/Inserts/2nd Unit	10	18,500.00		18,500.00
17.00	Location	11	485,763.00		485,763.00
18.00	Stage/Studio Operations	11	11,000.00		11,000.00
19.00	Publicity	11	15,000.00		15,000.00
20.00	Insurance/Taxes/Licenses	12	141,500.00		141,500.00
21.00	General Overhead	12	74,750.00		74,750.00
22.00	Miscellaneous	12	23,500.00		23,500.00
	TOTAL BELOW-THE-LINE				3,567,606.75
	TOTAL DIRECT COSTS				5,098,376.79
	Contingency				0.00
	Completion Bond				0.00
	GRAND TOTAL				5,098,376.79

Date Prepared July 7, 1985 Revised

From 122 Page Script Dated May, 1985

 43 Day Shooting Schedule at Distant Location(s)

Director Terry Winsor   Producer Steve Friedman

Budget by John Quill

Shoot Week is 90 Pay hours [40 @ straight time; 28 @ 1 1/2; 4 @ Double]

PICTURE BUDGET DETAIL

TITLE: HOMEFRONT   [IATSE, NY]   85002
                                                        PICTURE NO.

ACCT.#	DESCRIPTION	PAGE	TOTAL	TOTALS	TOTALS
1.00	Story/Screenplay	1	383,100.00		383,100.00
2.00	Producer/Staff	1	18,500.00		18,500.00
3.00	Director/Staff	1	114,764.80		114,764.80
4.00	Cast	2	829,963.93		829,963.93
5.00	Travel/Living	3	132,295.00		132,295.00
6.00	Fringe Benefits	3	52,146.31		52,146.31
	TOTAL ABOVE-THE-LINE				1,530,770.04
7.00	Production Staff	4A	304,630.74		304,630.74
8.00	Extras	4B	252,534.04		252,534.04
9.00	Production Operating Staff	5/6	892,659.20		892,659.20
10.00	Set Designing	7	169,958.17		169,958.17
11.00	Set Operations	8	444,775.00		444,775.00
12.00	Cutting/Film/Laboratory	9	429,495.69		429,495.69
13.00	Music	10	150,000.00		150,000.00
14.00	Sound	10	81,375.00		81,375.00
15.00	Transportation	10	325,434.49		325,434.49
16.00	Tests/Inserts/2nd Unit	10	18,500.00		18,500.00
17.00	Location	11	485,763.00		485,763.00
18.00	Stage/Studio Operations	11	11,000.00		11,000.00
19.00	Publicity	11	15,000.00		15,000.00
20.00	Insurance/Taxes/Licenses	12	141,500.00		141,500.00
21.00	General Overhead	12	74,750.00		74,750.00
22.00	Miscellaneous	12	23,500.00		23,500.00
	TOTAL BELOW-THE-LINE				3,820,875.33
	TOTAL DIRECT COSTS				5,351,645.37
	Contingency				0.00
	Completion Bond				0.00
	GRAND TOTAL				5,351,645.37

                    July 7, 1985 Revised
Date Prepared_____
             122   May, 1985
From_____Page Script Dated_____
             43   Distant Location(s)
_____Day Shooting Schedule at_____
             Terry Winsor   Steve Friedman
Director_____Producer_____
             John Quill
Budget by_____

    Shoot Week is 90 Pay hours [40 @ straight time; 28 @ 1 1/2; 4 @ Double]

PRODUCTION BUDGET

DATE: _____ July 26, 1985

NOTHING BUT THE TRUTH

TITLE: _____ Prod. No. _____ 85003

DAYS   Exec. Producer:
Travel: 2   Producer: Steve Friedman
Rehearse: 5   Director: Jim McBride
Distant: 47   Start Date: Oct. 21, 1985
Local Loc: Finish Date: Dec. 14, 1985
Holidays: 1   Script Dated: Feb. 25, 1985
TOTAL: 55   Script Pages: 123
UPM: Exec V.P. Prod: John E. Quill
1st AD:

ACCT.#	DESCRIPTION	PG.		TOTAL	TOTALS
1100	Story, Rights, & Continuity	1		368,000.00	368,000.00
1200	Producers Unit	1		31,300.00	31,300.00
1300	Direction	1		386,500.00	386,500.00
1400	Cast	2			2,104,650.00
1500	Travel and Living	3		221,500.00	221,500.00
1600	Miscellaneous	3		0.00	0.00
1900	Fringe Benefits	3		97,524.00	97,524.00
	TOTAL ABOVE-THE-LINE				3,209,474.00
2000	Production Staff	4		341,054.00	341,054.00
2100	Extra Talent	5		306,744.00	306,744.00
2200	Art Direction	6		128,500.00	128,500.00
2300	Set Construction	6		243,550.00	243,550.00
2400	Set Striking	6		5,400.00	5,400.00
2500	Set Operations	7		117,929.00	117,929.00
2600	Special Effects	8		141,850.00	141,850.00
2700	Set Dressing	8		206,975.00	206,975.00
2800	Property	9		103,709.00	103,709.00
2900	Men's Wardrobe	9		100,284.00	100,284.00
3000	Women's Wardrobe	10		67,260.00	67,260.00
3100	Make-up/Hairdressing	10		85,501.00	85,501.00
3200	Electric/Lighting	11		180,072.00	180,072.00
3300	Camera Operations	12		207,655.00	207,655.00
3400	Production Sound	12		76,347.00	76,347.00
3500	Transportation	13		281,540.00	281,540.00
3600	Location	14		457,640.00	457,640.00
3700	Production Film and Lab	15		154,551.00	154,551.00
3800	Stage Facilities	15		27,500.00	27,500.00
3900	Process and Rear Projection	16		0.00	0.00
4000	2nd Unit/Miniatures/Effects	16		30,000.00	30,000.00
4100	Tests	16		2,500.00	2,500.00
4900	Fringe Benefits	16		265,197.00	265,197.00
	TOTAL PRODUCTION PERIOD				3,531,758.00

Form Copyright (c) 1985, PENDRAGON FILM LTD.

ACCT.#	DESCRIPTION	PG.		TOTAL	TOTALS
5000	Editorial	17		220,926.00	220,926.00
5100	Music	18		175,000.00	175,000.00
5200	Post-production Sound	18		116,275.00	116,275.00
5300	Post-production Film & Lab	19		63,150.00	63,150.00
5400	Main and End Titles	19		27,500.00	27,500.00
5900	Fringe Benefits	19		40,425.00	40,425.00
	TOTAL EDITING PERIOD				643,276.00
6500	Publicity	20		22,500.00	22,500.00
6700	Insurance	20		180,000.00	180,000.00
6800	General Overhead	21		64,250.00	64,250.00
6900	Fringe Benefits	21		3,146.00	3,146.00
7500	Fees/Charges/Miscellaneous	21		60,000.00	60,000.00
	TOTAL OTHER CHARGES				329,896.00
	ABOVE-THE-LINE				3,209,474.00
	BELOW-THE-LINE				4,504,930.00
	DIRECT COSTS				7,714,404.00
	CONTINGENCY				0.00
	OVERHEAD FEE				
	COMPLETION BOND				0.00
			TOTAL		7,714,404.00
	DEFERMENTS TOTAL	22			
			TOTAL NEGATIVE COSTS (Deferments Included)		7,714,404.00

NIGHT AND THE CITY

Island Pictures, which had filmed *A Night in the Life of Jimmy Reardon* in the Chicago area on a budget of $3.6 million, was considering a similarly budgeted production of *Night and the City*, a remake of the 1951 film set in London, situated in either New York or Chicago. Several budgets were prepared to determine the cost difference between shooting in New York with a NABET crew or transposing the script to Chicago and filming there and in Los Angeles with a nonunion crew. At Island's request, the fixed above-the-line costs such as script, producer, director, and cast were excluded from consideration. Ultimately both budgets were in excess of the amount which Island was prepared to commit to the production at that time.

PRODUCTION BUDGET

REV. Jan. 27, 1987

DATE: _____

"NIGHT AND THE CITY"   (N.Y. - NABET)   IP 87-001

TITLE: _____ PICTURE NO. _____

DAYS   Exec Producer:
Travel: Producer:
Rehearse: Director:
Distant: Start Date:
Local Loc: 40   Finish Date:
Stage: Script Dated:
2nd Unit: Script Pages: 107
TOTAL: 40   Budget Prep: Alain Silver

ACCT.#	DESCRIPTION	PG.		TOTAL	TOTALS
1100	Story, Rights, & Continuity	3		4,500.00	4,500.00
1200	Producers Unit	3		0.00	0.00
1300	Direction	3		17,400.00	17,400.00
1400	Cast	4		0.00	0.00
1500	Travel and Living	5		52,000.00	52,000.00
1600	Miscellaneous	5		0.00	0.00
1900	Fringe Benefits	5		2,427.30	2,427.30
	TOTAL ABOVE-THE-LINE				1,076,327.30
2000	Production Staff	6		199,432.20	199,432.20
2100	Extra Talent	7		116,846.23	116,846.23
2200	Art Direction	8		60,000.00	60,000.00
2300	Set Construction	8		50,000.00	50,000.00
2400	Set Striking	8		0.00	0.00
2500	Set Operations	9		73,876.47	73,876.47
2600	Special Effects	10		24,122.80	24,122.80
2700	Set Dressing	10		84,701.10	84,701.10
2800	Property	11		75,001.22	75,001.22
2900	Men's Wardrobe	11		84,249.90	84,249.90
3000	Women's Wardrobe	12		20,006.00	20,006.00
3100	Make-up/Hairdressing	12		40,980.00	40,980.00
3200	Electric/Lighting	13		120,080.64	120,080.64
3300	Camera Operations	14		202,810.48	202,810.48
3400	Production Sound	14		53,369.80	53,369.80
3500	Transportation	15		236,858.65	236,858.65
3600	Location	16		144,500.00	144,500.00
3700	Production Film and Lab	17		180,164.59	180,164.59
3800	Stage Facilities	17		0.00	0.00
3900	Process and Rear Projection	18		0.00	0.00
4000	2nd Unit/Miniatures/Effects	18		15,000.00	15,000.00
4100	Tests	18		500.00	500.00
4900	Fringe Benefits	18		239,802.79	239,802.79
	TOTAL PRODUCTION PERIOD				2,022,302.87

NIGHT AND THE CITY (NY - Nabet) 27-Jan-87   Page 2

ACCT.#	DESCRIPTION	PG.		TOTAL	TOTALS
5000	Editorial	19		195,911.50	195,911.50
5100	Music	20		57,500.00	57,500.00
5200	Post-production Sound	20		72,778.00	72,778.00
5300	Post-production Film & Lab	21		54,587.50	54,587.50
5400	Main and End Titles	21		17,500.00	17,500.00
5900	Fringe Benefits	21		21,561.59	21,561.59
	TOTAL EDITING PERIOD				419,838.59
6500	Publicity	22		3,000.00	3,000.00
6700	Insurance	22		129,000.00	129,000.00
6800	General Overhead	23		47,650.00	47,650.00
6900	Fringe Benefits	23		15,626.73	15,626.73
7500	Fees/Charges/Miscellaneous	23		45,000.00	45,000.00
	TOTAL OTHER CHARGES				240,276.73
	ABOVE-THE-LINE				1,076,327.30
	BELOW-THE-LINE				2,682,418.19
	DIRECT COSTS				3,758,745.49
	CONTINGENCY		10 %		376,000.00
	OVERHEAD FEE				150,000.00
	COMPLETION BOND		6 %		225,524.73
			TOTAL		4,510,270.22
	DEFERMENTS TOTAL	24			0.00
			TOTAL NEGATIVE COSTS (Deferments Included)		4,510,270.22

PRODUCTION BUDGET

DATE:_____   Jan. 21, 1987

TITLE:_____
"NIGHT AND THE CITY" (Non-IATSE, LA/Chicago)   IP 87-001
PICTURE NO._____

DAYS		Exec Producer:	
Travel:	2	Producer:	
Rehearse:		Director:	
Distant:	10	Start Date:	
Local Loc:	30	Finish Date:	
Stage:		Script Dated:	
2nd Unit:		Script Pages:	107
TOTAL:	42	Budget Prep:	Alain Silver

ACCT.#	DESCRIPTION	PG.		TOTAL	TOTALS
1100	Story, Rights, & Continuity	3		4,000.00	4,000.00
1200	Producers Unit	3		0.00	0.00
1300	Direction	3		17,400.00	17,400.00
1400	Cast	4		0.00	0.00
1500	Travel and Living	5		41,962.50	41,962.50
1600	Miscellaneous	5		0.00	0.00
1900	Fringe Benefits	5		2,427.30	2,427.30
	TOTAL ABOVE-THE-LINE				1,041,962.50
2000	Production Staff	6		204,547.50	204,547.50
2100	Extra Talent	7		45,790.00	45,790.00
2200	Art Direction	8		60,000.00	60,000.00
2300	Set Construction	8		50,000.00	50,000.00
2400	Set Striking	8		0.00	0.00
2500	Set Operations	9		73,250.00	73,250.00
2600	Special Effects	10		22,600.00	22,600.00
2700	Set Dressing	10		84,900.00	84,900.00
2800	Property	11		69,000.00	69,000.00
2900	Men's Wardrobe	11		76,200.00	76,200.00
3000	Women's Wardrobe	12		14,250.00	14,250.00
3100	Make-up/Hairdressing	12		39,200.00	39,200.00
3200	Electric/Lighting	13		112,748.40	112,748.40
3300	Camera Operations	14		165,900.00	165,900.00
3400	Production Sound	14		42,300.00	42,300.00
3500	Transportation	15		203,795.30	203,795.30
3600	Location	16		265,730.00	265,730.00
3700	Production Film and Lab	17		182,779.16	182,779.16
3800	Stage Facilities	17		0.00	0.00
3900	Process and Rear Projection	18		0.00	0.00
4000	2nd Unit/Miniatures/Effects	18		15,000.00	15,000.00
4100	Tests	18		500.00	500.00
4900	Fringe Benefits	18		200,366.34	200,366.34
	TOTAL PRODUCTION PERIOD				1,928,856.70

NIGHT AND THE CITY (Non-IA) 21-Jan-87   Page 2

ACCT.#	DESCRIPTION	PG.		TOTAL	TOTALS
5000	Editorial	19		124,375.00	124,375.00
5100	Music	20		57,500.00	57,500.00
5200	Post-production Sound	20		85,578.00	85,578.00
5300	Post-production Film & Lab	21		60,811.50	60,811.50
5400	Main and End Titles	21		17,500.00	17,500.00
5900	Fringe Benefits	21		13,008.38	13,008.38
	TOTAL EDITING PERIOD				358,772.88
6500	Publicity	22		250.00	250.00
6700	Insurance	22		87,900.00	87,900.00
6800	General Overhead	23		38,650.00	38,650.00
6900	Fringe Benefits	23		13,066.00	13,066.00
7500	Fees/Charges/Miscellaneous	23		45,000.00	45,000.00
	TOTAL OTHER CHARGES				184,866.00
	ABOVE-THE-LINE				1,041,962.50
	BELOW-THE-LINE				2,472,495.58
	DIRECT COSTS				3,514,458.08
	CONTINGENCY		10 %		351,400.00
	OVERHEAD FEE				150,000.00
	COMPLETION BOND		5 %		175,722.90
			TOTAL		4,191,580.98
	DEFERMENTS TOTAL	24			
			TOTAL NEGATIVE COSTS		4,191,580.98

**Indicates Travel to Location

BEST SELLER

As with *Night and the City*, this budget was prepared before final approval of the project by Hemdale. Since much of the script was situated in New York, the producer and production company were primarily interested in determining how much of the picture could be shot there or, conversely, how much would have to be shot in non-descript locations around Los Angeles to prevent costs from exceeding $5.5 million. The production company also wanted certain post-production costs to be carefully considered because on their production of *Hoosiers* those costs exceeded the budgeted estimates. Using a breakdown which isolated scenes specifically keyed to New York landmarks and those which could be shot in Los Angeles, distant location days were adjusted to achieve the desired total. The process was quite similar to the one described below for *Gaslight*.

PRODUCTION BUDGET

                                                      Rev. Feb. 4, 1986
                                          DATE:_____

                "BEST SELLER"
TITLE:_____PICTURE NO._____

DAYS   Exec
Travel: 2   Producer: Carter DeHaven
Rehearse: Director: John Flynn
Distant: 16   Start Date:
Local Loc: 22   Finish Date:
Stage: Script Dated:
2nd Unit: Script Pages:
TOTAL: 40   Budget Prep: Alain Silver
1st A.D.   UPM:

ACCT.#	DESCRIPTION	PG.	TOTAL	TOTALS
1100	Story, Rights, & Continuity	3	223,750.00	223,750.00
1200	Producers Unit	3	380,350.00	380,350.00
1300	Direction	3	319,900.00	319,900.00
1400	Cast	4	1,142,427.00	1,142,427.00
1500	Travel and Living	5	56,900.00	56,900.00
1600	Miscellaneous	5	1,500.00	1,500.00
1900	Fringe Benefits	5	123,165.30	123,165.30
	TOTAL ABOVE-THE-LINE			2,247,992.30
2000	Production Staff	6	199,041.73	199,041.73
2100	Extra Talent	7	114,629.70	114,629.70
2200	Art Direction	8	52,300.00	52,300.00
2300	Set Construction	8	25,000.00	25,000.00
2400	Set Striking	8	3,000.00	3,000.00
2500	Set Operations	9	55,048.33	55,048.33
2600	Special Effects	10	30,500.00	30,500.00
2700	Set Dressing	10	66,925.00	66,925.00
2800	Property	11	68,385.00	68,385.00
2900	Men's Wardrobe	11	55,940.00	55,940.00
3000	Women's Wardrobe	12	15,230.00	15,230.00
3100	Make-up/Hairdressing	12	27,280.00	27,280.00
3200	Electric/Lighting	13	88,925.00	88,925.00
3300	Camera Operations	14	163,393.33	163,393.33
3400	Production Sound	14	25,830.00	25,830.00
3500	Transportation	15	297,929.57	297,929.57
3600	Location	16	295,491.83	295,491.83
3700	Production Film and Lab	17	144,945.41	144,945.41
3800	Stage Facilities	17	11,755.00	11,755.00
3900	Process and Rear Projection	18	0.00	0.00
4000	2nd Unit/Miniatures/Effects	18	7,500.00	7,500.00
4100	Tests	18	1,500.00	1,500.00
4900	Fringe Benefits	18	166,081.31	166,081.31
	TOTAL PRODUCTION PERIOD			1,916,631.21

ACCT.#	DESCRIPTION	PG.		TOTAL	TOTALS
5000	Editorial	19		183,250.00	183,250.00
5100	Music	20		0.00	0.00
5200	Post-production Sound	20		141,573.00	141,573.00
5300	Post-production Film & Lab	21		40,896.00	40,896.00
5400	Main and End Titles	21		17,500.00	17,500.00
5900	Fringe Benefits	21		12,051.00	12,051.00
	TOTAL EDITING PERIOD				395,270.00
6500	Publicity	22		12,750.00	12,750.00
6700	Insurance	22		120,000.00	120,000.00
6800	General Overhead	23		66,100.00	66,100.00
6900	Fringe Benefits	23		1,625.00	1,625.00
7500	Fees/Charges/Miscellaneous	23		51,500.00	51,500.00
	TOTAL OTHER CHARGES				251,975.00
	ABOVE-THE-LINE				2,247,992.30
	BELOW-THE-LINE				2,563,876.21
	DIRECT COSTS				4,811,868.51
	CONTINGENCY		10 %		481,186.85
	OVERHEAD FEE				
	COMPLETION BOND		6 %		288,712.11
			TOTAL		5,581,767.48
	DEFERMENTS TOTAL	24			
			TOTAL NEGATIVE COSTS (Deferments Included)		5,581,767.48

DISORDERLIES and CHECKING OUT

These budgets were prepared as part of a package submitted to secure funding for the productions. As with *Night and the City*, the budget for *Checking Out* excluded above-the-line from consideration. This is a common tactic in presentation budgets, particularly because it leaves the actors' salaries unspecified and places the burden of such costs directly on the distributor. Because of the attachments, *Disorderlies* succeeded at Warner Bros. On its initial submission, *Checking Out* did not, but, after different attachments were added, it, too, received backing from a different distribution company. *Disorderlies* was prepared with a budgeting program. Certain of these programs create detail pages by building up from account "modules." In other words, only after the preparer enters amounts in line items of the form do those lines become part of the detail pages and are added to accounts. There are two disadvantages in this method. First, depending upon the detail, accounts may not always appear on the same page and, thus, there is no "standard" form. Second and much more significant, certain lines which the preparer does not use are not even printed. Since part of the review process should address the possible need for items for which are no current allowances, not having those empty lines printed for reference can considerably complicate that review process.

```
PROD. # CP 86-001          PRODUCER                          STUDIO    15
TITLE    DISORDERLIES      DIRECTOR Michael Schultz          LOCAL     25
                           PREPARER Alain Silver             DIST       5
START DATE                                                   TRAVEL     2
PREPARED    March 3, 1986                                    TOTAL     47
```

Acct #	Category	Page #	Budgeted	Total
1100	STORY/RIGHTS/CONTIN	2	201,250	
1200	PRODUCERS UNIT	2	507,500	
1300	DIRECTION	3	390,300	
1400	CAST	4	600,460	
1500	TRAVEL & LIVING	5	38,100	
1600	MISCELLANEOUS	5	2,500	
1900	FRINGES	5	149,026	
TOTAL	ABOVE THE LINE	5	1,889,136	
2000	PRODUCTION STAFF	6	213,843	
2100	EXTRA TALENT	7	55,395	
2200	SET DESIGN	7	62,500	
2300	SET CONSTRUCTION	8	144,700	
2400	SET STRIKING	8	5,000	
2500	SET OPERATIONS	9	92,135	
2600	SPECIAL EFFECTS	10	80,000	
2700	SET DRESSING	10	101,800	
2800	PROPERTY	11	91,275	
2900	MEN'S WARDROBE	12	97,975	
3000	WOMEN'S WARDROBE	13	24,025	
3100	MAKE-UP/HAIRDRESSIN	14	47,825	
3200	ELECTRIC/LIGHTING	15	142,235	
3300	CAMERA	16	195,560	
3400	PRODUCTION SOUND	17	50,760	
3500	TRANSPORTATION	18	251,115	
3600	LOCATION	20	231,441	
3700	PROD. FILM & LAB	21	153,205	
3800	STAGE FACILITIES	22	58,225	
3900	PROCESS/REAR SCREEN	22	0	
4000	SECOND UNIT	22	0	
4100	TESTS	22	3,000	
4200	MISC. PROD. EXPENSE	23	0	
4300	FRINGES	23	135,652	
TOTAL	TOTAL PROD. PERIOD	23	2,237,666	
4500	FILM EDITING	24	229,435	
4600	MUSIC	25	200,000	
4700	POST PROD. SOUND	25	114,785	
4800	POST PROD. FILM/LAB	26	34,435	
4900	MAIN & END TITLES	26	17,500	
5900	FRINGE BENEFITS	26	13,145	
TOTAL	TOTAL EDITING PERIO	26	609,300	
6500	PUBLICITY	27	22,750	
6600	INSURANCE	27	134,125	
6800	GENERAL EXPENSE	28	47,000	
6900	FRINGE BENEFITS	28	0	
7500	FEES/CHARGES/MISC.	28	58,750	
TOTAL	TOTAL OTHER CHARGES	29	262,625	
TOTAL - BELOW THE LINE			3,109,591	
TOTAL ABOVE & BELOW THE LINE			4,998,727	
CONTINGENCY		10.0 %	499,872	
COMPLETION BOND		6.0 %	299,923	
GRAND TOTAL			5,798,522	

CP 86-001   DISORDERLIES

Acct#	Description	Time	Units	X	Rate	Amount	Total
	4600	**MUSIC**					
4601	COMPOSER(S)						75,000
	Underscore Package	1	Allow	1	75,000	75,000	
4675	CLEARANCE/ROYALTIES						125,000
	Allowance	1		1	125,000	125,000	
4685	OTHER RIGHTS						0
4689	STUDIO CHARGES						0
					TOTAL	4600	200,000

Acct#	Description	Time	Units	X	Rate	Amount	Total
	4700	**POST PROD. SOUND**					
4701	TRANSFER COSTS						5,000
	Allowance	1		1	5,000	5,000	
4711	ADR FACILITY						13,200
		48	Hours	1	275	13,200	
4715	FOLEY FACILITY						11,000
		40	Hours	1	275	11,000	
4721	MUSIC MIX						0
4731	MUSIC/FX STOCK						12,500
	Allow	250000	Feet	1	0.05	12,500	
4741	TEMP DUB(S)						5,000
	Allowance	1		1	5,000	5,000	
4745	PRE-DUB(S)						12,825
		27	Hours	1	475	12,825	
4751	MASTER DUB						49,500
		90	Hours	1	550	49,500	
4761	M & E DUB						1,500
	Transfer only	1		1	1,500	1,500	
4771	STOCK RENTALS						1,500
	Allowance	1		1	1,500	1,500	
4773	FULL COAT PURCHASED						1,200
		15000	Feet	1	0.08	1,200	
4781	1/4 INCH PROTECTION						60
		4	rolls	1	15	60	
4785	OTHER COSTS						1,500
	Miscellaneous	1	Allow	1	1,500	1,500	
4789	STUDIO CHARGES						0
							0
					TOTAL	4700	114,785

PRODUCTION BUDGET

DATE: Jan. 29, 1987

TITLE: "CHECKING OUT"   PICTURE NO.   IP 87-004

DAYS		Exec Producer:	
Travel:		Producer:	
Rehearse:		Director:	
Distant:		Start Date:	
Local Loc: 40		Finish Date:	
Stage:		Script Dated:	
2nd Unit:		Script Pages:	129
TOTAL:	40	Budget Prep:	Alain Silver

NOTE: The Above-the-line total includes a General Allowance of $1,150,000 for Talent and Fringe.

ACCT.#	DESCRIPTION	PG.		TOTAL	TOTALS
1100	Story, Rights, & Continuity	3		3,250.00	3,250.00
1200	Producers Unit	3		5,600.00	5,600.00
1300	Direction	3		18,900.00	18,900.00
1400	Cast	4		0.00	0.00
1500	Travel and Living	5		7,500.00	7,500.00
1600	Miscellaneous	5		0.00	0.00
1900	Fringe Benefits	5		1,339.20	1,339.20
	TOTAL ABOVE-THE-LINE				1,186,589.20
2000	Production Staff	6		201,091.50	201,091.50
2100	Extra Talent	7		41,377.50	41,377.50
2200	Art Direction	8		46,700.00	46,700.00
2300	Set Construction	8		40,000.00	40,000.00
2400	Set Striking	8		0.00	0.00
2500	Set Operations	9		72,600.00	72,600.00
2600	Special Effects	10		14,250.00	14,250.00
2700	Set Dressing	10		74,150.00	74,150.00
2800	Property	11		68,250.00	68,250.00
2900	Men's Wardrobe	11		57,800.00	57,800.00
3000	Women's Wardrobe	12		21,250.00	21,250.00
3100	Make-up/Hairdressing	12		36,950.00	36,950.00
3200	Electric/Lighting	13		100,448.40	100,448.40
3300	Camera Operations	14		122,450.00	122,450.00
3400	Production Sound	14		34,050.00	34,050.00
3500	Transportation	15		178,671.50	178,671.50
3600	Location	16		127,250.00	127,250.00
3700	Production Film and Lab	17		123,319.66	123,319.66
3800	Stage Facilities	17		31,950.00	31,950.00
3900	Process and Rear Projection	18		0.00	0.00
4000	2nd Unit/Miniatures/Effects	18		17,500.00	17,500.00
4100	Tests	18		500.00	500.00
4900	Fringe Benefits	18		149,306.36	149,306.36
	TOTAL PRODUCTION PERIOD				1,559,864.92

ACCT.#	DESCRIPTION	PG.		TOTAL	TOTALS
5000	Editorial	19		121,486.25	121,486.25
5100	Music	20		50,000.00	50,000.00
5200	Post-production Sound	20		66,988.00	66,988.00
5300	Post-production Film & Lab	21		37,945.95	37,945.95
5400	Main and End Titles	21		12,500.00	12,500.00
5900	Fringe Benefits	21		13,245.53	13,245.53
	TOTAL EDITING PERIOD				302,165.73
6500	Publicity	22		2,325.00	2,325.00
6700	Insurance	22		78,800.00	78,800.00
6800	General Overhead	23		31,450.00	31,450.00
6900	Fringe Benefits	23		0.00	0.00
7500	Fees/Charges/Miscellaneous	23		35,500.00	35,500.00
	TOTAL OTHER CHARGES				148,075.00
	ABOVE-THE-LINE				1,186,589.20
	BELOW-THE-LINE				2,010,105.65
	DIRECT COSTS				3,196,694.85
	CONTINGENCY		10 %		319,700.00
	OVERHEAD FEE				
	COMPLETION BOND		5 %		159,834.74
			TOTAL		3,676,229.59
	DEFERMENTS TOTAL	24			
			TOTAL NEGATIVE COSTS		3,676,229.59

THE RETURN OF BILLY JACK

Several budgets and topsheets were produced for a partial script. Because production on this project had begun but was shut down due to the extended illness of the lead actor, the budget was prepared to determine the cost of starting up production, using certain scenes already shot, and completing principal photography. Because of the money lost in the shutdown, the other significant consideration was a change of location and the use of non-IATSE craftspeople to reduce costs and, in fact, complete the picture for a lower amount than the original total cost projected before problems arose.

PRODUCTION BUDGET

DATE: June 4, 1987

TITLE: "THE RETURN OF BILLY JACK"

PICTURE NO. SR 87-011

DAYS			
Travel:	2	Exec Producer:	
Rehearse:		Producer:	
Distant:	3	Director:	
Local Loc:	17	Start Date:	
Stage:	20	Finish Date:	
2nd Unit:		Script Dated:	
TOTAL:	42	Script Pages:	110 (Approx)
		Budget Prep:	Alain Silver

ACCT.#	DESCRIPTION	PG.		TOTAL	TOTALS
1100	Story, Rights, & Continuity	3		4,000.00	4,000.00
1200	Producers Unit	3		0.00	0.00
1300	Direction	3		17,400.00	17,400.00
1400	Cast	4		0.00	0.00
1500	Travel and Living	5		3,400.00	3,400.00
1600	Miscellaneous	5		0.00	0.00
1900	Fringe Benefits	5		2,427.30	2,427.30
	TOTAL ABOVE-THE-LINE				1,027,227.30
2000	Production Staff	6		176,790.00	176,790.00
2100	Extra Talent	7		29,930.00	29,930.00
2200	Art Direction	8		40,850.00	40,850.00
2300	Set Construction	8		75,000.00	75,000.00
2400	Set Striking	8		0.00	0.00
2500	Set Operations	9		61,850.00	61,850.00
2600	Special Effects	10		15,600.00	15,600.00
2700	Set Dressing	10		60,550.00	60,550.00
2800	Property	11		53,500.00	53,500.00
2900	Men's Wardrobe	11		54,400.00	54,400.00
3000	Women's Wardrobe	12		17,250.00	17,250.00
3100	Make-up/Hairdressing	12		38,400.00	38,400.00
3200	Electric/Lighting	13		88,950.00	88,950.00
3300	Camera Operations	14		163,250.00	163,250.00
3400	Production Sound	14		37,715.00	37,715.00
3500	Transportation	15		159,904.10	159,904.10
3600	Location	16		116,971.60	116,971.60
3700	Production Film and Lab	17		147,691.13	147,691.13
3800	Stage Facilities	17		66,000.00	66,000.00
3900	Process and Rear Projection	18		0.00	0.00
4000	2nd Unit/Miniatures/Effects	18		0.00	0.00
4100	Tests	18		500.00	500.00
4900	Fringe Benefits	18		146,419.36	146,419.36
	TOTAL PRODUCTION PERIOD				1,551,521.19

THE RETURN OF BILLY JACK 10-Jun-87

ACCT.#	DESCRIPTION	PG.		TOTAL	TOTALS
5000	Editorial	19		104,680.00	104,680.00
5100	Music	20		57,500.00	57,500.00
5200	Post-production Sound	20		57,628.00	57,628.00
5300	Post-production Film & Lab	21		32,100.00	32,100.00
5400	Main and End Titles	21		17,500.00	17,500.00
5900	Fringe Benefits	21		10,099.80	10,099.80
	TOTAL EDITING PERIOD				279,507.80
6500	Publicity	22		250.00	250.00
6700	Insurance	22		90,800.00	90,800.00
6800	General Overhead	23		30,400.00	30,400.00
6900	Fringe Benefits	23		10,929.00	10,929.00
7500	Fees/Charges/Miscellaneous	23		36,500.00	36,500.00
	TOTAL OTHER CHARGES				168,879.00
	ABOVE-THE-LINE				1,027,227.30
	BELOW-THE-LINE				1,999,907.99
	DIRECT COSTS				3,027,135.29
	CONTINGENCY		10 %		302,700.00
	OVERHEAD FEE				150,000.00
	COMPLETION BOND		5 %		151,356.76
			TOTAL		3,631,192.05
	DEFERMENTS TOTAL	24			
			TOTAL NEGATIVE COSTS		3,031,192.05

**Indicates Travel to Location

RECENT EXAMPLES

THE COLORS and *FIGHTING CHANCE*

Not only are these both presentation budgets, but the first drafts were produced at such an early stage that they were from treatments rather than scripts. Obviously, without a script, shooting schedules are mostly conjecture; but the process is still valid. Personal experience has shown that even after the scripts are written and the films are shot, the subsequent discrepancies between real costs and first draft budgets from treatments may have been less significant than those caused by accommodating the limited availabilities of actors or locations.

PRODUCTION BUDGET

REVISED Nov. 21, 1991
DATE:_____

TITLE: "THE COLORS"_____

PICTURE NO. MBP 91-001_____

DAYS
Trvl/Hldy: 6   Producer: Milton Bagby, Jr.
Rehearse: Director:
Distant: 80   Finish Date:
Local Loc: Script Dated:
Stage: Budget Pages: 23
2nd Unit: Script Pages: 115
TOTAL: 86   Budget Prep: Alain Silver

ACCT.#	DESCRIPTION	PG.	TOTAL	TOTALS
1100	Story, Rights, & Continuity	3	258,000.00	258,000.00
1200	Producers Unit	3	755,000.00	755,000.00
1300	Direction	3	1,061,500.00	1,061,500.00
1400	Cast	4	4,709,646.70	4,709,646.70
1500	Travel and Living	5	514,360.00	514,360.00
1600	Miscellaneous	5	2,500.00	2,500.00
1900	Fringe Benefits	5	758,116.26	758,116.26
	TOTAL ABOVE-THE-LINE			8,059,122.96
2000	Production Staff	6	681,455.15	681,455.15
2100	Extra Talent	7	251,482.50	251,482.50
2200	Art Direction	8	122,600.00	122,600.00
2300	Set Construction	8	850,000.00	850,000.00
2400	Set Striking	8	0.00	0.00
2500	Set Operations	9	226,100.00	226,100.00
2600	Special Effects	10	342,950.00	342,950.00
2700	Set Dressing	10	146,800.00	146,800.00
2800	Property	11	359,650.00	359,650.00
2900	Men's Wardrobe	11	239,450.00	239,450.00
3000	Women's Wardrobe	12	109,500.00	109,500.00
3100	Make-up/Hairdressing	12	222,325.00	222,325.00
3200	Electric/Lighting	13	418,600.00	418,600.00
3300	Camera Operations	14	765,350.00	765,350.00
3400	Production Sound	14	180,250.00	180,250.00
3500	Transportation	15	1,034,861.25	1,034,861.25
3600	Location	16	1,594,264.00	1,594,264.00
3700	Production Film and Lab	17	421,497.00	421,497.00
3800	Stage Facilities	17	32,100.00	32,100.00
3900	Process and Rear Projection	18	25,000.00	25,000.00
4000	2nd Unit/Miniatures/Effects	18	250,000.00	250,000.00
4100	Tests	18	15,000.00	15,000.00
4900	Fringe Benefits	18	499,846.81	499,846.81
	TOTAL PRODUCTION PERIOD			8,789,081.71

Form SB002, Copyright (c) 1984, PENDRAGON FILM LTD.

ACCT.#	DESCRIPTION	PG.		TOTAL	TOTALS
5000	Editorial	19		534,325.00	534,325.00
5100	Music	20		400,000.00	400,000.00
5200	Post-production Sound	20		216,627.00	216,627.00
5300	Post-production Film & Lab	21		93,921.12	93,921.12
5400	Main and End Titles	21		45,000.00	45,000.00
5900	Fringe Benefits	21		41,833.93	41,833.93
	TOTAL EDITING PERIOD				1,331,707.05
6500	Publicity	22		62,500.00	62,500.00
6700	Insurance	22		422,700.00	422,700.00
6800	General Overhead	23		151,000.00	151,000.00
6900	Fringe Benefits	23		49,258.75	49,258.75
7500	Fees/Charges/Miscellaneous	23		347,000.00	347,000.00
	TOTAL OTHER CHARGES				1,032,458.75
	ABOVE-THE-LINE				8,059,122.96
	BELOW-THE-LINE				11,153,247.50
	DIRECT COSTS				19,212,370.46
	CONTINGENCY		10 %		1,921,200.00
	OVERHEAD FEE				0.00
	COMPLETION BOND		5 %		960,618.52
			TOTAL		22,094,188.99
	DEFERMENTS TOTAL	24			
			TOTAL NEGATIVE COSTS		22,094,188.99

DRAFT BUDGET TOPSHEET

TITLE: "FIGHTING CHANCE"   PFL 92-007
                                               PICTURE NO. _____

ACCT.#	DESCRIPTION	PG.		TOTAL	TOTALS
1.00	Story/Screenplay	2		12,000.00	12,000.00
2.00	Producer/Staff	2		30,000.00	30,000.00
3.00	Director/Staff	2		50,725.06	50,725.06
4.00	Cast	3		143,512.65	143,512.65
5.00	Extras	4		24,096.56	24,096.56
6.00	Travel/Living	4		500.00	500.00
7.00	Fringe Benefits	4		12,605.50	12,605.50
	TOTAL ABOVE-THE-LINE				273,439.77
8.00	Production Staff	5		104,941.78	104,941.78
9.00	Production Operating Staff	6		177,907.62	177,907.62
10.00	Set Designing	9		27,500.00	27,500.00
11.00	Set Operations	10		94,080.00	94,080.00
12.00	Cutting/Film/Laboratory	12		164,970.53	164,970.53
13.00	Music	14		25,000.00	25,000.00
14.00	Sound	14		54,900.00	54,900.00
15.00	2nd Unit/Tests/Inserts	14		2,750.00	2,750.00
16.00	Transportation	15		61,429.53	61,429.53
17.00	Publicity	15		1,250.00	1,250.00
18.00	Location	16		76,882.97	76,882.97
19.00	Stage/Studio Operations	16		0.00	0.00
20.00	Insurance/Taxes/Licenses	17		32,000.00	32,000.00
21.00	General Overhead	17		32,250.00	32,250.00
22.00	Miscellaneous	17		250.00	250.00
	TOTAL BELOW-THE-LINE				856,112.43
	TOTAL DIRECT COSTS				1,129,552.21
	Contingency		10.0 %		113,000.00
	Completion Bond		5.0 %		56,477.61
	GRAND TOTAL				1,299,029.82

REV. May 5, 1992
Date Prepared_____

From_____Page Script Dated_____
30   0   30   0
_____Day Schedule (Rehearse____Distant_____ Local Loc._____ Studio_____)
          Ron Walsh   James Allard
Director_____ Producer_____
          Alain Silver
Budget_____

Form SB001, Copyright (c) 1984, PENDRAGON FILM LTD.

FIGHTING CHANCE 01-Jun-92   Page 2

ACCT.#	DESCRIPTION	NO.	DAYS/WKS/ QUANTITY	RATE	TOTAL
	STORY/SCREENPLAY				
1.10	Story Purchase				
1.30	Screenplay Purchase				10,000.00
1.32	Writer(s)				
1.34	Revision(s)				
1.36	Polish				
	Deferment				
1.50	Stenographer/Secretary				
1.60	Copying				500.00
1.70	Research/Clearance		Allow		1,500.00
1.80	Script Timing				
1.90	W.G.A. Fringes		0.0 %		0.00
	TOTAL				12,000.00
	PRODUCER/STAFF				
2.10	Producer(s)				30,000.00
2.20	Executive Producer(s)		Allow		
2.30	Associate Producer(s)		Allow		
2.40	Supervising Producer(s)		Incl. Below Acct. 2.01		0.00
2.50	Secretary(ies)				0.00
2.60	Production Assistant(s)		Incl. Below		0.00
					0.00
	TOTAL				30,000.00
	DIRECTOR/STAFF				
3.10	Director		13.0 wks	7,190.95	93,482.35
	Deferment				(52,837.85)
3.50	Casting Director		Allow		5,000.00
3.60	Personal Assistant(s)		Incl.Above		0.00
3.90	D.G.A. Fringes		12.5 %		5,080.56
	TOTAL				50,725.06

ACCT.#	DESCRIPTION	NO.	DAYS/WKS/ QUANTITY	RATE	TOTAL
4.00	CAST:				
1	DANNY BRAVO		6.0 wks	1,785.00	10,710.00
2	CORY BREWSTER		6.0 wks	1,785.00	10,710.00
3	AARON EXLEY		3.0 wks	1,785.00	5,355.00
4	ARMANDO		4.0 wks	1,785.00	7,140.00
5	BIG "O" SAYLES		3.0 wks	1,785.00	5,355.00
6	KUJO		2.0 wks	1,785.00	3,570.00
7	LUIS		1.4 wks	1,785.00	2,499.00
8	PRESS BOOTH ANNOUNCER		1.0 dys	515.00	515.00
9	SIDELINE REPORTER		1.0 dys	515.00	515.00
10	GARY KUBY		3.0 dys	515.00	1,545.00
11	SECURITY MAN		1.0 dys	515.00	515.00
12	P.R. GUY		2.0 dys	515.00	1,030.00
13	GUARD		2.0 dys	515.00	1,030.00
14	MAJOR SUIT		2.0 dys	515.00	1,030.00
15	MINOR SUIT		2.0 dys	515.00	1,030.00
16	BARTENDER		1.0 dys	515.00	515.00
17	SACRAMENTO BEE REPORTER		1.0 dys	515.00	515.00
18-20	FRIEND #1/#2/#3	3	1.0 dys	515.00	1,545.00
21-22	SPORTS REPORTER #1/#2	2	1.0 dys	515.00	1,030.00
23	TRAINER		1.0 dys	515.00	515.00
24	DESK MAN		1.0 dys	515.00	515.00
25-26	LITTLE KID #1/#2	2	1.0 dys	515.00	1,030.00
27	ESPN REPORTER		1.0 dys	515.00	515.00
28-29	BAR GUY #1/#2	2	1.0 dys	515.00	1,030.00
30-31	TENNIS PLATER #1/#2	2	1.0 dys	515.00	1,030.00
32	DISC JOCKEY		1.0 dys	515.00	515.00
33-34	AGENT #1/#2	2	1.0 dys	515.00	1,030.00
35	ODDSMAKER		1.0 dys	515.00	515.00
	NON-SCRIPT LINES	6	Allow	466.00	2,796.00
4.60	Stunt Coordinator		6.0 wks	1,750.00	10,500.00
	Stunt Doubles	2	15.0 dys	466.00	13,980.00
	Supplemental		10.0 dys	466.00	4,660.00
	Utility Stunts		Incl. Above		
	Stunt Adjustments		Allow		12,500.00
	Adjustment for SAG Low Budget Agreement				(10,646.00)
4.80	Weekly Player Overtime		20.0 %	Allow	11,167.80
4.82	Daily Player Overtime		37.5 %	Allow	14,430.00
4.86	Fitting/ADR Days		5.0 dys	466.00	2,330.00
4.90	S.A.G. Fringe Benefits		12.5 %		18,945.85
	TOTAL				143,512.65

ACCT.#	DESCRIPTION	NO.	DAYS/WKS/ QUANTITY	RATE	TOTAL
	EXTRAS				
5.00	Stand-ins				
		2	30.0 dys	90.00	5,400.00
					0.00
5.10	Extras				
	General Atmos		150.0 dys	65.00	9,750.00
	Crowd Extras		Allow		3,000.00
	Adjustments		20.0 dys	10.00	200.00
5.60	Overtime		37.5 %		4,856.25
5.70	Casting Service Fee		5.0 %		890.31
5.80	Interviews/Fittings		Allow		0.00
5.90	Union Fringe Benefits		12.5 %		0.00
	TOTAL				24,096.56
	TRAVEL AND LIVING				
6.00	Fares				0.00
					0.00
6.10	Accommodations/Per Diem				0.00
					0.00
6.20	General Allowance				500.00
	TOTAL				500.00
	FRINGE BENEFITS				
7.10	Payroll Service Charges		1.5 %		1,231.81
7.20	Union Fringes (not included above)				
7.90	Government Fringes		13.85 %		11,373.69
	TOTAL				12,605.50

ACCT.#\	DESCRIPTION	NO.	DAYS/WKS/ QUANTITY	RATE	TOTAL
	PRODUCTION STAFF				
8.00	* Production Manager		18.6 wks	1,250.50	23,259.30
8.01	D.G.A Production Fee		6.0 wks	270.50	1,623.00
8.02	Saturday Adjustment		dys	198.39	0.00
8.05	* Unit Production Manager		10.0 wks	653.48	6,534.78
8.06	D.G.A. Production Fee				0.00
8.07					
8.10	* 1st Assistant Director		10.0 wks	1,187.50	11,875.00
8.11	D.G.A Production Fee		6.0 wks	219.50	1,317.00
8.12	Saturday Adjustment		dys	183.52	0.00
8.20	* Key 2nd Assistant Director		8.6 wks	796.00	6,845.60
8.21	D.G.A. Production Fee		6.0 wks	168.00	1,008.00
8.22	Saturday Adjustment		dys	125.74	0.00
8.25	* Additional Assistant(s)		8.0 wks	457.50	3,660.00
8.29	DGA Deferments		Incl. Above	(72,959.49)	
8.30	D.G.A. Trainee	70	7.0 wks	7.59	3,719.10
8.32	Script Supervisor		8.0 wks	1,000.00	8,000.00
8.40	Production Coordinator		12.0 wks	700.00	8,400.00
8.42	Production Secretary(ies)		8.0 wks	400.00	3,200.00
8.50	Casting Director		Allow		5,000.00
8.52	Casting Assistant(s)		Incl.Above		0.00
8.60	Choreographer		Allow		0.00
8.62	Assistant(s)				0.00
8.66	Technical Advisor(s)				0.00
8.70	Standby First Aid		Allow		2,500.00
8.72	Welfare Worker(s)				0.00
8.80	Production Accountant		18.0 wks	1,000.00	18,000.00
8.84	Assistant Accountant(s)				0.00
8.90	Government Fringe Benefits		13.9 %	Incl.Below	5,190.65
8.92	D.G.A. Fringe Benefits		13.0 %	Acct.	2,806.13
8.94	D.G.A. Vacation/Holiday Pay		7.7 %	9.93	1,548.99
	* Includes Severance				
	TOTAL				104,941.78

ACCT.#	DESCRIPTION	NO.	DAYS/WKS/ QUANTITY	RATE	TOTAL
	PRODUCTION OPERATING STAFF				
	CAMERA				
9.00	**Director of Photography		6.0 wks	2,750.00	16,500.00
9.01	Camera Operator				0.00
9.02	1st Assistant Cameraperson		7.0 wks	1,000.00	7,000.00
9.03	2nd Assistant Cameraperson		6.6 wks	600.00	3,960.00
9.04	Additional Operator(s)		3.0 dys	200.00	600.00
9.04	Additional Assistant(s)		3.0 dys	175.00	525.00
9.06	Loader(s)				
9.07	Camera Technician(s)				
	Steadicam		Allow		
9.08	Still Photographer(s)		6.0 wks	700.00	4,200.00
9.09	2nd Unit D.P.				0.00
	TOTAL CAMERA PERSONNEL				32,785.00
	PRODUCTION SOUND				
9.11	Mixer		6.0 wks	1,250.00	7,500.00
9.12	Boom Operator(s)		6.0 wks	700.00	4,200.00
9.13	Recordist(s)				0.00
9.14	Sound Utility				0.00
9.15	Cable Person				0.00
9.16	Audio Playback Operator				0.00
9.17	Video Playback Operator(s)				0.00
9.18	Video Technician(s)				0.00
	TOTAL SOUND PERSONNEL				11,700.00
	SET OPERATIONS				
9.21	Key Grip		7.0 wks	1,000.00	7,000.00
9.22	Grip Best Boy		6.8 wks	700.00	4,760.00
9.23	Set Operations Grip(s)				0.00
9.24	Extra Grip(s)		6.6 wks	600.00	3,960.00
9.25	Dolly Grip(s)		Incl.Above		0.00
9.26	Crane Crip(s)				0.00
9.27	Construction Grip(s)				0.00
	TOTAL SET OPERATIONS PERSONNEL				15,720.00

ACCT.#	DESCRIPTION	NO.	DAYS/WKS/ QUANTITY	RATE	TOTAL
	ELECTRICAL				
9.31	Gaffer		7.0 wks	1,000.00	7,000.00
9.32	Best Boy Electric		6.8 wks	700.00	4,760.00
9.33	Special Equipment Operator				0.00
9.34	Lamp Operator(s)	2	6.0 wks	600.00	7,200.00
9.35	Extra Lamp Operator(s)	2	10.0 dys	110.00	2,200.00
9.36	Generator Operator(s)				0.00
9.37	Rigging Gaffer		Allow		0.00
9.38	Rigging Electricians		Allow		0.00
	TOTAL ELECTRICAL PERSONNEL				21,160.00
	MAKEUP/HAIR				
9.41	Makeup--Department Head		6.0 wks	1,000.00	7,200.00
9.42	Key Makeup Person(s)				0.00
9.43	Effects Make-up Person(s)				0.00
9.44	Hairdresser--Department Head		6.0 wks	900.00	6,000.00
9.45	Key Hairdresser(s)				0.00
9.46	Additional Hairdresser(s)				0.00
9.47	Wigmaker/Stylist				0.00
9.48	Body Make-up Person(s)				0.00
	TOTAL MAKEUP/HAIR PERSONNEL				13,200.00
	WARDROBE				
9.51	Costume Designer		Allow		
9.52	Coordinator		12.0 wks	900.00	10,800.00
9.53	Set Costumer (Men)		8.4 wks	600.00	5,880.00
9.54	Set Costumer (Women)				0.00
9.55	Assistant Set Costumer(s)				0.00
9.56	Checker(s)				0.00
9.57	Fitter(s)				0.00
9.58	Tailoring				0.00
	TOTAL WARDROBE PERSONNEL				17,880.00
	SPECIAL EFFECTS				
9.61	Special Effects Foreperson		PACKAGE		7,500.00
9.62	Effects Assistant(s)				0.00
9.63	Effects Rigger(s)				0.00
9.64	Powderperson(s)				0.00
9.65	Plumber(s)				0.00
	TOTAL EFFECTS PERSONNEL				7,500.00

ACCT.#	DESCRIPTION	NO.	DAYS/WKS/ QUANTITY	RATE	TOTAL
	PROPERTY/SET DRESSING				
9.70	Property Master		9.0 wks	900.00	8,100.00
9.71	Assistant Property Master(s)		7.6 wks	600.00	4,560.00
9.72	Additional Prop Assistant(s)				0.00
9.73	Propmaker(s)				0.00
9.74	Set Decorator		10.0 wks	900.00	9,000.00
9.75	Assistant Set Decorator(s)				0.00
9.76	Leadperson		8.0 wks	600.00	4,800.00
9.77	Swingperson(s)				0.00
					0.00
9.78	Greensperson(s)				0.00
9.79	Draper(s)				0.00
	TOTAL PROP/SET PERSONNEL				26,460.00
	STANDBY LABOR				
9.81	Craft Service		6.4 wks	400.00	2,560.00
9.82	Craft Service Assistant(s)				0.00
9.83	Set Laborer(s)				0.00
9.84	Assistant Set Laborer(s)				0.00
9.85	Production Assistant(s)		8.0 wks	400.00	3,200.00
			4.0 wks	350.00	1,400.00
			6.0 wks	350.00	2,100.00
					0.00
					0.00
	TOTAL STANDBY LABOR				9,260.00
	PRODUCTION OPERATING STAFF SUB-TOTAL				155,665.00
	FRINGE BENEFITS				
9.91	Overtime Allowance				0.00
9.93	Union Fringe Benefits - DGA				4,355.12
9.95	Rate Adjustment Allowances				
9.96	Government Fringe Benefits		13.85 %		17,887.50
	TOTAL FRINGE BENEFITS				22,242.62
	PRODUCTION OPERATING STAFF TOTAL				177,907.62

ACCT.#	DESCRIPTION	NO.	DAYS/WKS/ QUANTITY	RATE	TOTAL
	SET DESIGNING				
10.01	Production Designer		Allow		10,000.00
10.02	Art Director(s)				0.00
10.04	Assistant Art Director(s)				0.00
10.06	Draftperson(s)				0.00
10.08	Construction Coordinator				0.00
10.09	Assistant Coordinator				0.00
10.19	Fringe Benefits - Labor		0.0 %		0.00
	[SUB-TOTAL - LABOR]				10,000.00
	SET CONSTRUCTION		LABOR	MATERIAL	
10.20	Rigging Allowance		Incl.Below		
10.22	Backings		Incl.Below		
10.24	Greens		Incl.Below		
10.26	Parallels		Incl.Below		
10.30	Striking Allowance		Incl.Below		
10.40	Drafting Materials/Supplies		Incl.Below		
10.50	Sets				
	General Allowance				17,500.00
	TOTAL				27,500.00

ACCT.#	DESCRIPTION	NO.	DAYS/WKS/ QUANTITY	RATE	TOTAL
	SET OPERATION EXPENSES				
11.01	Camera Equipment Rental		6.0 wks	3,500.00	21,000.00
11.03	Additional Camera(s)	0	Incl.Above		0.00
	Special Equipment		Allow		0.00
11.05	Camera Expendables		Allow		750.00
11.10	Production Sound Equipment		6.0 wks	750.00	4,500.00
11.12	Production Playback		Allow		0.00
11.13	Wireles Microphones				0.00
11.14	Walkie-talkies	8	6.0 wks	60.00	2,880.00
11.16	Video Playback Equipment		0.0 dys		0.00
11.18	Sound Expendables		Allow		500.00
11.20	Electrical Equipment Rentals		6.0 wks	2,750.00	16,500.00
11.21	Supplementary Equipment		Allow		1,500.00
11.23	Globe Breakage		Incl.Above		0.00
11.24	Burn Time (HMI)		Incl.Above		0.00
11.26	Generator		Incl.Below		0.00
11.28	Electrical Expendables		Allow		2,500.00
11.29	Box Rental(s)				0.00
11.30	Grip Equipments Rentals		6.0 wks	750.00	4,500.00
11.31	Supplementary Equipment		Allow		0.00
11.32	Dolly Rental		6.0 wks	450.00	2,700.00
11.33	Crane Rental		5.0 dys	475.00	2,375.00
11.34	Car Mounts		Allow		0.00
11.35	Grip Expendables		Allow		750.00
11.39	Box Rental(s)				0.00
11.40	Make-up Expendables		Allow		350.00
11.42	Hairdressing Expendables		Allow		350.00
11.43	Hairdressing Rentals		Allow		300.00
11.49	Box Rentals				0.00

ACCT.#	DESCRIPTION	NO.	DAYS/WKS/ QUANTITY	RATE	TOTALS
11.50	Prop Rentals		Allow		3,500.00
11.51	Prop Purchases		Allow		5,000.00
11.52	Prop Expendables		Allow		500.00
11.53	Animals				0.00
11.54	Set Dressing Rentals		Allow		5,000.00
11.55	Set Dressing Purchases		Allow		2,500.00
11.56	Set Dressing Expendables		Allow		1,250.00
11.57	Supplementary Allowance		Allow		2,500.00
11.58	Loss/Damage		Allow		2,000.00
11.59	Box Rental(s)				0.00
11.60	Wardrobe Rentals		Allow		1,000.00
11.62	Wardrobe Purchases		Allow		2,500.00
11.64	Wardrobe Maintenance		Allow		1,250.00
	Fitting/Tailoring		Allow		1,000.00
11.66	Wardrobe Expendables		Allow		500.00
11.69	Box Rental(s)				0.00
11.70	Special Effects Rentals		Incl.Above		0.00
11.72	Special Effects Purchases		Acct. 9.60		0.00
11.74	Ritters				0.00
11.76	Expendables		Allow		0.00
11.79	Box Rentals				0.00
11.80	Craft Service Rentals		Incl.Below		0.00
11.82	Craft Service Purchases		Incl.Below		0.00
11.84	Set Food/Water/Ice		30.0 dys	200.00	6,000.00
11.86	Craft Service Expendables		Allow		0.00
11.89	Box Rentals				0.00
11.90	Miscellaneous Rentals		Allow		0.00
11.92	Miscellaneous Purchases		Allow		0.00
	TOTAL SET OPERATIONS				94,080.00

ACCT.#	DESCRIPTION	NO.	DAYS/WKS/ QUANTITY	RATE	TOTAL
	CUTTING/FILM/LABORATORY				
12.01	Editorial Supervisor				0.00
12.03	Editor(s)		15.0 wks	1,200.00	18,000.00
12.05	Assistant Editor(s)		15.0 wks	600.00	9,000.00
12.07	Apprentice Editor(s)		6.0 wks	450.00	2,700.00
12.11	Sound Effects Editor(s)		Incl. Below Acct. 14		0.00
12.12	Assistant Sound FX Editor(s)				0.00
12.13	Foley Editor(s)				0.00
12.14	ADR Editor(s)				0.00
12.15	Music Editor(s)		Allow		2,000.00
12.17	Negative Cutter(s)		Allow		4,000.00
12.18	Post-production Supervisor				0.00
12.19	Fringe Benefits		%		0.00
	[SUB-TOTAL LABOR]				35,700.00
12.20	Negative (Rawstock) - Type 1		120000 ft	0.4100	49,200.00
12.21	- Type 2		ft		0.00
12.22	Process Negative		108000 ft	0.12	12,960.00
12.23	Forced Developing		ft	0.05	0.00
12.25	One-light Workprint		81000 ft	0.16	12,960.00
12.27	Timed Workprint		ft		0.00
12.29	Reprints		2500 ft	0.16	400.00
12.30	Production Sound (1/4 inch)		20 rls	6.25	125.00
12.32	Mag Stripe - Production		89100 ft	0.08	7,128.00
12.34	Transfer from 1/4 inch		Incl.12.32		0.00
12.38	Video Transfers				0.00
12.40	Mag Stripe - Music		Incl. Below		0.00
12.41	Mag Stripe - Effects		Incl. Below		0.00
12.43	Transfers				0.00
12.44	Full Coat/3 Stripe - Dubs		8400 ft	0.08	672.00
12.45	- M&E		8400 ft	0.08	672.00
12.46	Protection				
12.48	Optical Neg - Shoot		8400 ft	0.07	588.00
12.49	- Process		8400 ft	0.18	1,512.00

Appendix 3

ACCT.#	DESCRIPTION	NO.	DAYS/WKS QUANTITY	RATE	TOTAL
12.50	Dirty Dupe(s)		Allow		1,200.00
12.52	Video Transfers (24 frame)		Allow		0.00
12.54	Optical Effects		Allow		2,500.00
12.56	Titles - Main and End		Allow		7,500.00
12.58	Foreign Textless Titles				
12.60	First Trial Print		ft		0.00
12.61	Answer Print		8400.0 ft	0.860	7,224.00
12.62	A/B Surcharge		ft		0.00
12.63	Master Interpositives		ft		0.00
12.65	C.R.I.(s)		ft		0.00
12.67	Release Prints		ft		0.00
12.69	Video Master (1 inch)		Allow		0.00
12.70	Cutting Room Rentals		15.0 wks	1,000.00	15,000.00
					0.00
12.73	Off-line rental				0.00
					0.00
12.76	Equipment Rentals		Incl.Above		0.00
12.78	Reels/Leader/Fill		Allow		1,250.00
12.79	Expendables		Allow		750.00
12.80	Coding		Allow		0.00
12.81	Stock Footage		Allow		0.00
12.83	Process Plates		Allow		0.00
12.85	Projection - Dailies		29.0 hrs	Incl. Above	0.00
12.86	Projection - Assemblies		6.0 hrs	80.00	480.00
12.87	Miscellaneous		Allow		0.00
12.90	Sales Tax		0.0825 %		7,149.53
	PRODUCTION - TOTAL				82,773.00
	POST-PRODUCTION - TOTAL				39,348.00
	CUTTING/FILM/LABORATORY TOTAL				164,970.53

ACCT.#	DESCRIPTION	NO.	DAYS/WKS QUANTITY	RATE	TOTAL
	MUSIC				
13.01	Composer (Underscore)		PACKAGE		25,000.00
13.11	Orchestrator(s)				
13.21	Music Supervisor				
13.31	Scoring – Labor				
13.41	– Rentals				
13.51	– Materials				
13.61	Video				
13.71	Royalties				
13.90	Fringe Benefits				
	TOTAL MUSIC				25,000.00
	SOUND				
14.01	Mix	9	10.0 dys	450.00	40,500.00
14.11	ADR	9	2.0 dys	325.00	5,850.00
14.21	Foley	9	2.0 dys	325.00	5,850.00
14.24	Foley Artists	2	2.0 dys	300.00	1,200.00
14.30	Pre-Dub(s)		Incl.Above		0.00
14.40	Master Dub		Incl.Above		0.00
14.44	Stereo Surcharge		Incl.Above		0.00
14.50	Stock/Equipment Rentals		Allow		750.00
14.60	Transfer Time		Allow		750.00
	SOUND TOTAL				54,900.00
	2ND UNIT/TESTS/INSERTS				
15.01	Helicopter				0.00
15.10	Local Hires				0.00
15.20	Production Staff				0.00
15.30	Prod. Operating Staff				0.00
15.40	Set Operations				0.00
15.50	Travel/Living				0.00
15.60	Miscellaneous				0.00
15.70	L.A. Operations Rebate				0.00
15.80	Pre-production Tests				2,000.00
15.90	Post-production Inserts		Allow		750.00
	TOTAL				2,750.00

ACCT.#	DESCRIPTION	NO.	DAYS/WKS/ QUANTITY	RATE	TOTAL
	TRANSPORTATION				
16.01	Transportation Coordinator		8.0 wks	1,200.00	9,600.00
16.02	Driver Captain(s)		5.0 wks	750.00	3,750.00
16.03	Driver(s) - 1		5.0 wks	600.00	6,000.00
16.08	Additional Driver(s)	2	20.0 dys	65.00	2,600.00
16.11	**Honeywagon Driver(s)		6.0 wks	950.00	5,700.00
16.14	Crane Driver				0.00
16.16	Insert Car Driver				0.00
16.21	Camera/Sound Van		6.0 wks	350.00	2,100.00
16.22	Prod. Van (Grip/Electric)		Incl.Above		0.00
16.23	Prop/FX Truck		8.0 wks	275.00	2,200.00
16.25	Set Dressing Truck		8.0 wks	275.00	2,200.00
16.27	Wardrobe Trailer		8.0 wks	175.00	1,400.00
16.31	Utility Pick-up(s)		8.0 wks	150.00	1,200.00
16.33	Utility Station Wagon(s)		2.0 wks	150.00	300.00
16.35	Maxivan(s)		2.0 wks	225.00	450.00
16.37	Bus(es)				0.00
16.41	Honeywagon(s)/Cast Trailer(s)		6.0 wks	1,200.00	7,200.00
16.43	Generator		6.0 wks	650.00	3,900.00
16.47	Insert Car				0.00
16.50	Miscellaneous Equipment		Allow		0.00
16.60	Picture Cars/Boats		Allow		1,500.00
	Helicopter(s)		Allow		0.00
16.70	Car Allowances				0.00
16.80	Gasoline/Repairs		Allow		7,500.00
16.90	Fringe Benefits (Labor)		13.9 %		3,829.53
16.94	Union Fringes		0.0 %		0.00
	TOTAL TRANSPORTATION				61,429.53
	PUBLICITY				
17.01	Unit Publicist(s)				
17.10	Advertising		Allow		
17.20	Stills - Supplies		Allow		500.00
17.24	Stills - Lab Charges		Allow		750.00
17.30	Trade Paper Subscriptions		Allow		
17.40	Preview(s)		Allow		
17.50	Entertainment		Allow		
17.90	Miscellaneous		Allow		
	TOTAL PUBLICITY				1,250.00

ACCT.#	DESCRIPTION	NO.	DAYS/WKS/ QUANTITY	RATE	TOTAL
	LOCATION				
18.01	Location Manager(s)		10.0 wks	1,200.00	12,000.00
18.02	Asst. Location Manager(s)				0.00
18.11	Police Officers	18	14.0 hrs	36.00	9,072.00
18.14	Fire Safety Officers		Allow		5,000.00
18.18	Contact Person(s)		Allow		
18.20	Meals - Prep/Scout		Allow		750.00
18.24	Meals - Production	70	30.0 dys	9.50	19,950.00
18.30	Meals - Excess Allowance		Allow		1,500.00
18.40	Site Rentals		Allow		25,000.00
18.40	Permits		Incl. Abov		0.00
18.46	Gratuities		Allow		0.00
18.50	Dist. Loc. - Office/Overhead				0.00
18.52	- Police/Fire				0.00
18.54	- Telephone				0.00
18.60	Fares				0.00
					0.00
18.70	Accommodations				0.00
					0.00
18.80	Penalties				0.00
18.90	Miscellaneous		Allow		
18.96	Fringe Benefits (Labor)		13.9 %		3,610.97
	TOTAL LOCATION				76,882.97
	STAGE/STUDIO OPERATIONS				
19.01	Stage Rental - Prep/Strike				0.00
19.04	Stage Rental - Light/Shoot				0.00
19.08	Additional Stage Rental				0.00
19.10	Stage Telephone				0.00
19.20	Storage Rooms				0.00
19.30	Air Conditioning				0.00
19.40	AC Power				0.00
19.50	DC Power				0.00
19.60	Backlot Rentals				0.00
19.70	Dressing Rooms				0.00
19.80	Trash/Security/Deliveries				0.00
19.90	Miscellaneous				0.00
	TOTAL STAGE/STUDIO				0.00

Appendix 3

ACCT.#	DESCRIPTION	NO.	DAYS/WKS/ QUANTITY	RATE	TOTAL
	INSURANCE/TAXES/LICENSES				
20.01	Cast Insurance		2.5 %		32,000.00
20.02	Negative Insurance				
20.03	Public Liability Insurance				
20.04	Errors and Omissions				
20.06	Other Insurance				
20.09	Workmen's Compensation				
20.10	FICA/UI (Not included above)				
20.20	Union Fringe (not inc above)				
20.30	Payroll Service Fees				
20.35	Business Licenses				
20.40	MPAA Code Certificate				
20.90	MIscellaneous Taxes/Fees				
	TOTAL INSURANCE/TAXES/FEES				32,000.00
	GENERAL OVERHEAD				
21.01	Corporate/Partnrship Expense		Allow		
21.10	Office Allowance		4.0 mos	1,800.00	7,200.00
21.14	Additional Office(s)		2.0 mos	900.00	1,800.00
21.20	Furniture Rental		Incl.Above		0.00
21.30	Equipment Rental		Incl.Above		0.00
21.32	Additional Rentals/Computer		Incl.Above		0.00
21.36	Miscellaneous Office Expense		Allow		1,000.00
21.40	Telephone/Telegraph		Allow		3,500.00
21.46	Postage/Express Mail		Allow		1,000.00
21.48	Messenger Service		Allow		750.00
21.50	Copying		Allow		2,500.00
21.60	Executive Entertainment		Allow		1,000.00
21.64	Executive Travel		Allow		1,000.00
21.70	Records Storage		Allow		
21.74	CBC Representative		Allow		0.00
21.80	Legal Fees		Allow		12,500.00
21.90	Miscellaneous Overhead Costs		Allow		0.00
	TOTAL GENERAL OVERHEAD				32,250.00
	MISCELLANEOUS				
22.10	Guild/Union Bonds				100,000.00
22.20	Deposits - Service Vendors				25,000.00
22.30	Deposits - Stage/Office				
22.60	Recoverable Costs				(125,000.00)
22.90	Unclassified Expenses				250.00
	TOTAL MISCELLANEOUS				250.00

MOVIE-OF-THE-WEEK - *GASLIGHT*

With the advent of made-for-cable movies, the potential outlets and budget ranges of "movies-of-the-week" have expanded considerably. At the high end, motion pictures made for overseas theatrical release and domestic premieres on HBO or Showtime usually cost $5 million, which is considerably more than the $3 to 3.5 million standard for shows destined for the three major networks. At the low end, MOWs for the Fox or Turner Networks or such basic cable outlets as USA or Lifetime cost between $1.5 and 2.5 million.

The sample was commissioned as part of the development process by the independent production Guber-Peters Television in affiliation with Columbia Pictures Television on a project already approved by a network to determine the actual cost versus the network licensing fee. If that projected cost exceeds the licensing, as is normally the case, the production company must then decide if potential revenues from possible video release, syndication, overseas sales, etc. justify the expense.

In most cases, the budget preparer is provided with certain above-the-line parameters. The object is not only to determine if the project can be made for the amount specified but the possible impact on schedule, which, because of actor availabilities, is often in flux. Even in the most abstract case of an uncast, "unlocated," and even unscheduled script, budgeting strategies will always depend on assumptions. These assumptions, in turn, will determine whether "best case," "worst case," or, as is likelier, something in between, must be presented as part of the complete budget.

The draft negative cost of the sample budget was $3,359,456.76. The following notes were submitted with it and the production board:

PRODUCTION BUDGET

First Draft 9/17/90

DATE: _____

"GASLIGHT"

TITLE: _____PICTURE NO. _____

DAYS
Trvl/Hldy:	2	Producer:	
Rehearse:		Director:	
Distant:	5	Start Date:	
Local Loc:	20	Finish Date:	
Stage:		Script Dated:	
2nd Unit:		Script Pages:	
TOTAL:	27	Budget Prep:	Alain Silver

ACCT.#	DESCRIPTION	PG.		TOTAL	TOTALS
1100	Story, Rights, & Continuity	3		75,000.00	75,000.00
1200	Producers Unit	3		150,000.00	150,000.00
1300	Direction	3		119,932.00	119,932.00
1400	Cast	4		757,633.75	757,633.75
1500	Travel and Living	5		56,356.00	56,356.00
1600	Miscellaneous	5		0.00	0.00
1900	Fringe Benefits	5		152,761.52	152,761.52
	TOTAL ABOVE-THE-LINE				1,311,683.27
2000	Production Staff	6		148,525.20	148,525.20
2100	Extra Talent	7		40,115.38	40,115.38
2200	Art Direction	8		25,000.00	25,000.00
2300	Set Construction	8		0.00	0.00
2400	Set Striking	8		0.00	0.00
2500	Set Operations	9		57,505.00	57,505.00
2600	Special Effects	10		35,000.00	35,000.00
2700	Set Dressing	10		70,350.00	70,350.00
2800	Property	11		57,450.00	57,450.00
2900	Men's Wardrobe	11		46,450.00	46,450.00
3000	Women's Wardrobe	12		21,225.00	21,225.00
3100	Make-up/Hairdressing	12		33,150.00	33,150.00
3200	Electric/Lighting	13		102,610.00	102,610.00
3300	Camera Operations	14		112,775.00	112,775.00
3400	Production Sound	14		33,717.50	33,717.50
3500	Transportation	15		148,192.50	148,192.50
3600	Location	16		254,990.00	254,990.00
3700	Production Film and Lab	17		116,329.73	116,329.73
3900	Process and Rear Projection	17		0.00	0.00
4000	2nd Unit/Miniatures/Effects	18		0.00	0.00
4100	Tests	18		7,500.00	7,500.00
4200	Stage Facilities	18		0.00	0.00
4300	Fringe Benefits	18		98,345.20	98,345.20
	TOTAL PRODUCTION PERIOD				1,409,230.50

GASLIGHT 17-Sep-90   Page 2

ACCT.#	DESCRIPTION	PG.		TOTAL	TOTALS
4500	Editorial	19		83,775.50	83,775.50
4600	Music	20		72,500.00	72,500.00
4700	Post-production Sound	20		59,578.00	59,578.00
4800	Post-production Film & Lab	21		40,683.00	40,683.00
4900	Main and End Titles	21		12,500.00	12,500.00
5200	Fringe Benefits	21		8,795.99	8,795.99
	TOTAL EDITING PERIOD				277,832.49
6500	Publicity	22		9,250.00	9,250.00
6700	Insurance	22		79,300.00	79,300.00
6800	General Overhead	23		50,750.00	50,750.00
7400	Fringe Benefits	23		710.50	710.50
7500	Fees/Charges/Miscellaneous	23		34,500.00	34,500.00
	TOTAL OTHER CHARGES				174,510.50
	ABOVE-THE-LINE				1,311,683.27
	BELOW-THE-LINE				1,861,573.49
	DIRECT COSTS				3,173,256.76
	CONTINGENCY - Below-the-line Only		10 %		186,200.00
	OVERHEAD FEE				0.00
	COMPLETION BOND				0.00
			TOTAL		3,359,456.76
	DEFERMENTS TOTAL	24			
			TOTAL NEGATIVE COSTS		3,359,456.76

** Indicates Travel to Distant Location

Form SB002, Copyright (c) 1984, PENDRAGON FILM LTD.

```
*** DAY OUT OF DAYS ***

    GASLIGHT
```

COMPUTER GENERATED DAY OUT OF DAYS

```
        Start Date:
        Month:
           Date: ! 5! 6! 7! 8! 9!10!11!12!13!14!15!16!17!18!19!20!21!22!23!24!25!26!27!28!29!30! 1! 2! 3! 4!
```

ID	Character	1	2	3	4	5	6	7	8	9	10	11	12	13	14	15	16	17	18	19	20	21	22	23	24	25	26	27	28	29	30	W	H	T	HL	TOT
1	PAULA	SW	W	W	W	W	W	W	W	W	W	W	W	W	W	W	W	W	W	W	W	W	W	W	W	W	WF					25	1	0	0	26
2	GREGORY	SW	W	W	W	W	W	W	H	W	W	W	W	W	W	W	W	W	W	H	W	H	W	WF								22	4	0	0	26
3	LITTLE PAULA								SW	W	WF																					3	0	0	0	3
4	BRIAN CAMERON		SW	W	W	W	H	H	W	H	W	H	W	H	W	H	W	H	H	W	H	H	H	W	WF							11	13	0	0	24
5	MARLA	SF											SW	W	H	H	H	W	H	H	WF											4	5	0	0	9
6	AMY															SW	H	H	H	H	W	H	WF									3	5	0	0	8
7	PRESIDENT		SW	WF																		SW	W	WF								5	0	0	0	5
8	PSYCHIATRIST							SF																								1	0	0	0	1
9	MAITRE D'						SF																									1	0	0	0	1
10	CLERK				SF																											1	0	0	0	1
11	HANNAH																			SF												1	0	0	0	1
12	LAWYER									SF																						1	0	0	0	1
13	ATTENDANT								SF																							1	0	0	0	1
14	DESK OFFICER																						SF									1	0	0	0	1
15	GRANDMOTHER (V						SW	WF																								2	0	0	0	2
16	DR. COLLINS						SF																									1	0	0	0	1
17	BANK OFFICER								SF																							1	0	0	0	1
18	HOMELESS MAN	SF																														1	0	0	0	1
19	DETECTIVE #1																		SF													1	0	0	0	1
20	DETECTIVE #2																		SF													1	0	0	0	1
21	SECRETARY																			SF												1	0	0	0	1
22	POLICEMAN																					SF										1	0	0	0	1
23	SUPERIOR																					SF										1	0	0	0	1
24	WIFE		SW	WF																SF												3	0	0	0	3
25	ELIZABETH							SW	H	H	H	W	W	W	H	WF																5	4	0	0	9

1. Schedule

The basic assumption is a five week, 25-day shooting schedule with two travel days. The first travel day is in pre-production. There is one week of distant location with five shooting days and the sixth day used for turnaround and travel. The four remaining weeks are all local location. For a 100 5/8 page script, the average page-counts are four per day or twenty per week.

The primary selection criteria for distant location scenes were those keyed to locales unique to New Orleans. There were several swing scenes such as the Bank and the Ballroom. If the overall schedule were reduced, these might be added to the New Orleans work.

Wherever possible, weeks, days, and portions thereof are in continuity. Since most of the night scenes are in New Orleans, the major turnaround problem is solved with a late-departure travel day. So as not to have to resort to cover sets late in the schedule, all but one of the exterior scenes are to be shot by Day 13. The last one, involving Marla, was placed with interior scenes at the same location and moved back to allow for ten intervening days for a drop-and-pickup on that actress.

Week 1 contains the lightest page-count for several reasons: (1) most of the night exteriors are set in New Orleans so the week begins with two split days and then three days of night work; (2) there are two action sequences—the murder attempt on the boat and the pursuit during Mardi Gras; (3) large numbers of extras and/or non-paid crowds are involved in the background of the Mardi Gras scenes; (4) the Creole Queen, used as a picture boat actually moving on the river, will likely present unusual logistical problems, hence two nights are allowed there.

Week 2 contains most of the local exteriors, beginning with the beach resort scenes, which are the first script scenes involving the two leads, and ending with a split day that includes the only local night work. While the character of Paula is not in the last scene on Day 11, there may be a slight turnaround problem on her going into Week 3.

There are two main considerations in scheduling the "1961" mansion scenes: (1) ample time to redress both the interiors and exteriors between the 1961 and 1991 scenes; and (2) the limited work hours for the character of Little Paula. The latter is scheduled over three days to work in scenes containing 1 2/8, 2 1/8, and 2/8 pages respectively. The last day of her work (the exterior mansion scene after the killing) will act as a contingency day for the interior scenes. Day 5 assumes that the "1991 Porch" can be shot without major redressing to the full "1961" exteriors because there are not enough "1961" scenes to make up a full day.

Week 3 begins with a day away from the mansion to allow three days (weekend plus one) for a full redressing of the exteriors and interiors. After Day 13 finishes the mansion exteriors, Days 14, 15, and 16 are high page-count days containing almost entirely one- and two-character scenes inside the mansion.

Week 4 finishes the interior mansion scenes with four more high page-count days. Day 21 is an ambitious day, which contains Marla's murder and the aftermath in her charred studio, and may go long. However, since Paula is not involved in the last part of the day, there will not be an actor turnaround problem.

Week 5 completes the shooting. There are several light days. The two days of work at the Police Station, for example, might be accomplished in one-half day less. Being the final week, this is the ultimate contingency on the rest of the schedule and should allow for simple pickups, retakes, or added scenes to be accomplished without resorting to a second unit or added days.

2. Budget

Since distant location is scheduled for only one week, the budget assumes: (1) travel of all department heads and main seconds, with one week distant location prep for most of them; (2) separate equipment packages (distant location is 80% night work and will have higher requirements) and set dressing packages (only some props, the most significant of which is the cathedral window, work both distant and local location); (3) local hires for both lower echelon crew and Day Players who work only in New Orleans.

The key issue in local schedule is the mansion, particularly whether or not to shoot interiors on a sound stage. The types of exteriors described in the script should readily be found in local neighborhoods such as Hancock Park, although night filming restrictions should be kept in mind when scouting. As to the interior, the script describes a multi-story (lower, upper, and top floor) structure. If the scenes following Little Paula and grown Paula up and down stairs are to be accomplished (via steadicam or other device), a multi-story set would be required. Given less then unlimited means, finding and making over an actual multi-story structure would be much less expensive than constructing a multi-level set on a high-grid sound stage. This would also facilitate the many scenes containing transitions from exterior to interior or tying in an exterior view through a window.

The least detailed area is the above-the-line. The Supporting and Day Players have been filled in, based on the schedule, with ballpark salaries. The travel is also detailed, but the only allowance made for star perquisites are one extra round-trip for each of the two leads.

CALL SHEETS

The Stage Report Call Sheet from Cry Devil aka Night Visitor was manually assembled from a legal-size, one-sided master form. Certain cast and crew members were typed onto the master. Handwritten additions and corrections are used for changes in personnel, day players, etc. The Location Call Sheet from Hold Me, Thrill Me, Kiss Me was produced using a template and a computer at the location office. Even in this case, certain last-minute, hand-written notations are in evidence.

PENDRAGON FILM LTD.

CALL SHEET

UNIT ____

20TH DAY OF SHOOTING

730A CREW CALL

8A SHOOTING CALL

PICT. "CRY DEVIL."

PRODUCER ALAIN SILVER

DATE FRIDAY AUGUST 26, 1988

PFL NO. 88-002 DIRECTOR RUPERT HITZIG

SET	SCS.	cast	D/N	pages	LOC.
SET					LOC. STAGE 2
SET INT. WILLARD HOUSE-BASEMENT	scs 126pt, 127, 129,	1, 2, 3, 4, 5,	D7	2⅛	LOC. CULVER STUDIO
SET	scs 131, 133, 135,	3x, 4x, 5x, XX			LOC.
SET	scs 139, 141, 143				LOC.
SET	scs 144, 145				LOC.
SET	scs				LOC.
SET INT. WILLARD HOUSE-RITUAL RM	scs 119C, 123, 125	1, 3	D7	1⅞	LOC.
SET	scs				LOC.
SET INT. WILLARD HOUSE- RITUAL RM	scs 69Bpt, 70pt	4, 5	N5 (1⅜)		LOC.
SET	scs.				LOC
SET	scs.		TOTAL	5⅜	LOC.

CAST AND DAY PLAYERS	PART OF	MAKEUP	SET CALL	REMARKS
1. DEREK RYDALL	BILLY	730A	8A	REPORT TO STAGE 2
2. TERESA VANDER WOUDE	KELLY	7A		
3. ELLIOTT GOULD	DEVEREAUX	730A		
4. ALLEN GARFIELD	WILLARD			
5. MICHAEL J. POLLARD	STANLEY			
3x	DBL. DEVEREAUX			
RAY GABRIEL	UTILITY STUNT			
KATHRYN KIMLER	UTILITY STUNT	↓	↓	↓
		THRU GATE		
2 Standins Mohrhoff/Osborn		730A		Report to STAGE

PROPS: BRIEFCASE, SHOTGUN, CORPSE, WHISKEY BOTTLE, TOOLS OF TORTURE, DEVIL BOOK, DEVIL MASK, KNIFE, ETC.

NOTES MU: BLOOD, 2ND CORPSE (KK.)

Prod. Office-(213) 559-0346

F/X: RIG "WALL" TO COLLAPSE, CHAINSAW GAG

ART/SET DR.: TRYPTICH, ALTAR STUFF, CURTAINS, ETC, DEAD CAT, SMALL MOLLUSKS, OAT MEAL, PEAS, SCISSORS, PIZZA, TAP SHOES, SLUG SUN, RED RIBBON, LARGE RIBBON, KNIFE,

PLEASE NOTE: NO SMOKING, FOOD OR DRINKS ON SETS / NO VISITORS W/O A.D. APPROVAL

ADVANCE SCHEDULE

ITEM	LV.	NO.	ITEM	LV.	NO.	ITEM	LV.	
CAMERAMAN Jensen	730A	1	MAKEUP Clark	6½A				
OPERATOR		1	MU/Hair Perkins	↓		INSERT CAR		
ASSISTANT 1 PORTER	715A				1	Camera/Sound trk		
ASSISTANT 2 Goldman	↓				1	Prop 5-ton		
EXTRA CAMERA	W/N				1	Set Dressing van		
EXTRA OPERATOR	↓							
Set Tech Janosi	715A	1	COSTUMER Scott	6½A	1	Cargo van		
		1	Cost Asst Smith	↓		PICTURE CARS		
KEY GRIP Pickens	730A							
2ND GRIP Rapini	↓	1	SP EFX	730A				
EXTRA GRIPS Neinhaus	↓							
		1	GAFFER McClain	718A				
CRAB DOLLY	X	1	BEST BOY Cragoe					
CRAFT SERVICE Reynolds	7A	2	Elec. Gibson/West	↓	6	DRESSING ROOMS		
SOUND MIXER Oldfield	715A	1	PROPERTY Reach					
BOOM Heusey		1	ASST.PROP. Fong	↓	1	MU/Ward trlr		
		1	Art Dr Sovago	O/C				
		1	SET DEC Cordova	O/C				
SCRIPT Dreiling	↓	1	Lead Henderson	O/C				
				O/C				
STILL Ward	8A	1	Swing Adae	O/C				
LOC MGR FEDER	W/N	1	EXTRA ELEC.	730A	1	Trans coord Ear		
					1	Barbera		

TRANSPORTATION DEPT.

ASSISTANT DIRECTOR L. RACE/G. LaDUE

UNIT PROD. MANAGER R. ABRAMITIS

"HOLD ME, THRILL ME, KISS ME" **CALL SHEET**

Thrill Me Productions, Inc.

9713 Santa Monica Blvd., Suite 215

Beverly Hills, CA 90210

213/559-0346 Fax: 213/559-0348

6A

Trailer Park Production Phone

818-448-0662

DATE: Friday, Sept. 13, 1991

DAY 5

Crew Call: **6:00 AM**

ALL CREW REPORT TO DRIVE-IN

Shooting Call: **7:30 AM**

Producers: Martin Ira Rubin, Travis Swords, Alain Silver

Director: Joel Hershman

Sunrise: 6:35 AM

Sunset: 7:03 PM

Weather: AM clouds clearing by late morning

light winds, high 80°

Mileage: 64 miles RT

SET	SCENES	CAST	D/N	PGS	LOCATION
COMPLETE EXT. DRIVE-IN / JONES'S CAR	116	1, 2, 7, 8, S1, S2, S3, S	D-9	4 - 1/8	Edward's Drive-In 714-721-7170
Jones lays out the plan for Bud's getaway.					4469 Live Oak Road, @ Peck
					Arcadia, CA
EXT. DRIVE-IN PARKING LOT	118	1	D-9	1/8	
Bud charges into storage area.					
EXT. DRIVE-IN PARKING LOT	120	1, 2	D-9	6/8	
Bud waits while Dannie finishes off Twinkle.					
INT. DRIVE-IN STORAGE AREA	117	2, 7	D-9	4/8	
Twinkle tries to kill Dannie.					
INT. DRIVE-IN STORAGE AREA	119	1, 2, 7	D-9	2/8	
Bud shoots Twinkle.				5 - 6/8	TOTAL PAGES

#	CAST		PART OF	MAKE-UP	ON SET	REMARKS
1.	Max Parrish	(W)	Bud / Eli	6:30 A	7:30 A	Report to Set @ 6:30 AM
2.	Adrienne Shelly	(W)	Dannie	6:00 A	7:30 A	Nectar P/U @ 5:15 AM
7.	Sean Young	(W)	Twinkle	6:30 A	7:30 A	Report to Set @ 6:30 A
8.	Timothy Leary	(WF)	Mr. Jones	6:30 A	7:30 A	P/U @ 5:45
S1.	Bob Cota	(W)	Stunt Coord./Double Max	6:00 A	7:30 A	Report to Set @ 6:00 AM
S2.	Ralph Ramirez	(SWF)	Twinkle drive double	6:00 A	7:30 A	Report to Set @ 6:00 AM
S3.	Sheryl Rusa	(SWF)	Stunt Double	6:00 A	7:30 A	Report to Set @ 6:00 AM
S4.	Chris Palomino	(SWF)	Stunt Double Twinkle	6:00 A	7:30 A	Report to Set @ 6:00 AM

ATMOSPHERE	PROPS & SETS	PICTURE CARS	SPECIAL INSTRUCTIONS
Stand-in (Carrie) Report to Drive-In @ 6 A	Jones's Military sunglasses		SPFX: As needed for fights, blood & car crash
	Bud's Duffelbag	Motorcycle	STUNTS: Safety & Rigging crew Rpt. @ 6 A
Mr. Jones photo double @ 6 A.	Bud's false mustache	Stunt Double Cycle	
	Birth Certificate (Fritz Westenberger)		WARDROBE: Dannie's Sabra outfit, falsies
	Twinkle's Gun (must work)		Bud's 'after crash' outfit
	Cash in Jones's pockets		Wardrobe for Stunt Doubles
	Bud's Passport	Mr. Jones' Car	MAKE-UP: Tattoo, False mustache on Twinkle
			Blood on Bud
			SPECIAL EQ: Apollo Crane Rpt. @ 3P
		Dannie's Sabra look	Hair extensions

ADVANCE SCHEDULE				
SHOOTING DATE	SET NAME	SCENES	D/N	LOCATION
SATURDAY, 9/14	I/E Social Security Office	72, 71	D-5	3380 Flair Drive 818-288-3122
				El Monte, CA
	COMPANY MOVE >>			
	Ext. Statue of Liberty	105	D-7	11234 Valley Blvd. 818-575-4101
	Federal Bldg.	A105	D-7	" " "
	COMPANY MOVE >>			
	I/E Pet Cemetery	93 thru 97	D-6	18300 Figueroa, Gardena 213-321-0191
SUNDAY, 9/15 OFF	Whatever set you'd like			
MONDAY, 9/16	Int. Illusions Bar	8, 26, 59	N-1, 2, 4	Illusions Bar 818-444-8119
	Ext. Illusions Bar	7, 60	N-1, 4	12121 Valley, Blvd., El Monte

Assistant Directors: M. Proust, R. Allen, Steve Day (213) 827-0516   U.P.M.: Nick Redman

OTHER FORMS

In the course of producing a feature film, the full range of forms that the production manager and assistant directors typically handle is extremely varied. The standard-format sign-out sheet for members of the Screen Actors Guild and the carbons of camera reports filled out by the camera assistants are entirely unrelated to one another. And, yet, the second assistant director must extract detailed information from both to use in completing the production report. The same is true of extra vouchers, the script supervisor's report, a caterer's receipt, and sundry timecards. In many cases, the assistant directors are relying on others for the accuracy of figures that tally items as diverse as raw stock used, pages shot, and lunches eaten. The form samples given here are intended merely to complement the variety of material already reproduced by illustrating some of the subsidiary paperwork.

The breakdown sheets are alternate formats to the examples in the main text. The Summary of Production Costs is the cost report topsheet that matches the long-form standard budget.

The DGA has an alternate deal memo designed for use on low-budget features which qualify for partial deferments. A similar form is used for directors of such features and both forms are provided to producers by the DGA in the package of signatory documents. The weekly and daily actor contracts are commercially available in quadruplicate, color-coded sets. As was noted, because the SAG rules require contracts to be tendered before services are rendered, assistant directors should have blank day-players contracts available for actors who are called in unexpectedly or upgraded extra performers. When circumstances require them, SAG Taft-Hartley reports should be filled out immediately because late reporting can result in fines being levied against the company. Extra vouchers comprising information on work time and photographic releases are normally provided by the extra casting agency. In those cases where, for any reason whatsoever, other persons appear in a shot, assistant directors are expected to have them sign a standard photo release. Legally, persons in public streets, sidewalks, et al have given implied consent to being photographed, but many production companies prefer that formal releases be obtained whenever possible.

Crew and location deal memos are also available commercially and vary considerably. The two examples are particularly suited to low-budget productions and may, with slight alteration, be used for either salaried employees or individuals and companies who contract for services. Of course, employees must also complete standard W-4 and I-9 forms and should provide tax identification numbers so that the proper reporting via W-2 or 1099 Misc. can be accomplished later.

The significance of the SAG sign-out sheet, script supervisor's report, and camera reports has already been discussed. The correlation of these forms to the production report is a critical task, and the preparer's work is simplified if the layout of the information that the report duplicates is similar to that on the subsidiary forms. For instance, the sample script supervisor's report given here mirrors the configuration on Production Report Illustration No. 2 on page 101.

BREAKDOWN SHEET

SHEET No. _____

PICTURE No. _____

NAME _____

SCENE

COSTUME No.

DAY NO N PE PAGES	SCENE NO	DESCRIPTION	No.	CAST
TOTAL				

PROPS	ATMOSPHERE	BITS

CARS – LIVE STOCK	SPECIAL EFFECTS	MUSIC

PRODUCTION TITLE			PAGE NO
SET		TOTAL SEQUENCES	LOCATION
PERIOD	SEASON	TIME ALLOWED	TOTAL SCRIPT PAGES
CAST	BITS	EXTRAS	ANIMALS
			SPECIAL PROPS

SEQUENCES · SCENES · SYNOPSES :

SUMMARY PRODUCTION COSTS						
PRODUCTION NUMBER	TITLE				DATE	
PRODUCER		ASSOCIATE PRODUCER			DIRECTOR	
CAST			WRITER		CAMERAMAN	
DATE STARTED			SCHEDULED FINISH DATE		FINISH DATE	
ACCT. No.	CLASSIFICATION	BUDGET	COST TO DATE	ESTIMATED COST TO COMPLETE	ESTIMATED TOTAL COST	OVER OR (UNDER) BUDGET
01	Story					
02	Supervisors					
03	Cast					
04	Direction					
	Total Above the Line Costs					
05	Director's Staff					
06	Camera					
07	Set Operations					
08	Set Construction Cost					
09	Set Design					
10	Set Dressings					
11	Special Effects					
12	Process					
13	Miniature					
14	Draperies					
15	Props					
16	Live Stock — Handlers and Eqpt.					
17	Locations					
18	Transportation					
19	Lighting					
20	Wardrobe					
21	Make-up and Hairdressing					
22	Film and Laboratory					
23	Sound Recording					
24	Sound Royalties					
25	Sound Dubbing and Scoring					
26	Film Editing					
27	Titles and Inserts					
28	Music					
29	Studio Rentals					
30	Tests and Pre-production					
31	Studio General					
	Total Below the Line Costs					
	Total Direct Cost					
40 - 000	Contingency					
50	General Studio Overhead					
	TOTAL COST					

Remarks:

Film Budgeted   Feet Film Shot   Feet

Signed   Signed

Producer   Production Dept.

EXHIBIT "B"
UNIT PRODUCTION MANAGER & ASSISTANT DIRECTOR DEAL MEMORANDUM
FOR THEATRICAL PICTURE COSTING $3,000,000 OR LESS

Name: _____   SS#: _____

Loanout: _____   Tel.: _____

Address: _____

_____

____ Unit Production Manager   ____ First Assistant Director

____ Key 2nd Assistant Director   ____ Second 2nd Assistant Director

____ Second Unit   ____ Added Scenes or Reshoots

Salary: $_____ per week/per day (cross out one)

Production Fee: $_____ per week/per day (cross out one)

of which _____ % is payable when services are performed

and   _____ % is deferred under the "Low Cost" Sideletter

Current Title of Picture: _____

Start Date: _____   Guar. Period: _____

Guar. Prep: _____   Guar. Shoot: _____   Guar. Wrap: _____

Studio or Local Location/Distant Location/Combination (Cross
out if not applicable)

Estimated Production Cost (Check One):

         _____ A. Under $1,800,0000
         _____ B. $1,800,0000 to $3,000,000

Other Terms (e.g., Credit, Suspension, Per Diem, etc.): _____

_____

_____

This employment is subject to the provisions of the DGA Basic
Agreement (including the Sideletter for pictures costing $3,000,000
or less).

Accepted and Agreed: Signatory Co.: _____

Employee: _____   By: _____

Date: _____   Date: _____

C310/111287

DEAL MEMORANDUM

Between PENDRAGON FILM LTD. and _____

This will confirm our agreement to engage your services in connection with a motion picture tentatively entitled **The Hunting Ground.** Said services shall consist of:

_____

The commencement date for the rendering of said services shall be:

_____

_____ Payment for said services shall be:

_____ dollars per week/day (cross out one).

You shall perform your services at such locations as the Producer may designate for the duration of the production. All weekly employment is on a week-to-week basis, with weeks consisting of any five days out of seven at Producer's discretion. All partial weeks upon completion of assignment will be paid on a pro rata basis. Weekly or daily salary is based on an open-ended work day. Unless otherwise noted below or unless the weekly or daily guarantee is less than would be due if the actual hours of work were compensated at the minimum hourly rate set by statute, no overtime shall be payable. For purposes of tax reporting and claims of unemployment compensation, your employer of record shall be CD Payroll.

You grant to us all rights of any kind in and to the results and proceeds of your services as herein comtemplated. This Memorandum incorporates by reference all provisions normally found in agreements of this type in the motion picture and television industry in Los Angeles, California. You grant to us and our assignees and licensees in perpetuity and throughout the universe, the right to use any likeness, performance, and/or the results and proceeds of your services for any purposes in connection with the motion picture. No inadvertent failure to comply with any credit provisions shall constitute a breach of this Memorandum agreement. We shall use our good faith efforts to prospectively cure any error within a reasonble time after receiving written notice from you of such error. You shall not be entitled to injunctive or any similar type of relief in the event of any errors in these credit provisions. This will further confirm that you agree to keep confidential the terms of this agreement and the material content of the motion picture, **The Hunting Ground** including, but not limited to financial information, the budget thereof, or the material content of the motion picture, **The Hunting Ground.**

Credit provisions and other terms, if any, shall be:

Agreed to and accepted this date: _____, 1992.

By_____
for PENDRAGON FILM LTD.

and_____
for the Employee
Tax I.D./Soc. Sec. No._____

Address:_____

_____ Phone_____

THRILL ME PRODUCTIONS, INC.
9713 Santa Monica Boulevard, Suite 215
Beverly Hills, California 90210
(213) 275-4150

MEMORANDUM OF AGREEMENT FOR SERVICES AND/OR FACILITIES

Between THRILL ME PRODUCTIONS, INC. and

_____

This will confirm our agreement to engage your services in connection with a motion picture tentatively entitled **Hold Me, Thrill Me, Kiss Me.** Said services shall consist of:

_____.

The commencement date for the rendering of said services, if at other than your own discretion shall be:

_____. Payment for said services shall be:

_____ dollars per week/day (cross out one)

You shall perform your services at such locations as the Producer may designate for the duration of the production. All weekly employment is on a week-to-week basis, five or six-day weeks at Producer's discretion. All partial weeks upon completion of assignment will be paid on a pro rata basis. Weekly or daily salary is based on an open-ended work day. Unless otherwise noted below or unless the weekly or daily guarantee is less than would be due if the actual hours of work were compensated at the minimum hourly rate set by statute, no overtime shall be payable. For purposes of tax reporting, payment for your services shall be made by Thrill Me Productions, Inc.

You grant to us all rights of any kind in and to the results and proceeds of your services as herein comtemplated. This Memorandum incorporates by reference all provisions normally found in agreements of this type in the motion picture and television industry in Los Angeles, California. You grant to us and our assignees and licensees in perpetuity and throughout the universe, the right to use any likeness, performance, and/or the results and proceeds of your services for any purposes in connection with the motion picture. No inadvertent failure to comply with any credit provisions shall constitute a breach of this Memorandum agreement. We shall use our good faith efforts to prospectively cure any error within a reasonable time after receiving written notice from you of such error. You shall not be entitled to injunctive or any similar type of relief in the event of any errors in these credit provisions. This will further confirm that you agree to keep confidential the terms of this agreement and the material content of the motion picture, **Hold Me, Thrill Me, Kiss Me** including, but not limited to financial information, the budget thereof, or the material content of the motion picture, **Hold Me, Thrill Me, Kiss Me.**

Credit provisions and other terms, if any, shall be:

Agreed to and accepted this date: _____, 1991.

By_____
for THRILL ME PRODUCTIONS, INC.

and_____
for the Service Vendor
Tax I.D. (Soc. Sec. or Fed. Emp. [95]) No._____

Address:_____

_____ Phone_____

**THE ARTIST MAY NOT WAIVE ANY PROVISION OF THIS CONTRACT
WITHOUT THE WRITTEN CONSENT OF SCREEN ACTORS GUILD, INC.**

SCREEN ACTORS GUILD, INC. MINIMUM FREE LANCE CONTRACT

Continuous Employment - Weekly Basic - Weekly Salary - One Week Minimum Employment

THIS AGREEMENT, made this .... day of ...., 19 ...., between

...., hereinafter called "Producer", and

...., hereinafter called "Player".

1. PHOTOPLAY, ROLE, SALARY, AND GUARANTEE. Producer hereby engages Player to render services as such in the role of......................

....

in a photoplay, the working title of which is now...........................

....

at the salary of $... ($..........................)

per week. Player accepts such engagement upon the terms herein specified. Producer guarantees that it will furnish Player not less than ....

.............................week's employment (if this blank is not filled in, the guarantee shall be one week).

2. TERM. The term of employment hereunder shall begin on ....

.... on or about*...............................

..........................., and shall continue thereafter until the completion of the photography and recordation of said role.

3. BASIC CONTRACT. All provisions of the collective bargaining agreement between Screen Actors Guild, Inc. and Producer, relating to theatrical motion pictures, which are applicable to the employment of the Player hereunder, shall be deemed incorporated herein.

4. PLAYER'S ADDRESS. All notices which the Producer is required or may desire to give to the Player may be given either by mailing the same addressed to the Player at ....

...., or such notice may be given to the Player personally, either orally or in writing.

5. PLAYER'S TELEPHONE. The Player must keep the Producer's casting office or the assistant director of said photoplay advised as to where the Player may be reached by telephone without unreasonable delay. The current telephone number of the Player is.......................

....

6. MOTION PICTURE AND TELEVISION RELIEF FUND. The

Player (does) (does not) hereby authorize the Producer to deduct from the compensation hereinabove specified an amount equal to .... per cent of each installment of compensation due the Player hereunder, and to pay the amount so deducted to the Motion Picture and Television Relief Fund of America, Inc.

7. FURNISHING OF WARDROBE. The (Producer) (Player) agrees to furnish all modern wardrobe and wearing apparel reasonably necessary for the portrayal of said role; it being agreed, however, that should so-called "character" or "period" costumes be required, the Producer shall supply the same.

8. ARBITRATION OF DISPUTES. Should any dispute or controversy arise between the parties hereto with reference to this contract, or the employment herein provided for, such dispute or controversy shall be settled and determined by conciliation and arbitration in accordance with the conciliation and arbitration provisions of the collective bargaining agreement between the Producer and Screen Actors Guild relating to theatrical motion pictures, and such provisions are hereby referred to and by such reference incorporated herein and made a part of this Agreement with the same effect as though the same were set forth herein in detail.

9. NEXT STARTING DATE. The starting date of Player's next engagement is..

10. The Player may not waive any provision of this contract without the written consent of Screen Actors Guild, Inc.

11. Producer makes the material representation that either it is presently a signatory to the Screen Actors Guild collective bargaining agreement covering the employment contracted for herein, or, that the above-referred-to photoplay is covered by such collective bargaining agreement under the provisions of the current Producer-Screen Actors Guild Codified Basic Agreement applicable to independent producers.

ADDITIONAL CLAUSES NOT PART OF STANDARD FORM

12. Producer shall have the exclusive right to make one or more promotional films of twelve (12) minutes or less and to utilize the results and proceeds of Player's services therein upon all of the terms and provisions set forth in the SAG Agreement. Player agrees to render such services for said promotional films during the term of his employment hereunder as Producer may request and Player further agrees to the use by Producer of film clips and behind-the-scenes shots in which Player appears in such promotional films. Provided Player appears therein, Producer shall pay to Player the applicable day player minimum scale sum within ten (10) days after the first use of each such promotional film on television or before a paying audience.

13. Producer shall have the exclusive right to use and to license the use of Player's name, sobriquet, photograph, likeness, character portrayed by Player in the photoplay, voice and/or caricature and shall have the right to simulate Player's voice, signature and appearance by any means in and in connection with the photoplay and the advertising, publicizing, exhibition and/or other exploitation thereof in any manner and by any means and in and in connection with commercial advertising and publicity tie-ups.

14. Producer is also granted the further exclusive right and license, but only in connection with the role portrayed by Player in the photoplay, to use and to license the use of Player's name, sobriquet, photograph, likeness, character portrayed by Player in the photoplay, caricature and/or signature (collectively referred to herein as "name and likeness") in and in connection with any merchandising and/or publishing undertakings. In consideration therefor, Producer shall pay to Player a pro-rata share (payable among all players whose name, etc. is used) of 2¾% of the gross monies actually derived by Producer as a license fee for the use of such name, etc. on merchandising and publishing items which so utilize Player's name and likeness, other than in a listing of cast credits.

15. Producer is also granted the further exclusive right to use and to license the use of and to advertise and publicize the use of Player's voice from the sound track of the photoplay on commercial phonograph records and albums and the exclusive right to use Player's name and likeness on jackets and labels of such commercial phonograph records and albums. If Producer issues or authorizes the issuance of such record or album using Player's voice, Producer shall pay to Player a sum equal to applicable AFTRA scale.

16. Player acknowledges that Player has read the final printed script of the Photoplay and agrees to perform such scenes of nudity as are included in that script, in accordance with Paragraph 43 of the Producer-Screen Actors Guild Supplement Agreement of 1971.

17. If Producer should desire to obtain cast insurance on Player, Player agrees to cooperate with Producer in obtaining such insurance and agrees to submit to the usual and customary medical and other examination requisite therefor, prior to or during the term hereof. Said insurance shall be obtained at the expense of Producer and for Producer's sole benefit during the term hereof. If Player fails to appear for the requisite examinations at the time and place designated by Producer, or if as a result of any such examination, Producer is unable to obtain insurance covering Player at rates normal to Player's age and sex or without any exclusions or without any limitation of liability on the part of the insurer, then in any such event Player shall be deemed incapacitated and Producer shall thereupon have the immediate right to terminate Player's engagement hereunder. For the period commencing two weeks prior to the start date, until completion of all services required hereunder, Player shall not ride in any aircraft other than as a passenger on an airliner flown by a United States or major international air carrier maintaining regularly published schedules, or engage in any extra-hazardous activity without Producer's written consent in each and every case.

IN WITNESS WHEREOF, the parties have executed this agreement on the day and year first above written.

PRODUCER. . . . .   PLAYER. . . . .

BY . . . .   Social Security Number . . . .

*The "on or about" clause may only be used when the contract is delivered to the Player at least seven days before the starting date. See the applicable Schedules of the current Producer-Screen Actors Guild Codified Basic Agreement; otherwise a specific starting date must be stated.   FORM 7-1-75

**THE ARTIST MAY NOT WAIVE ANY PROVISION OF THIS CONTRACT
WITHOUT THE WRITTEN CONSENT OF SCREEN ACTORS GUILD, INC.**

**SCREEN ACTORS GUILD
DAILY CONTRACT
(DAY PLAYER)
FOR THEATRICAL MOTION PICTURES**

Company _____   Date_____

Date Employment Starts _____   Actor Name _____

Production Title _____   Address:_____

Production Number _____   Telephone No.: ( )_____

Role _____   Social Security No. _____ — _____ — _____

Daily Rate $_____   Date of Birth:_____

Weekly Conversion Rate $_____   Legal Resident of (State): _____

Complete for "Drop-And-Pick-Up" Deals ONLY: Citizen of U.S. _____ Yes _____ No

Firm recall date on _____ or   Wardrobe supplied by actor _____ Yes _____ No

on or after* _____   If so, number of outfits _____ @ $ _____

("On or after" recall only applies to pick-up as Weekly Player.)   (formal) _____ @ $ _____

As ☐ Day Player ☐ Weekly Player   Date of Actor's next engagement _____

*Means date specified or within 24 hours thereafter.

The employment is subject to all of the provisions and conditions applicable to the employment of DAY PLAYERS contained or provided for in the Producer-Screen Actors Guild Codified Basic Agreement of 1983 as the same may be supplemented and/or amended.

The Player (does) (does not) hereby authorize the Producer to deduct from the compensation hereinabove specified an amount equal to _____ per cent of each installment of compensation due the Player hereunder, and to pay the amount so deducted to the Motion Picture and Television Relief Fund of America, Inc.

Special Provisions:

PRODUCER_____PLAYER_____

BY _____

Production time reports are available on the set at the end of each day.
Such reports shall be signed or intialed by the Player.

Attached hereto for your use is Declaration Regarding Income Tax Withholding.

NOTICE TO ACTOR: IT IS IMPORTANT THAT YOU RETAIN A COPY OF THIS CONTRACT FOR YOUR PERMANENT RECORDS.
THE ARTIST MAY NOT WAIVE ANY PROVISION OF THIS CONTRACT WITHOUT THE WRITTEN CONSENT OF SCREEN ACTORS GUILD, INC.

ENTERPRISE PRINTERS & STATIONERS, HOLLYWOOD, CALIF. Telephone: 876-3530   PRINTED ON NCR PAPER, NO CARBON REQUIRED. FORM NO. 39

SCREEN ACTORS GUILD

TAFT/HARTLEY   REPORT

ATTENTION:_____ ATTACHED: RESUME_____ PHOTO_____

PLAYER INFORMATION

NAME _____ SS#_____

ADDRESS _____

AGE (IF MINOR) _____ PHONE (   ) _____

TYPE OF EMPLOYMENT _____

DATE (S) OF EMPLOYMENT_____ SALARY _____

ADVERTISING AGENCY (COM'LS) _____ PHONE (   ) _____

STUDIO _____ PHONE (   ) _____

PRODUCTION COMPANY_____ PHONE (   ) _____

PRODUCTION TITLE AND/OR #_____

REASON FOR HIRE (BE SPECIFIC)_____

_____

_____

_____

_____

_____

_____

_____

Employer is aware of General Provision, Section 14 of the 1977 Codified Basic Agreement and the 1977 Television Agreement (as amended by the 1980 Television and Basic Agreements); and Schedule B of the 1979 Commercials Contract wherein Preference of Employment shall be given to qualified professional actors (except as otherwise stated). Producer will pay to the Guild as liquidated damages, the sums indicated for each breach by the Producer of any provision of those sections.

DATE_____

SIGNATURE _____
        Producer or Casting Director - Please indicate which.

PRINT NAME _____ PHONE (   ) _____

RELEASE

AUTHORIZATION TO REPRODUCE PHYSICAL LIKENESS

For good and valuable consideration, the receipt of which from _____

is acknowledged, I hereby expressly grant to said_____
and to its employees, agents, and assigns, the right to photograph me and use my picture, silhouette and other
reproductions of my physical 'likeness (as the same may appear in any still camera photograph and/or motion
picture film), in and in connection with the exhibition, theatrically, on television or otherwise, of any motion
pictures in which the same may be used or incorporated, and also in the advertising, exploiting and/or publicizing
of any such motion picture, but not limited to television or theatrical motion pictures. I further give the said company the right to reproduce in any manner whatsoever any recordations made by said company of my voice and all
instrumental, musical, or other sound effects produced by me.

I hereby certify and represent that I have read the foregoing and fully understand the meaning and

effect thereof and, intending to be legally bound, I have hereunto set my hand this _____day of

_____ , 19____.

WITNESS: _____

_____   _____

CREATURE FEATURES

SCREEN ACTORS GUILD
ACTORS PRODUCTION TIME REPORT

EXHIBIT G

PICTURE TITLE: _____

PROD. NO. _____

DATE: _____

CAST	CHARACTER	W S R T	H S F T	Makeup Wdrb.	WORK TIME			MEALS		TRAVEL TIME				Stunt Adjust.	ACTORS SIGNATURES
			TR		Report On Set	Dismiss On Set		1st MEAL	2nd MEAL	Leave For Location	Arrive On Location	Leave Location	Arrive At Studio		

NORMAL — W   REHEARSAL — R   FINISHED — F
STARTED — S   HOLD — H   TEST — T
TRAVEL — TR

Assistant Dir. _____

```
                    SCRIPT SUPERVISOR'S DAILY REPORT
Series:_____Prod. No._____Title:_____

Date:_____Shooting Day_____Status:_____
                                                   (Pgs. Behind Sched.)
===============================================================================

              SCENES      PAGES     MINUTES      SETUPS

TODAY:        _____     _____     _____     _____

PREVIOUS:     _____     _____     _____     _____

TOTAL TO DATE: _____    _____     _____     _____

TOTAL IN SCRIPT: _____  _____

TO BE TAKEN:   _____    _____
_____

Scene Numbers Taken Today:_____

_____

Special Notes:_____

                    Script Supervisor_____
```

CAMERA REPORT

№ 5743

Company _____

Address _____

Phone _____

Production _____

Customer P.O. _____

Date _____ Camera Report No. _____
(TO ENSURE CONTINUITY OF DAILIES INDICATE)

Director _____ Cameraman _____

Magazine No. _____ Roll No. _____

UNLESS OTHERWISE INDICATED ALL DAILIES WILL BE PRINTED AS ONE-LIGHT COLOR.

EMULSION NO.	CIRCLE ONE				FILM TYPE
	A Camera	B Camera	C Camera	D Camera	

SCENE NO.	PRINT CIRCLED TAKES				DAY OR NIGHT	REMARKS	INT. OR EXT.
	1^5	2^6	3^7	4^8			

FORCE DEVELOP:	ONE STOP	TWO STOPS

Glossary

Above-the-line—The creative elements of the production (i.e., writer, producer, director, actors), the fees for whose services appear in the upper half of the budget top-sheet, literally above the dark line which divides the page.

Air date—In television production, the specific date on which a movie-of-the-week or series episode is to be televised and by which post-production on the show must be completed.

Art director—See *production designer*.

Associate producer—Normally refers to the person who acts as liaison between the production company and the personnel involved in post-production. In television film production, the associate producer supervises the post-production and is responsible for meeting the air date. In features, the "title" is often given to a writer, actor, or other creative element as part of a billing arrangement. Increasingly, production managers and editors are also being credited as associate producers.

Atmosphere—The extras who are staged and photographed to portray the normal human traffic needed to add realistic detail in numerous script situations.

Background—See *atmosphere*.

Below-the-line—The production staff and technical elements of a project, the cost of which appears in the bottom half of the budget top-sheet, literally below the dark line which divides the page.

Bit—A minor part. The term may refer to a "bit player" actor who speaks only a few lines, or to a "silent bit" extra who pantomimes and performs a significant action.

Box rental—A fee or allowance paid to a crew member for providing his or her own equipment or apparatus to be used on production.

Breakdown—The process of isolating the discrete units in a shooting script and noting the significant elements of each such unit.

Call Sheet—A form specifying all the scenes to be filmed and all the personnel and equipment required to film them on a certain day.

Camera Blocking—Noting the changing position of the camera, lens size, and focus during a scene. In three-camera format, this involves noting the relevant information for three or more cameras simultaneously.

Cameraman, -person—See *cinematographer*.

Carry Day—Any day for which cast or crew are paid but not required to perform any actual work.

Cinematographer—The camera and lighting supervisor on any production. Besides overseeing the work of the camera crew (camera operator and assistants), the cinematographer is also assisted by the grips and electricians in preparing the technical aspects of recording an image on film.

Completion Bond—A guarantee that principal photography on a given production will be completed. The bonding agent indemnifies the production against unforeseen costs of any sort, whether or not they result from problems covered by insurance.

Contingency—A percentage of the budget—either the total amount or a designated subtotal—which is added in anticipation of potential cost overruns. This is not the same as a completion bond, although many bonding agents require the production company to cover or post the contingency amount from their own production funds.

Coverage—The more detailed shots of indeterminate number which are filmed to be intercut with a "master" scene.

Cover Set—A location, usually weatherproof, which is prepared to serve as an alternate to planned work in case of inclement or inappropriate weather conditions.

Dailies—The first assembly of camera and sound footage usually viewed the day following that on which the footage work is photographed and recorded.

Day-Out-of-Days—A form designating the workways for various cast members of a given production.

Day's Work—A term used to refer to the total work shown on the call sheet which the shooting company expects to complete on a given day.

Deal Memo—A form, varying in detail, which lists the pertinent details of salary, guaranteed conditions, etc., of the work agreement negotiated between a member of the cast or crew and the production company.

DGA—The Directors Guild of America, a collective bargaining unit which represents directors, assistant directors, production managers, and videotape personnel (associate directors, stage managers, production associates, production assistants).

Director of Photography—See *cinematographer*.

Downtime—Time when a single malfunctioning or ill-prepared element of production keeps all the other elements waiting.

Flat—An agreement to perform work or provide a service for a fixed wage or fee not to be affected by overtime restrictions or unexpected costs.

Forced Call—Under union conditions, when a person is recalled to work before a minimum number of hours have elapsed to constitute an acceptable rest period. Penalties for a forced call vary from a single fine to a doubling of hourly work rates depending on the guild or union jurisdiction.

Gaffer—The chief electrician, who supervises set lighting in accordance with the requirements of the cinematographer.

Golden Time—a.k.a. gold time, any overtime period for IATSE members during which they are paid at two or two and one-half times their base rate of pay.

Guest Shot—A term used to refer to a director hired to direct a single episode of a television series.

IATSE—The International Alliance of Theatrical and Stage Employees, which represents most of the film technicians through various locals and is their collective bargaining agent.

Industry Experience Roster—A qualifications list maintained by the Contract Services Trust Administration for various motion picture crafts. In the western United States, there is a qualifications list for production managers and assistant directors.

Key Grip—The chief grip, who works with the gaffer in creating shadow effects for the set lighting and who supervises camera cranes, dollies, and platforms as well as "wild wall" movements according to the requirements of the cinematographer.

Light Plot—Used in three-camera format to list the lighting effects (day or night) in each scene.

Line—The dark line drawn across the budget top-sheet to separate creative and technical production costs and personnel.

Line Producer—An often-used but ill-defined term. It appears infrequently as a formal designation, usually in episodic television, to indicate the person(s) supervising all the physical aspects of production. Originally, the term indicated a line relationship to the studio chief, and it retains that meaning at some of the major studios.

Location Manager—Normally, the person charged with discovering potential locations for review by the director and producer and negotiating the terms for use of those locations that prove acceptable. The location manager may also be charged by the production manager to secure permits and hire police and fire safety personnel as required.

Master—The camera setup or angle which provides the widest or most comprehensive view of continuous action. The "master" may represent several scenes, a single scene, or only a portion of a scene depending on script-designated action.

Meal Penalty—Under union conditions, failure to permit a meal period for cast and crew before a maximum number of work hours have elapsed.

Night Premium—An adjustment made to the basic rate of pay for work performed after a certain hour, usually 8 P.M., but varying according to the guild or union jurisdiction.

Packaging—A combination of several creative elements such as script, actor(s), and director to attract the interest of a production company and/or private investors, and often to the advantage of entertainment agents who benefit from developing a package comprised entirely of their own clients.

Page Count—The length of a given script or scene in pages and eighths of pages. This term may also refer to the "page count" of the day's work (see above) or of the total shooting completed to any specific date.

Pan—A horizontal or side-to-side movement of the camera on a fixed axis.

Pay or Play—A clause in a deal memo or contract which commits the production company to compensating a cast or crew member for a project whether or not that project ever goes into production. Many "pay or play" clauses have cutoff dates, at which a company must either go ahead with production or make payment in full.

Performance History—A production company's record of having complied with union conditions and made prompt payment of salaries and fringes.

Picture Deal—A contract or deal memo which sets salary or compensation based on the total requirements of a production rather than on a weekly basis.

Pick-up Shot—Reshooting a portion of a scene, the rest of which was acceptably filmed in a previous take. Pick-ups may be made of either masters or coverage (see above). In three-camera format, the demands of the continuous action occasionally require a planned overlap in the filming. See Appendix I.

Production Board—A series of strips representing all the master scenes of a given production organized according to the planned sequence in which they will be filmed.

Production Coordinator, Secretary—This person assists the unit production manager in the production arrangements. Additionally, this person is usually responsible for preparing copy-ready versions of the shooting schedule and any schedule revisions.

Production Designer—The person responsible for the design of the sets, whether on stage or practical locations, whether exterior or interior. The production designer normally supervises the work of the construction crew, set decorating crew, and property department in conjunction with the director and cinematographer.

Production Report—The detailed record of the personnel, the equipment used, scenes shot, and the hours expended on a given day of production.

Props—Any inanimate object (other than wardrobe) that is designated by the script or the director to be used by an actor in a scene.

Report to—A crew call which requires the set personnel to report directly to a location rather than to a studio for filming.

Run of the Picture—A cast member whose work period may include any of the days scheduled for principal photography without incurring liability for additional compensation.

SAG—The Screen Actors Guild which is the collective bargaining agent for actors (including stuntpeople, singers, and pilots) who work in the film medium.

Scene—A portion of the script which has been given its own number designation. Such a scene may or may not coincide with the continuous action of a master sequence.

SEG—The Screen Extras Guild, the collective bargaining agent for extras who work in the film medium.

Sequence—A term with no formal meaning in the film industry. Usually, this refers to a group of master scenes that form part of an identifiable larger unit such as a dance number or battle scene. For example, the "Dirty Harry" sequence in *The Creature Wasn't Nice* consists of several master scenes that together constitute the preview watched by the spaceship crew.

Set Dressing—Any items of set decoration, such as furniture, drapery, carpeting, and any hand props which are not designated in the script or by the director as part of a specific action.

Set-up—Each discrete position of the camera, excluding those changes in position which may occur when a dolly or crane is used to move the camera during filming.

Shooting Schedule—A comprehensive listing of the units of a given script and their respective production requirements organized according to the order in which they are filmed.

Shooting Script—A term whose meaning varies among production companies. The fundamental distinction between a shooting script and any other format is that the shooting script must have consecutive numbers identifying the individual scenes. Once assigned, a scene's number may not change.

Striking—When referring to a camera setup: breaking down the position of the camera and lights preliminary to preparing the subsequent setup. When changing location: securing equipment at the end of the day. When referring to a set: removing the set dressing. When referring to stage construction: disassembling the walls.

Strip—The sections of the production board used to record information for each master scene.

Talent—A general term for above-the-line personnel, which is often used to refer specifically to the cast.

Temp Dub—A preliminary mixing of dialogue, music, and sound effects, usually so that a first cut may be viewed with all these sounds at their proper audio level.

Tilt—A vertical or up and down movement of the camera on a fixed axis.

Top-sheet—Literally the top page of the various pages which constitute the complete budget. The top-sheet normally lists only the total of the major accounting categories along with applicable contingencies, deferments, completion bonds, etc., which combine to form the budget's grand total.

Working the Set—A term for the job function of the first assistant director which is used to contrast it with that of the production manager who, although often present on the set, might technically be said to "work the production office."

Wrap—Usually refers to securing equipment at the end of the day. May also refer to finishing work on a particular set, sequence, or location. See *striking*.

Index

Italic page numbers indicate illustrations. "n" indicates footnote. Entries after semicolon indicate glossary.